OUT
ON THE
LAND

Bloomsbury Publishing
An imprint of Bloomsbury Publishing Plc

50 Bedford Square	1385 Broadway
London	New York
WC1B 3DP	NY 10018
UK	USA

www.bloomsbury.com

BLOOMSBURY and the Diana logo are
trademarks of Bloomsbury Publishing Plc

First published in 2016
© Ray Mears and Lars Fält, 2016
Photography © Ray Mears, except
where credited on page 6, 2016
Map on page 17 and diagram on page 231
© John Plumer

Ray Mears and Lars Fält have asserted
their right under the Copyright, Designs
and Patents Act, 1988, to be identified as
Authors of this work.

British Library Cataloguing-in-
Publication Data
A catalogue record for this book is
available from the British Library.

Library of Congress Cataloguing-in-
Publication data has been applied for.

ISBN: HB: 978-1-4729-2498-8
       ePub: 978-1-4729-2499-5
       ePDF: 978-1-4729-2500-8

2 4 6 8 10 9 7 5 3 1

Designed by Austin Taylor
Typeset in Spectrum MT
Printed and bound in China by C&C
Offset Printing Co.

To find out more about our authors
and books visit www.bloomsbury.com.
Here you will find extracts, author
interviews, details of forth-
coming events and the
option to sign up for
our newsletters.

RAY MEARS & LARS FÄLT

OUT
ON THE
LAND

Bushcraft Skills from the Northern Forest

BLOOMSBURY
LONDON · OXFORD · NEW YORK · NEW DELHI · SYDNEY

Dedication

We dedicate this work
to the memory of
Samuel Hearne

Between 1769 and 1772 Hearne made three overland expeditions to reach the Coppermine River from the Prince of Wales Fort on Hudson's Bay. Travelling on foot, he covered some 8,000km (4,971 miles), exploring an estimated 650,000 sq km. Experience taught him that to succeed he would have to adopt the skills and methods of his Dene guides, learning to rely on the land itself for his sustenance.

In 1795, three years after his death, his journal was published, *A Journey from Prince of Wales's Fort in Hudson's Bay to the Northern Ocean*. This remains one of the finest written works of anthropology, providing a vivid portrait of the harsh life and skills of a Dene band as they traversed both boreal forest and barren lands. It also contains early, accurate and detailed accounts of the wildlife he encountered.

Although the Coppermine River would ultimately prove to have only small significance, his methods would profoundly influence all of the significant explorers of Canada who were to follow him.

Perhaps because we understand intimately the land and the skills he discovered, we trust him. In an age where the terms 'expert' and 'explorer' have been too often appropriated by braggarts and self-publicists, Hearne's humility is a refreshing example of how to live when travelling 'Out on the Land'.

Contents

Picture credits

Acknowledgements

We are mindful of the many generous people who have assisted us on our paths of learning.

In Sweden we thank Per-Anders Hurri, Per-Nils Päiviö and Britt-Marie Labba, and Rune Stokke for sharing their experiences of traditional Sami life. Peter Gustavsson, CO, Swedish Armed Forces Survival School 2009–11. Jan Waernberg, from the Swedish military library, Dr Anders Holmström, for his medical expertise, advice and comments on cold injuries. The staff and management of Gränsfors axe forge. Bosse Weslien, Head of Sjövik outdoor craft and leadership school and the Tyresö fungi girls, hopefully they have left some fungi for the rest of us to collect.

In Finland we would like to thank Sergei and Matleena Fofonoff, for introducing us to the traditions of the Skolt Sami. Turkka Aaltonen, our old friend and the No. 1 in Finland for good advice. Mika Kalakoski, trusted friend and expert outdoorsman for welcoming us to his fire and Hannu Tikkanen for assisting us with our research in northern Finland.

In Siberia we are indebted to the Evenki reindeer brigade who welcomed us to their nomadic life in the taiga, for both of us a profoundly moving experience.

In Canada we thank the elders and families at Behchoko and Gameti for sharing Tłįchǫ traditions and staying strong as two people. At La Ronge, Sally Milne for demonstrating a Cree love for the forest. On Bear Island, Virginia McKenzie, for opening an Anishnabe sweat lodge. Always, our dear friends: Pinnock Smith who keeps Algonquin traditions alive, Jeremy Ward, who curates our favourite museum, the Canadian Canoe Museum, and Becky

Mason and Reid McLachlan, the finest exponents of traditional Canadian canoe technique.

Special thanks go also to Daniel Hume and Keith Whitehead, instructors at Woodlore School of Wilderness Bushcraft, for their enthusiastic support. Big thanks to Jackie Gill.

Finally, and most importantly, we thank our wives: Ruth Mears and Louise Fält. Without your love, patience and tireless support this publication could not have been possible, thank you.

The Authors

Ray Mears

Over the course of my life I have had the amazing fortune to be involved with the art of bushcraft, and this abiding professional and personal interest has enabled me to explore some of the remotest and most beautiful wilderness locations on our planet.

I was born in 1964 in the south of London. My interest in bushcraft was sparked early in my childhood when, wanting to sleep out while on the trail of some foxes I had been tracking, a World War II veteran suggested that I did not need camping equipment but could instead rely upon survival skills, as he had during the Burma campaign. This and subsequent experiences, coupled with a chance encounter with a book about the Pygmies of central Africa, made me realise how important indigenous bushcraft methods are.

For years I travelled outdoors without a sleeping bag, practising and acquiring new skills as I went. After every journey I would assess what I had achieved and search for answers to the inevitable questions that presented themselves. This entailed spending long hours in museums and anthropological libraries leafing through old texts and assimilating ancient wisdom.

Living far from wilderness, I had no alternative but to shoulder my pack and travel in search of further knowledge – something I still do. I have been around the globe many times, through deserts and jungle, savannah and steppe. Living out on the trail with heat, cold, lightning, sand storms and insects has proven to be the best way to fully understand techniques and to recognise their significance, and this has greatly informed my work as a wilderness guide and bushcraft instructor.

As a film-maker, I have been able to further pursue my interest in indigenous methods by documenting the traditional living skills of many First Nation groups. In so doing, I have unwittingly frequently found myself recording the wisdom of the last generation of elders who have lived fully as hunter-gatherers – lifestyles that may seem simple to a casual observer but which are in fact incredibly complex. These have been fascinating and humbling experiences, and the faces and the wisdom so willingly shared remain with me to this day.

More than fifty years into my life journey I realise that while I love remote, wild places and the peoples I meet there, it is in forests that I find the greatest joy. It is the great circumpolar boreal forest of the north that calls to me most. I love to travel there, particularly by canoe, often alone, discovering a quietude that is enchanting. Here is a landscape where all the component parts – trees, insects and animals – combine to create one great living entity. It is a landscape in which bush knowledge and, to an even greater extent, experience really count, allowing me to harmonise with the chorus of the wild and to become a part of the forest itself.

Lars Fält

I was born in 1945 in the south of Sweden. In 1963 I joined the Swedish Army and in 1965 I was posted to the Army Ranger School in Kiruna, Sweden's northernmost city, situated in Lapland some 200km (124 miles) north of the Arctic Circle. At that time, my experience of extreme cold and skiing in winter and of mosquitoes during summer was very limited but, fortunately, I was trained by officers adept at imparting their considerable knowledge to green 19-year-olds. We had no motorised snow transport, relying instead upon skis, dogs and horses, so the going was tough.

After a few years I was given responsibility for the training of 30 young Sami recruits. This is when my interest in First Nation people began. During long training periods in the wilderness I found myself learning from them and I realised that living in these conditions was a way of life for these people. So we learned from each other, and I must have been doing something right because after one year of training a Sami soldier told me, 'You are not such a good skier, but we appreciate that you are interested in our culture and we like the way that you teach the military way of doing things.'

After five years I was posted to the Army Parachute Ranger School in Karlsborg. Here I was to have yearly contact with World War II veterans from the Finnish Long-range Patrol Unit and the Norwegian Resistance. These encounters kindled my interest in how to survive in the boreal forest for long periods of time in both summer and winter.

In the early 1980s I was tasked with overseeing the founding of a Swedish military survival-training unit. To achieve this, I attended many specialist courses in Arctic survival skills, which provided me with the opportunity to work with other First Nations, including the Inuit.

In 1989 I founded the Swedish Armed Forces Survival School, where I had the privilege of training Victoria, Crown Princess of Sweden, in survival skills.

Since retiring from the Army I have been able to indulge my love of the outdoors with frequent canoeing trips in Canada. I also continue to lecture and have written ten books on wilderness-living skills. I am currently enjoying teaching my grandson how to live outdoors.

Introduction

Join us as we enter a long-deserted cabin in winter. A deep melancholy chills every dark corner, but we kindle a flame in the stove and a cheery glow soon suffuses the space with light and warmth. Out too come a kettle and some coffee to warm us from within. The essentials dealt with, now let us begin.

This book has been 30 years in the making.

It's a collaborative effort by two friends who share a passion for the north woods, its people and its wildlife. Through our work in our respective countries we are both fortunate to be acknowledged authorities on bushcraft and survival skills, and for more than 20 years we have worked together teaching these skills in Arctic Lapland.

Independently, we have travelled widely in the boreal forest in search of the ancient knowledge of how to live in what can be a difficult region. What we have been taught has inevitably shaped our outlook and attitude, influencing our every decision before and during our travels into the remotest corners of the north woods.

In the following pages we have recorded the best of the modern and traditional knowledge and skills we have come to rely upon, pooling them to create a guide that will hopefully both inspire you and enable you to visit and enjoy the wilder regions of the boreal forest in safety. But more than this, we are sharing with you our philosophy and love for this wonderful landscape.

This is also our humble tribute to the many wise elders we have had the privilege to learn from. It is our fervent wish to inspire future generations to seek out such expertise and experience and to preserve them before they are lost forever.

In Canada, First Nation bands go out on the land to camp in summer and winter. This provides them with the opportunity to reconnect with their country, and to pass down culture, traditions and skills to the next generation. In our professional lives, we both agree that it is only by going 'Out on the Land', far from the convenience of the workshop or woodcraft camp, that we can meet the unforeseen challenges of bush life and test our knowledge, skills and ideas. This has been our world for over 30 years. Now we invite you to join us on our journey…

The Boreal World

'FROM A SATELLITE orbiting high above Earth, the taiga appears as a dark mantle draped across Earth's shoulders, a robe glistening with aquamarine lakes. This forest-green cloak declares to the rest of the solar system that this planet is the home of living things.'

J DAVID HENRY *Canada's Boreal Forest*

'The best thing in life is moving on'
Traditional Evenk saying

Right At one with the forest. For this man, the boreal forest is his home, his provider and he looks to the forest for the things he needs to live. He has no sense of isolation. He is a simple talker.

Join us in the very far north-east of Finland, where we are doing the necessary research to help us complete the book you have just opened. It is 2°C (36°F) on 1 April 2015 and we are standing in snow made wet by this year's uncommonly warm weather, conditions that bring many problems for the local inhabitants. Around us is a forest of birch and pine trees. The silence of winter has already been broken by birdsong from crossbills, heralding the onset of spring.

This is the boreal forest or taiga, the Earth's largest terrestrial biome where just less than one-third of all the trees to be found on our planet grow. Draped like a giant blanket around the shoulders of the continents of the northern hemisphere, the taiga encompasses the Arctic Circle, stretching from Alaska, Canada and the northern states of the USA to Iceland, Scotland, Norway, Sweden, Finland, Russia, Mongolia and northern Japan. It extends southwards to 50°N latitude in the continents of North America and Eurasia and pushes northwards to 70°N latitude in Scandinavia, driven by the warmth of the Gulf Stream. To the south are temperate forests and to the north tundra

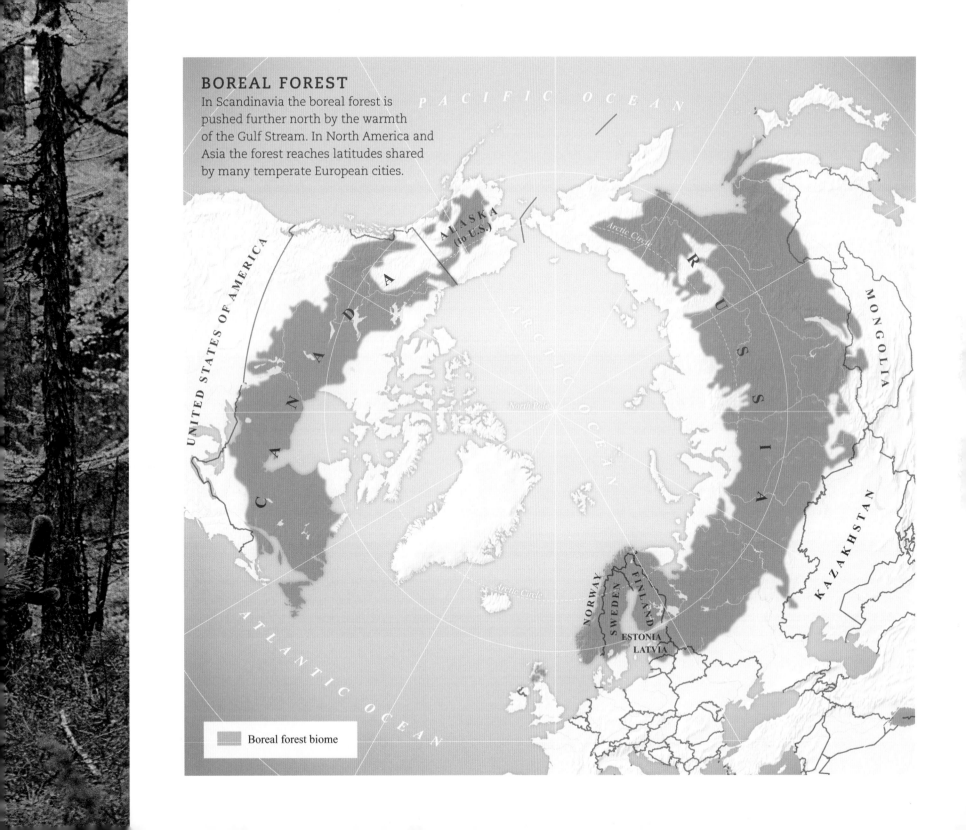

BOREAL FOREST

In Scandinavia the boreal forest is
pushed further north by the warmth
of the Gulf Stream. In North America and
Asia the forest reaches latitudes shared
by many temperate European cities.

PACIFIC OCEAN

ALASKA
(to U.S.)

Arctic Circle

CANADA

UNITED STATES OF AMERICA

R U S S I A

MONGOLIA

North Pole

ARCTIC OCEAN

KAZAKHSTAN

Arctic Circle

NORWAY

SWEDEN

FINLAND

ESTONIA
LATVIA

ATLANTIC OCEAN

Boreal forest biome

or barren lands. If, like us, you are a lover of untamed wilderness then this is an incredible landscape to explore, home to astonishing natural beauty.

The boreal forest itself seems to be one great living entity rather than, as logic would suggest, a conglomeration of many tiny parts. It is a land of extremes, of sultry heat and paralysing cold, of fire and water, sometimes alive with the sound of a billion insects and yet at other times profoundly silent – a truly awe-inspiring and majestic environment. To watch a lightning storm raging across the canopy of the trees is to gaze upon the immense power of nature, while the hypnotic scrolling of the Northern Lights across the skies reminds us that the forest is but a tiny speck in the greater cosmos.

The forest varies significantly from region to region. In its southern reaches, it is tight-packed and species-rich. This 'closed boreal forest' is a dark place that is difficult to walk through, though it is rich in wildlife, with trees such as white cedar and Jack pine being common. At the northern edge, the trees grow less high and are widely spaced, making travel easier. This is the 'open boreal forest', predominantly comprising of pine and black spruce, where fewer species grow and the wildlife is thinner on the ground.

In central Siberia, we have travelled with Evenk reindeer-herders through forest consisting mostly of larch, a species that predominates due to its ability to cope with the shallow soils found above the permafrost. In the autumn, after a dazzling display of colour, these coniferous trees drop their needles and the Siberian forest becomes a wind-chilled landscape. To cope with these challenging conditions the Evenk have devised special skills, such as ways of tying knots that ensure that their fingers are exposed to the cold for the least possible amount of time. Gloves are sometimes even permanently attached to sleeves, for, as one Evenk told us, 'If you lose your gloves in winter, you lose your life.'

Life in the forest

This region of our planet has always been a challenging place in which to live. Most of the birds that arrive to enjoy the seasonal glut of summer insects will be temporary visitors, departing for more temperate climes before the frost once again exerts its grip on the land. Any creature that lives here year round must have a means of coping with the great challenge of winter. These include the beaver, which works throughout the summer to construct a strong, well-insulated lodge that is sealed with an airlock to prevent predators from entering it. Just outside is a raft of food that is accessed throughout the winter from beneath the water. Bears, meanwhile, sleep through the cold months in hibernation, relying on body fat gained during the summer. The sows give birth to tiny cubs during the latter part of winter in the secrecy of their cosy dens before emerging in the spring. Above ground, the lynx preys upon the hare, the wolf upon the reindeer, and the few humans there are upon them all; this has never been a region heavily populated by people since food is so difficult to find.

Human societies within the boreal forest were once inescapably bound to the welfare of the animals upon which they depended, most importantly the caribou or reindeer. Today, we know that the population density of wildlife within this ecosystem has cyclical highs and lows. For example, the willow grouse population fluctuates from low to high density every eight or more years. The same is true for the woodland caribou population, which cycles from boom to bust over a period of approximately 40 years. For the forest Indian, this meant that perhaps once in every human lifetime there would be years of starvation. To prepare for this, the native inhabitants of the Scandinavian forests, the Sami, brought their reindeer into semi-domestication, watching over their newborn calves at the end of May and guarding them from their most significant threat, the European brown bear – a custom that continues to this day.

During the course of our experiences in the forest we have learned to respect the skill and knowledge of the First Nations. Quiet people all, they call a landscape that others consider a threatening wilderness 'home'. There are many similarities in the ways of life and attitudes beween the different nations to be found in this wilderness, but perhaps the greatest is also the least

Opposite and right

1 Once a common sight, a fur-trade canoe is here being poled and lined upstream on the French River, Ontario. Today, we follow the same routes, stumble at the same obstacles and sweat up the same steep portage trails that the voyagers once knew well.

2 During the golden years of the Canadian fur trade, 11m-long (36ft-long) birch-bark canoes like this were the power behind the industry that would lead to the exploration of even the remotest regions of Canada's boreal forest.

3 Enthusiasts from the Canadian Canoe Museum, Peterborough keep alive the skills of the voyagers. Here they are portaging a fur-trade canoe past rapids too shallow to paddle; a reminder of the hard life of the traveller.

tangible: the profound stoicism that they demonstrate while enduring times of extreme hardship. Using only the simplest of toolkits, they look to the forest to provide the resources necessary for life. Indeed, in Sweden there is an old saying that 'the forest is the poor man's overcoat'.

Throughout the region, indigenous communities have had to find clever solutions to the difficult realities of forest life and travel. Their ingenuity has given the world many wonderful inventions, such as the canoe, the ski and the snowshoe, to name just a few. Across the forest, native societies value the skills of self-reliance and craftwork, creating tools that are necessary for

life while also being objects of great beauty. This latter attribute both helps to establish cultural identity and demonstrates respect for the forest. In Labrador, for example, an Innu man going hunting would once have donned a beautiful white coat carefully made by his wife in order to show respect to the caribou he was hunting. He would have believed that failure to do this could have resulted in poor successive hunts as the animals would have refused to allow themselves to be hunted. In a modern sense, this may seem like simple superstition, but then again, who knows best how to live and survive in this forest?

Showing respect for older forest traditions is part

Above and Right Cree lady Sally Milne biting thin birch bark to form beautiful patterns. This entertaining pastime had a practical origin: designs made in this way were used as patterns for decorating garments with applied porcupine quill-work and, later, bead-work.

Top left Typical Sami craftwork, including: *nåjd* or shaman drum; root basket; reindeer-skin pouch; *kåsa* or cup; needle case; knife; wooden box; antler-strap weaving loom; large *kåsa*. The Sami have a word to convey the concept of being very skilled at handicraft – *duodji*. Today, this has become a familiar hallmark on authentic Sami craftwork.

Bottom left A Tłįchǫ (Dogrib) elder scrapes fat and hair to clean caribou skin with a scraper made from a caribou leg bone; the animal provided both the skin for leather and the tools with which that skin is worked. Bone was also traditionally made into the needles that were used for sewing the hides into clothing, while the tendons provided the sinew threads. The hard work involved with the process is predominantly carried out by the remarkable women of the north.

Below Traditional forest-Sami basket woven from birch roots. Time-consuming crafts such as this are very often the first to be lost in modern life.

of the way in which we have chosen to travel in the forest. First Nations have taught us that nothing in nature comes for free, that every resource harvested comes at a price and, for this reason, careful consideration and profound respect must be shown to all things of the forest.

To live successfully here requires courage, intelligence, strength and, above all else, teamwork. In many parts of the boreal forest communities were deliberately small, just one or two families living together for most of the year in a mutually supportive way. These groups only gathered together for large social events during the summer, when food was plentiful. The basic unit of life was the husband and wife, each of whom needed, supported and respected the other's contribution.

With ground unsuitable for agriculture, it is only relatively recently that outsiders from southern lands ventured into the boreal forest – Christian missionaries in search of souls to save, traders in search of fur. Today, exploration continues, often in the quest for oil and valuable minerals. The earliest explorers of the boreal forest had to learn to adopt the local techniques and methods in order to travel in it. There is no better example of this than Samuel Hearne of the Hudson's Bay Company, who late in the 18th century journeyed with a band of Dene people from Prince of Wales Fort (near present-day Churchill) to the Coppermine River and back. His account of this journey remains essential reading for northern travellers.

Opposite top left In the winter, the forest can seem a rather hostile environment to the unprepared traveller.

Opposite top right Bears are the largest predator in the boreal forest. Grizzly bears inhabit its northern reaches.

Opposite bottom A Tłı̨chǫ summer camp. Today, modern materials are utilised in harmony with traditional knowledge. Going out on the land in this way gives families time to enjoy each other's company. Camping demands cooperation and teamwork – behaviours that benefit everyone.

The traders and settlers from the south brought with them high-quality steel tools that were greatly valued in the forest. The axe and the gun are the most obviously useful ones, but consider the impact of the arrival of a copper cooking pot on households in which water was boiled using heated stones in a birch-bark cooking basket. Progress comes at a price, however, and today much boreal knowledge and culture has been lost, which is a great shame. Despite this, the people of the forest – both native and non-native – still exhibit a deep spiritual connection with their surroundings and the seasons. Forest craftwork is still alive and popular and people still enjoy gathering berries and wild mushrooms, albeit for pleasure rather than for subsistence.

As modern recreational travellers, we have a broad interest in the historic human lore of the forest. We have adopted many First Nations' techniques, but the greatest of their teachings has been the importance of looking to the forest itself for answers. As our dear and now sadly departed forest-Sami friend, Par Anders Hurri, once said: 'Naturen är en tyst men rättvis lärare.' (Nature is a quiet but fair teacher.)

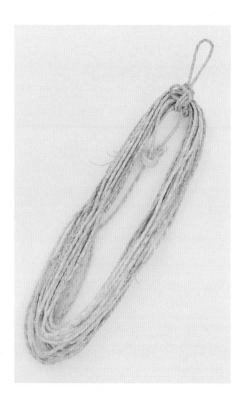

Above The lasso is the item that most strongly represents the cultural identity of the reindeer-herding communities. Originally fashioned from rawhide, like this Skolt Sami one, today they are made from modern materials, and there are even different lassos to suit differing temperatures.

Right A Tłįchǫ (Dogrib) elder prepares to feed the fire. Offerings of valuable items such as food and tobacco will be burned with religious ceremony to honour the ancestors and to ensure that the time out on the land will pass without difficulty.

Top right Less nomadic than the mountain Sami, the forest Sami constructed sturdy wooden cabins called *kåta*. The typical pyramidal construction combines the qualities of the skin tent with the available timber for construction. With a small floor area and a low ceiling, they were easily warmed and fuel-efficient. Here, our friend Rune Stokke kindles a cooking fire on which to boil coffee.

Bottom right The sauna was important to life across the boreal forest, and there remain many traditions of sweat-cleansing. Among the First Nations of North America, the sweat lodge was a place of spiritual as well as bodily cleansing, as it is here for the Anishinaabe (Ojibwe) in northern Ontario. To be invited to a sweat lodge is a great privilege.

Below Totally a child of nature, this Evenk infant photographed in 1996 may be one of the last natives of the boreal forest to have been raised in the traditional forest way. Travelling in the cradle board for safety, here propped up so that he can observe his parents as they erect their *chum* (Evenk tipi), he is surrounded by the sights and sounds of the forest that he will come to know intimately as home – an immersive experience of nature at which we can only wonder.

Below right Evenk skin-working tools and components for winter boots: reindeer shin-skins that are tanned with larch wood, scraped and softened, and then sewn into boots with sinew threads. These traditional skills survive even today because the garments they produce remain better than the modern alternatives.

Opposite top Life in the Evenk *chum* (hut) is simple but good. During the autumn, preparations are made for winter, including drying reindeer-leg skins so they can be made into warm winter boots. Thinking ahead is a golden principle of surviving life in the northern forests.

Opposite bottom A respected Montagnais elder with his drum. These instruments remain a heartbeat in aboriginal communities throughout the boreal forest, where they are used for entertainment but also as an essential part of ceremonial and spiritual life. In times past, the community shaman could locate a caribou herd using drumming. Once found, the shaman would sing a magic song to hold the caribou in that place until the hunters could intercept them.

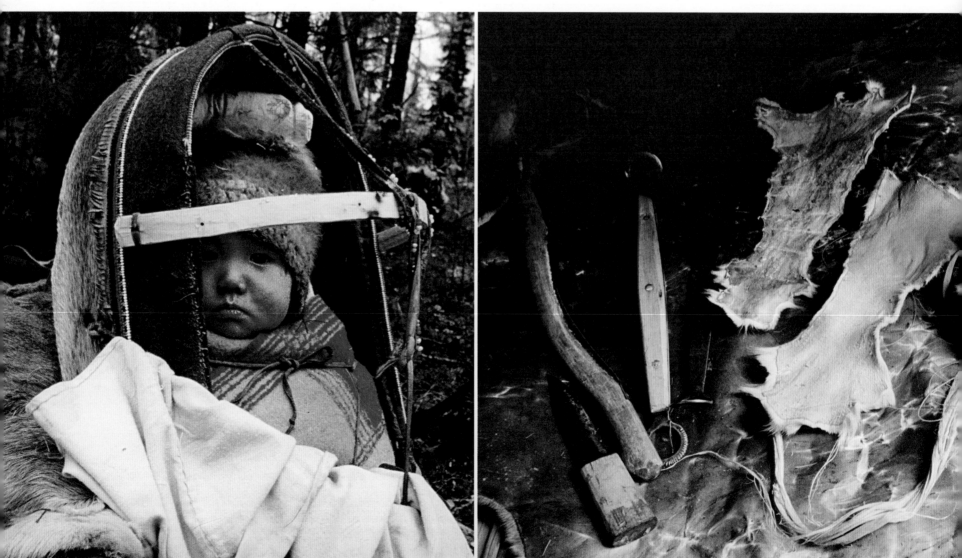

'Without the caribou there is no hunter. Without the hunter there is no caribou.'
Traditional Innu saying

Above A respected Montagnais elder extracts the brains from a caribou. This will be used to tan the animal's skin for clothing and footwear. In forest culture, nothing was wasted – every part of the animal's body had a value, from nose to tail. This traditional woman grew up in a world where respect for the animals hunted was of paramount importance. A concept that, in many cases, differentiates the native from the non-native hunter.

The Boreal World

Left The considerable amount of specialised clothing and equipment needed for winter was stored in the forest in an *ajjte* (storage hut). Note the use of tree stumps to keep vermin from entering the cache and destroying the contents.

Opposite Time spent out on the land provides an opportunity to pass on essential forest knowledge to the next generation. Here, the manufacture of a traditional deadfall trap.

Below At Lappstaden in Arvidsjaur, Swedish forest Sami meet each year at the summer's end for a church weekend. Here, a village of family *kåta* that has been owned by Sami families since the 18th century.

Left Reindeer bones fashioned into a Skolt Sami toy-reindeer herd and *akja* sled.

Above When the reindeer calve at the end of May they must be watched night and day by the Sami herders to protect the newborn animals from predation by wolf, lynx, wolverine, bear and eagle.

Opposite page top left
Weaving a basket with pine roots.

Opposite page top right
Traditional Swedish-forest craftwork.

Opposite page top middle
The sewing machine was a life-changing revolution when it was introduced to the forest peoples, meaning that communities could now more quickly fashion clothing and express their artistry in design and decoration.

Opposite page bottom Despite the changes brought by modern life, the Skolt Sami in northern Finland maintain their cultural traditions and crafts. They told us that they still feel themselves to be an integral part of the forest itself.

Below In the forests of Scandinavia you can sometimes find beautiful rustic cabins like this one, made by forest-workers.

Below and right Mushroom-picking in the Scandinavian forest remains a popular pastime, providing a reason to be out enjoying the delights of the forest in the autumn.

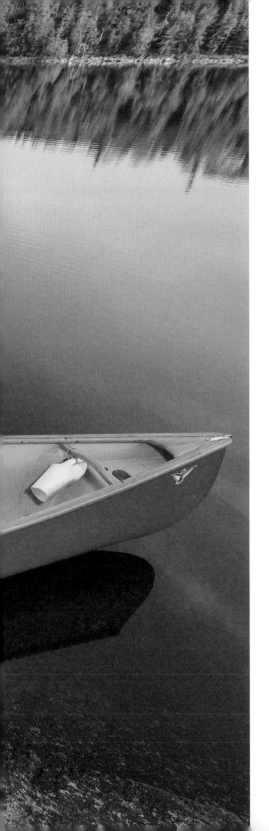

Outfit and Clothing

'IT SEEMS HARDLY NECESSARY to say that the best way to travel across country in summer is the Indian way; with an absolute minimum. An Indian would sooner live hard and carry a light pack than live well and carry a heavy one. A few pounds of dried meat, a very light woollen blanket, a .22 rifle, and enough tea to last him at the rate of three cups per day is all he will take.'

MICHAEL H MASON *The Arctic Forests*

Our outfit is our life-support system in the bush and the clothing choices that we make prior to setting out will determine how we live on the trail. Wherever possible it should be kept simple and light, and be versatile. What it is depends on several factors, including our ability, experience and personal preference. We both share a habit of taking a fairly spartan outfit with us, preferring simplicity to the fuss that attends complex baggage. Others may prefer more fancy equipment that promises greater comfort. There is no right or wrong; if you are prepared to carry extra kit then by all means do so. Our nuts-and-bolts approach, however, will at least be a good starting point from which you can go on to build your own outfit.

Getting organised

As you assemble your apparel for an excursion, remember the US-Navy principle: KISS, which stands for Keep It Simple, Stupid. It is far too easy to keep adding items to your packing pile, so have a plan and, at the end of each trip, re-evaluate your choices: was there anything you were in want of and, more importantly, which items did you carry that you didn't use or could easily have lived without?

For travel in the most remote wilderness, organise your outfit in a modular way. There are items that should always be carried on your body. There are things that may be needed throughout the day and thus should be kept in your daypack or, if hiking, in the outside pockets of your pack. Lastly, there are the items you only need at the end of the day, and your back-up kit, which should travel in the main compartment of your pack or, if canoeing, in your main packsack.

Never keep all of your eggs in one basket – spread your emergency equipment around your outfit in case

Below Ray's outfit for solo canoe travel for two weeks, including food. Longer trips will require an extra pack for food.

Previous pages When heading into remote wilderness, our outfit should be simple, versatile and contain nothing that is unnecessary.

'Victory awaits him, who has everything in order – luck we call it. Defeat is definitely due for him, who has neglected to take the necessary precautions – bad luck we call it.'

ROALD AMUNDSEN

of problems. For example, if you consult the canoe-expedition packing list (see page 69) you will see that should you wipe out in rapids you can survive with what you carry on your body. You can live quite comfortably with either the contents of your daypack or the main pack in isolation, if you have to. However, in a crisis the daypack is the one to grab as it also contains emergency communication equipment. It is also most likely to be within reach in such circumstances.

When travelling solo by canoe it is possible to carry more than a week's worth of food in a dry bag in the main canoe pack. For longer trips, however, at least one separate food pack will be necessary, the number depending on the duration of the journey.

The daypack is important. It should be set up so that the larger main packs need not be opened until you need to pitch camp. This means that navigation equipment, first-aid gear, waterproof clothing, a warm jacket and bug protection need to be in the daypack, along with a water bottle, water purifier and lunch. We favour a large daypack that also enables us to carry a tarp and a brew kit. Inevitably, there will be times when we have to wait for a storm to pass and in this circumstance the contents of the daypack alone can provide shelter, food and a warm drink. It is more efficient to have just one pack to reach for at these times.

Every item of your outfit should have a home within the baggage as a whole, but achieving this only comes with time; even the most experienced travellers find that it usually takes two days for the system of the trip to establish itself. If you find your system starting to slip during the course of a journey, it is a sure sign that you need to have a day off from travelling in order to clean up and reorganise yourself. In the past, when long expeditions lasting several months were more common, it was normal to rest each Sunday, which provided the traveller with just such an opportunity to regroup.

The safety equipment that we carry, such as ropes, rescue gear and our Personal Flotation Devices (PFDs), should be regularly maintained and retired when they begin to show signs of wear. Note also that matches and a field dressing are carried in our PFDs. If there is an accident on the water or portage trail, having a field dressing immediately to hand can be a real advantage. Military dressings are packaged in fully waterproof durable packaging that is ideal for the task. Note also that the PFD is permanently equipped with a rescue light and whistle, a legal requirement in many places. While being stored between trips, remove the batteries from the rescue light to prevent corrosion and store them in an envelope clipped to the PFD.

Assembling the outfit is a critical stage in preparation that requires careful thought and attention to detail. In many ways, it is at this stage of the process that the success of your entire trip will be determined.

Shouldering responsibility

When travelling, we have a golden rule: each person packs and loads their own equipment. Novices sometimes try to be helpful by picking up someone else's pack. This is a recipe for a forgotten pack. On an expedition, each person should assume responsibility for their own outfit and some other part of the communal load. If everyone follows this process, everything will be fine. If, however, on the portage trail a pack is lifted by a helpful soul they may miss the fishing rod that was carefully placed beside it as a reminder to its caretaker to take it with them. Only much later, usually at the day's end, are such losses discovered. Once again then: each person packs and loads their own equipment.

The other cause of many problems is 'assumption'. Never assume anything. If you do hear the word, alarm bells should start ringing. Always check, re-check and check again. For example, if you rent your camping equipment from an outfitter, open the tent and pitch it there and then to ensure that all of the necessary parts are included. The last thing you need to experience while out on the trail is a tent that has components missing or has been packed with ones that belong to a different model altogether. Check before you go.

In fact, the NEVER ASSUME rule reaches way beyond the outfit, keeping us safe in all aspects of our travels. We have lost count of the number of times that planned departures have been delayed by weather or other circumstances beyond our control. Always plan for the worst-case scenario, while hoping for the best. Oh yes, and then check everything just one more time!

Above NEVER ASSUME. Always check equipment prior to departure.

Opposite A dry bag containing a sleeping mat, sleeping bag, warm fleece, dry socks, boots for camp and a wash kit provides almost everything you need for life in camp.

What to pack?

Clothing for summer

In the summer, our clothing needs are straightforward. Our attire will need to provide versatility in terms of insulation, should be quick-drying, give protection from biting insects and be tough.

Underwear

Choose comfortable items that will dry extremely fast and not cause any chafing. For men, swimming shorts work well, since they are extremely light and can be washed and dried in minutes, even on cloudy days.

Socks

While canoeing or portaging, we prefer neoprene socks that provide insulation and keep us warm in the inevitably cold, wet conditions. Using these is generally a better option than trying to keep other types of sock dry. In camp, we use woollen socks or woollen foot wraps that can easily be dried if they become wet. Waterproof socks are also very useful. If our feet have been wet and cold all day, we wash them back at camp, massage each foot for five minutes, don dry socks and then put waterproof socks over the top. In 10 minutes our feet are toasty warm and thoroughly dried out and refreshed. In bad weather, waterproof socks can also be used in your camp shoes to keep your under-socks dry.

Always invest in your feet; there is nothing more miserable than being on a wilderness trip with constantly cold, wet feet.

Trousers

Your trousers are going to have a very hard life; you will wear them out four times faster than shirts and much more quickly than jackets. For this reason, try to avoid very expensive ones. You will need trousers made from a fabric that dries fast yet is very tough and woven tightly enough to resist the probing bite of mosquitoes. We willingly trade some drying speed for the latter criterion. Waist and cargo pockets are desirable, as are proper belt loops.

Belt

A good 'old-fashioned' leather belt is perfect; it will cope with the wet and provides support for your trousers as well as your knife. It can also be used to strop the edge of your knife.

Shirt

Your shirt also needs to be quick-drying and resistant to mosquito bites, but can be lighter in fabric weight than your trousers. We like ones with two breast pockets and, if possible, a deep internal map pocket. Good fabric also provides protection from harmful ultraviolet.

Undershirt

In the summer, a thin short-sleeved merino-wool undershirt is excellent. It will provide comfort on days that are chilly as well as on days when the temperature fluctuates wildly.

Bandanna

We always carry several light cotton bandannas that are 80cm (31in) square. Weighing virtually nothing, a bandanna can be worn to protect the neck from the sun and bites. They can also be used in endless ways – as emergency bandages or for protecting hands when lifting hot pots from the fire – and make the perfect bush towel, which can be washed by being boiled in a pot and then dries in minutes.

Boots

These are all about personal choice, but in truth the perfect boot has yet to be made. We use lightweight boots designed for use in water. They drain well, dry fast and have good grip, which is very important when carrying heavy loads across muddy portage trails or slippery rocks. They also provide adequate protection for toes and ankles, which is necessary when you are lining a canoe through shallow rock gardens.

In spring or autumn conditions, waterproof canoe boots that come high up the calf can be cosy. For hiking in the forest, we prefer high-leg pac boots.

In camp, a pair of old training shoes or some moccasins are good choices for comfort, and wearing them will give your feet and your canoeing boots time to dry out.

Hats

A hat is very important when canoeing, protecting you from sun, insects and rain. A wide-brimmed felt one is a traditional choice, or there is the wonderful Tilley hat, which is possibly the perfect canoeing hat. In the evening or early morning, a lightweight wool beanie is ideal. This can also be worn when sleeping in cold weather.

Opposite When the insects are at their worst, the Original Bug Shirt is your best friend. It's also wise to tuck your trousers into the top of your boots. Gloves and trousers that are sufficiently tightly woven to prevent blood-sucking penetration are also essential.

Below When travelling in the boreal forest we encounter swamps and wet ground, circumstances in which pac boots – constructed with a leather upper for stability and with a rubber base – are ideal. The leather can be waxed, providing an effective waterproof layer.

Insect protection

At the very least you should carry an insect head net with you. The distraction caused by insects can cause accidents, and although insect repellent keeps them away some of the time, a head net always works. Better still, equip yourself with an Original Bug Shirt. Designed in the Algonquin region of Ontario, it is the best insect protection that we have found.

We always carry some work gloves for safely handling hot kettles and pots, and these can double up to provide mosquito protection.

Top right A selection of the tools that can be used to safely remove ticks, at least one of which should be carried.

Bottom right Just a few of the varieties of insect repellent available. One bottle should always be carried in your top pocket.

Warm layers

In camp in cool weather a wool shirt is a comforting friend that is not bothered by sparks from the campfire. For emergency clothing, a dry bag containing a Buffalo Mountain Shirt and Salopettes is excellent for warming a chilled canoeist who has capsized on a cold day. It is easy to underestimate how many warm garments you may need on a summer canoe trip. Bear in mind that the weather can change from sultry heat to icy hailstorms overnight.

Waterproofs

Avoid ultra-lightweight waterproofs, which tend to cling too tightly to the body. A better option is a more robust breathable waterproof jacket that is long enough to reach to mid-thigh, combined with bib-over trousers. These styles of waterproofs provide the protection necessary to cope with the exposure to the elements that is experienced when canoeing. Good waterproofs are not cheap, but they are key to the success and enjoyment of your trip. All too often we have watched others suffer while we are comfortable. The old adage that 'there is no such thing as bad weather, only bad clothing' is certainly true.

Other items

A cotton T-shirt and lightweight shorts can prove comfortable in camp on hot days, while a swimming costume is useful when you want to cool off with a dip during very hot weather. In the spring and autumn, a lightweight windproof smock will provide comfort in cold, dry weather.

Clothing for winter

Clothing in winter is of the greatest importance, and getting it right takes time. It is not as simple as merely putting on a really thick jacket, for as soon as we start moving we generate both heat and moisture. If we become overheated it becomes almost impossible to function and we sweat heavily. Moisture then condenses in our clothing as a result of sweating and this reduces the insulation provided by the clothing, resulting in later chilling. Once again, our wardrobe must be versatile in order to cope with moments of high exertion, such as when skiing cross country or snowshoeing, and times when we are hardly moving and are exposed to extreme cold, such as when driving a snowmobile. We must therefore take care to anticipate these changes of activity level and adjust our clothing in readiness. In practice, this is much easier said than done.

In extreme cold – -20°C (-4°F) and below – breathable clothing reduces in its effectiveness, and consequently the vapour given off from our bodies tends to condense inside our outer layers. At first this

Opposite Winter
clothing made up of
many layers under
a Ventile windproof
overjacket.

moisture is subtle, its presence difficult to recognise, but with experience you will notice the reducing efficacy of your insulation as vapour levels build up.

For northern trappers bivouacking under a tarp to enable fast and light travel, this was a problem. Although warmed by their campfire at night, in a bivouac it is difficult to dry clothing efficiently. If they were caught out by a sudden drop in temperature or an ice storm, the reduced effectiveness of the insulation in their clothing and sleeping system could prove fatal. For this reason it is vitally important that our clothing is designed to facilitate drying, with layers that can easily be separated for this purpose. For example, never choose gloves with insulation that cannot be removed for drying.

It is equally important to avoid the fastest-drying fabrics, since these can cause chilling by rapid evaporation and are prone to melting if they are too closely exposed to a fire or a wood-burning stove. Herein lies a dilemma: when travelling in the forest we are exposed to both extreme cold from the elements and extreme heat when working with open fires and wood-burning stoves. In many ways, wool-based clothing is the perfect solution: it is comfortable to wear, provides warmth when damp and, if worn in many thin layers, can easily be separated for drying.

Underwear

Cotton underwear is fine and is sanitary as it can be washed at a high temperature. Although wool-mix underwear is equally good.

Base layers

The base layers we have been using for at least the last 20 years are modern knitted wool-blend garments produced by a company called Woolpower. These are very durable, comfortable and resist becoming smelly, unlike their totally synthetic counterparts. The layers nearest to the skin are made from the lightest fabric and they increase in weight layer by layer.

If you know that you will be exerting yourself then there is much to be said for wool-mesh base layers manufactured by Brynje, which are superb for allowing sweat to dissipate from the skin, meaning that there is always a layer of dry air close to the body. They can also be dried very easily in the field.

We each use a slightly different combination of layers that best suits our individual needs, which vary with age, individual physique, fitness and the type of activity we intend to be engaged in. Working this out takes time and experimentation. If you anticipate heavy exertion, you will obviously need to be clad lightly and should carry spare dry base layers to change into when your activity ceases.

Mid-layer

This can be an extension of the base layers and may be a heavy woollen pullover or wool shirt. We very much favour a lightweight down jacket, the slippery windproof surface of which allows snow to be easily brushed off and facilitates easy donning and removal of the outer layer of clothing.

Trousers

Just as for summer, trousers for the winter need to be tough. For versatility, we prefer to use lightweight windproof trousers that are large enough to accommodate several base layers, the latter of which we can adjust to provide the appropriate level of insulation. Heavy wool trousers are wonderful but can be very hot and slow to dry when wet, and they collect snow particularly when they are slightly damp with perspiration. If used, they must be protected from snow with a pair of thin windproof overtrousers.

Overtrousers

These are a real boon when the mercury drops, and should be insulative, windproof and large enough to be worn easily over all other layers. Long side zips that allow them to be put on or off without requiring the removal of footwear is essential. Ideally, they should reach up high enough up the back provide warmth to the kidneys.

Opposite top Part of
the secret to dressing
in the cold is to wear
layers appropriate to
your level of activity.
Here, outer layers
have been removed to
reduce sweating, but a
smooth windproof shell
is retained to prevent
snow from penetrating
woollen insulating
layers.

Opposite bottom
In winter we carry
a minimum of two
hats, often three. This
enables us to regulate
our body temperature
by changing them,
and prevents hats
from becoming
soaked with sweat.

Right Clear goggles
that provide a high
degree of impact- and
UV-protection enable
us to travel safely in
very bad weather.

Shirt

A shirt such as that used for canoeing can be worn in cabins or as a lightweight windproof top layer over a thin base layer when chopping wood on a fine day.

Windproof items

Our insulative base layers function by providing space in which pockets of warm air can be trapped. Without a windproof outer-garment, these pockets are constantly displaced by cold air, which is why a windproof outer layer is vitally important. We prefer over-the-head anorak designs, which are highly efficient and do not hinder movement. Our preferred fabric is Ventile, a tightly woven cotton fabric that also provides a significant degree of shower protection.

Headwear

Heat loss from the head and neck area is very significant and certainly cannot be ignored in the winter. It is not unusual to need to change hats for different activities, matching their insulative properties to exertion levels. For the head, we use a variety of different hats, the most important of which is our fur-trimmed warmest hat. It is important to ensure this is a good fit: wearing one that is even slightly too tight will cause a headache, while one that is too loose will slip annoyingly over your eyes when you are wearing a hood or snowmobile goggles. Some prefer to wear this style of hat over a peaked cap. A wool beanie is good for use in the tent or cabin and while sleeping. A peaked cap made of wool is also useful in the

spring or autumn, since it works well under the hood of a waterproof and is comfortable to wear when skiing.

A balaclava is another essential item, particularly on long journeys by snowmobile. For neck protection, tubular neck-warmers are perfect.

Handwear

We take our manual dexterity for granted, but in extreme cold we can lose the use of our hands to the cold alarmingly quickly. Our handwear is therefore of paramount importance, for without the use of our hands we cannot carry out any of the tasks that are vital for our life support in the wilderness.

You should always buy quality gloves from long-established glove specialists, such as Hestra. The folly of

not doing so was made plain to us one winter when we worked with a friend equipped with a top-model winter glove made by a well-known brand. At -50°C (-58°F), the gloves' surface broke like peanut brittle and they disintegrated. Fortunately, we had spare ones, so his hands came to no harm from the cold; the only damage was to his ego as a result of the sharp humour that ensued…

There is no one glove that can cope with all conditions; instead we rely upon a versatile system of handwear, as outlined below:

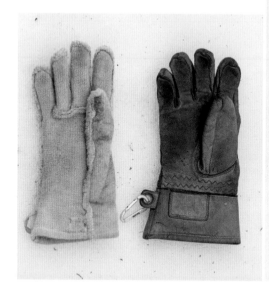

CONTACT GLOVES These are thin gloves that provide a barrier to the cold when you are handling cold items such as metal. They are thin enough to allow you to carry out fiddly tasks and are a real help if you happen to be repairing a snowmobile. You can choose between thin leather flying gloves and nitrile gloves, as used by paramedics.

MAIN GLOVES These are our workhorse gloves. They need to be very strong as they will be constantly pressed into hard service, from chopping and moving firewood to erecting shelters – in fact, they are used for about 90 per cent of everyday tasks during the winter. We prefer five-finger leather gloves, with knitted wool liners. We carry spare liners so that we always have dry ones to hand. Never use liners of any kind on their own; they are designed to insulate and will quickly be destroyed without the protection of the outer layer. The outers can be used on their own for greater dexterity

when skiing or using a knife. If you choose lined gloves, these should be equipped with a means by which they can be tied together and suspended for drying.

MITTENS These are our most important handwear for extreme cold. We prefer hand-knitted Lovikka mittens, which have a legendary reputation in northern Scandinavia. To protect these liners we use extremely tough-wearing ex-Swedish-army leather overmitts. When constructing snow shelters or otherwise handling snow for any length of time, it is wise to also wear waterproof overmitts. These can be used with any of the other glove/liner combinations above. They are very light and roll up to occupy next to no space. We favour short mitts with the cuffs rolled down,

'Where butter melts, leather melts.'
LARS FÄLT

Above In winter, we carry three pairs of gloves: five-finger gloves made of leather with a wool liner; woollen mittens with leather overmitts; and lightweight breathable waterproof overmitts. These layers can be configured to suit many different circumstances.

Below The footwear
we prefer in winter is
a rubber-and-leather
boot with a wool-felt
liner, combined, when
necessary, with a
fleece-lined overboot.

which prevents interference with your sleeve. It is also important that the mitts are very easy to put on; tight-fitting ones can be impossible to don if your hands are very cold. Attention to detail is everything.

GLOVE CARE Always take good care of your gloves and mitts. Whenever you come indoors, be in the habit of removing the liners, attaching them together with the outers and hanging them up to dry. Frequently treat the leather to some glove balm or proprietary leather dressing to prevent the leather from becoming dry and brittle. Wet gloves should always be dried slowly, away from direct heat. Should they stiffen, simply stretch the gloves across your knee or the edge of a table until they

are flexible again. Cared for in this way, your gloves will last many years. If you slice the leather of your glove with a knife or axe it can be sutured with a needle and thread. If the slice has not pierced the leather it is frequently possible to repair the damage with some strong glue.

Footwear

Our feet are the parts of our body in the most constant contact with the cold, and they are also at the furthest extremity. As a result of both these factors, they require the most careful protection to prevent cold injury. To further complicate matters, footwear needs to be able to contend with dry cold, cold water and slippery surfaces, and enable us to attach skis or snowshoes to our feet or drive a snowmobile. Sometimes we may encounter all of these demands in one day!

BOOTS Our choice of footwear reflects these requirements, and we prefer a boot with a rubber last and a leather upper, lined with wool-felt insoles and liners. The protection such boots offer is exceptional, protecting us from the cold and water, and they can also be fitted to the bindings of a forest ski.

Although designed to be roomy, boots should be purchased a size larger than normal. Even a slight constriction of the foot caused by wearing too many socks, over-tight laces or simply a boot that is too small can result in lack of circulation and frostbite. We always carry two pairs of liners so one pair can be dried while the other is being worn.

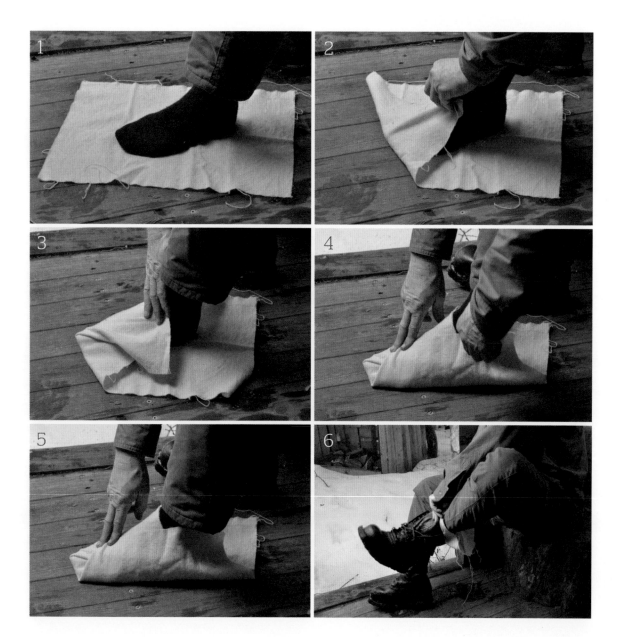

Left Traditional woollen foot wraps are easy to use, comfortable and, most importantly, very easy to dry if they become wet. They can be made quickly from a rectangle of thin woollen blanket, as shown in this sequence.

SOCKS We favour standard wool hiking socks coupled with a woollen foot wrap. These were once standard military issue in many northern armies and they have many advantages over regular socks. Despite how they appear, they are very comfortable and, most importantly, they can be dried in the field very easily by being held in front of a campfire or wrapped around our torsos while sleeping – a vital quality for winter clothing.

GAITERS These are a very good purchase and prevent snow from entering boot tops. We use the Sami shoe band, which like a narrow puttee binds our trouser hems to the top of our boots. These, like so many First Nation inventions, are superb. In very cold weather, rather than trying to increase the insulation inside a boot, it is preferable to add another exterior layer. For this we use fleece-lined overboots that easily fasten with hook Velcro.

Below A Sami shoe band is a wonderful gaiter that effectively prevents snow from entering the top of the boot. We have used these for many years and have found nothing to better them. To wear them, securely fasten one end by threading it through the laces of your boots, then wrap the shoe band around the bottom of your trousers and secure it in place as shown, tucking in the loose end.

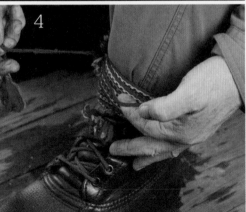

BEST FOOT FORWARDS

The effectiveness of correct footwear is illustrated by an incident that occurred some winters past, when we set out to make a three-hour snowmobile journey to a craft worker in Lapland. We checked on the driving conditions with a local guide, who informed us that the trails were all in a good state and that he had just driven the route. This was not in fact true, and what should have been an easy journey turned into a nine-hour challenge as we negotiated lake after lake awash with 60cm (24in) of overflow. Most of the day was spent towing the novice drivers accompanying us out of the slush and chipping ice from the frozen drivetrains of swamped snowmobiles.

At the outset of the journey, some sixth sense had prompted us both to don our overboots. Throughout the journey, despite repeatedly having to wade through deep water, we were comforted by the fact that at any stage we could if necessary stop and dry our foot wraps. Fortunately that wasn't necessary. By the journey's end, an exhausted party – buoyed by the sense of achievement that comes from having overcome adversity – shared a beer at the cabins while changing out of iced clothing. Our feet were encased in 3cm (2⅛in) of crystal-clear ice as a result of repeated soaking and freezing and it took more than an hour to break this free from our feet. Amazingly, once we stripped down to bare feet we discovered they were perfectly dry; the overboots had really earned their keep that day.

TRADITIONAL FOOTWEAR

The aboriginal societies inhabiting the boreal forest developed a variety of footwear. In Canada, mukluks produced from smoke-tanned caribou and moose hides were used in dry cold, while sealskin boots (often traded from Inuit communities) were worn in the wet. In Scandinavia and across Siberia, boots made from the shin- and face-skins of reindeer were used, sometimes in double layers with dried sedge in place of socks. These boots seem primitive compared to modern footwear but are in fact wonderful – light, comfortable and very warm.

Damp conditions have always been the greatest challenge, and one solution was to wear mukluks with rubber overboots. Until 20 years ago, we also used native footwear for much of the time. However, in recent years changing weather patterns have resulted in a much more moist north, a state of affairs that has resulted in our current footwear preferences.

Mothership

This is an important item of clothing, an overjacket large enough to be worn on top of your other layers. It is used when you are standing still, for example when ice-fishing, when travelling by snowmobile or just when the weather is extremely cold.

As ever, clothing needs to match exertion level. Say, for example, that you are skiing cross-country in

Opposite An over-sized Army great coat makes an excellent 'mothership' to wear in extreme cold.

Below A Skookum parka is a very good outer layer when travelling long distances by snowmobile.

-40°C (-40°F) conditions. You'd wear your mothership while you are setting up your skis and poles and for the first 10 minutes of your journey. Now well warmed up, you'd place the mothership in your daypack and continue, clad very lightly to match the exertion of your skiing. Stopping for lunch would allow some sweat out of your light layers and, as you start to feel the chill reaching you, on would go your mothership and you'd have a hot drink from your vacuum flask.

Facewear

Travelling in strong wind at low temperatures places a great demand on the adaptive response of our faces. This is particularly noticeable when travelling by snowmobile. If you are not wearing a helmet and integral face mask then it is wise to carry some face protection.

HEAT-EXCHANGE FACE MASK
A recent invention, heat-exchange face masks contain copper mesh that is warmed as you exhale. As you breathe in, the cold, dry air is warmed and humidified by the mesh. The manufacturers claim they help to reduce the overall chilling of the cold, and can help those who suffer from cold-induced asthma. We cannot

comment on this, but our own use has shown that they do seem to reduce dehydration from breathing super-dry air and definitely maintain facial warmth.

GOGGLES These protect our eyes from snow, and branches when skiing or snowmobiling, and simply enable us to function in a blizzard. Choose military-spec goggles that have clear visors with UV protection, since these can be used in the low light of the Arctic winter and some models have insulated visors. When snowmobiling, travel for a few minutes to allow your face to cool and dry before putting on the goggles. This will help to prevent them misting up. If they do become misty and frozen, dry them over the warm-air outlet of your snowmobile.

Floating overall

If we have to travel by snowmobile during seasons when the strength of the ice of rivers and lakes is suspect, we use a floating overall. These provide adequate warmth, although a mothership jacket will still be needed on long journeys or in extreme cold. Originally designed for sailors, as the name suggests, floating overalls contain buoyancy that can prove a lifesaver for self-rescue should the ice break beneath you. If a floating overall is not available, consider wearing a canoe buoyancy aid at such times.

Equipment

There are a few essential items we should never be without when travelling in the bush. The most important of these are a fire-starter, compass and whistle, all of which should be carried on the body at all times. The easiest way to achieve this is to string them on a cord and hang it around the neck. In this way, we are constantly aware of their presence and they are always with us, whatever changes we make to our clothing layers. We add a small torch to the cord along with a tiny set of tweezers, which are useful for removing splinters and ticks.

In a shirt pocket, we carry our main compass, a small notebook and pencil and, if we have a deep pocket, a head net and small sharpening stone. On our belt, we always carry a knife and sometimes a folding saw.

Miniature compass

A miniature compass is intended as a back-up tool for navigation and can be used to ensure your main compass is reading true. In practice, however, it is in almost constant use simply because of its convenience. Despite its small size and simplicity, it works to a surprising degree of accuracy, although generally it will primarily be called upon during a quick direction check, to give a rudimentary bearing or so you can orient your map to the land surface. Some miniature compasses are adjusted for local declination (see Navigation chapter) but we prefer an unadjusted one. Whichever you choose, this compass needs to be robust and reliable; beware cheap imitations. Like any tool, it must be used in training ahead of the time when it will be most needed.

You can create a reference mark by drawing it on using a soft pencil or scribing a line on the outer case, although the traditional way to use such a compass is to hold it as shown with the reference mark located at the point where your index fingers meet. Keep your elbows tucked into your waist and turn your

'There is more danger that a man take too much than too little into the wilderness.'
STEWART EDWARD WHITE
Camp and Trail

Left Microlite, tweezers, fire-starter, compass and whistle should be carried on a cord around the neck whenever travelling in remote wilderness.

Opposite A compass and a map are vital pieces of equipment for travelling in the wilderness, and should be looked after well.

body to face in your direction of travel. Read off the bearing or, having determined the bearing, turn until you are facing in the required direction.

A good compass can be energised with torchlight so that the face/card can be read in the dark.

Main compass

Your compass is your key to the wilderness. The baseplate compass is an essential tool for navigation. In fact the map and compass are often called the 'woodsman's friends'. Try to obtain a compass that has a globally balanced needle and a facility to offset the local magnetic declination. Your compass is a fragile precision instrument and will need to be looked after, treated gently and kept away from insect repellent, which might cause it damage.

Whistle

Every member of a party should have a whistle on their person. The international code for signalling with a whistle is:

One blast – Where are you?
Two blasts – Come to me
Three blasts – I need help
Response – One blast

If a member of a party becomes lost and signals with a whistle for help, you should *not* immediately answer. It is more important to point at once towards the sound and, if possible, fix a bearing on the direction from which the sound is coming using a compass. Two such bearings taken from different places can give a triangulation that pinpoints the location of the whistle blast. If instead you immediately answer, it is frequently the case that the lost party will stop whistling and you miss the opportunity to take the bearing. The lost party should of course continue signalling until they are reached, as this will enable a rescue party to home in on their position.

Torch

A head torch is a fundamental wilderness tool. Choose one with a range of settings, from low to high power, and a strobe facility. Always carry spare batteries and refresh these before any major expedition.

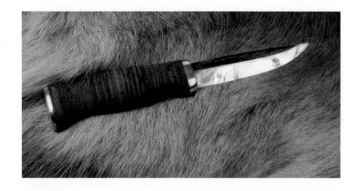

Knife

In the forest, a knife can literally mean life. It is as essential to remote forest travel as the ice axe is in alpine mountaineering. Choose a small, strong sheath knife. The classic puukko style from Scandinavia with a 10cm (4in) blade is ideal. Keep it sharp and clean.

> 'All puukkos are knives.
> Not all knives are puukkos.'
> TRADITIONAL FINNISH SAYING

Folding saw

The folding saw is light and safe to use. It can be used to cut firewood, to help with camp craft and repair, and for rescue. Choose a design with a strong blade such as the Bahco Laplander.

Axe

In the boreal forest, the axe is the master tool, without which most First Nation people never travel. It enables us to clear portage trails, split firewood and much else beside. In winter, it is arguably the single most important item of equipment.

Bucksaw

Safe and easy to use, a bucksaw greatly eases the task of cutting firewood and is the perfect partner to the axe. We carry a convenient folding bucksaw.

Expedition medical kit

This is your main first-aid kit, with the addition of

Top left A wilderness axe and a frame saw are ideal trail companions on a summer canoe trip; for winter travel, they are essential tools.

Top right A variety of axes suited to wilderness travel in the boreal forest. *From left to right*: Velvicut ¾ axe or 'boy's axe'; Gränsfors Bruks Scandinavian Forest Axe; Snow and Nealley Hudson Bay Axe; Woodlore Wilderness Axe; Gränsfors Bruks Outdoor Axe; and Gränsfors Bruks Wildlife Hatchet.

Left A puukko made by Ray Mears. This traditional Finnish knife is a workhorse design that remains superlative in the forest.

Right The tarp stretched in this way is perfect when travelling in summer, providing protection from the rain yet offering a clear 360-degree view of the forest.

Below A typical summer camp comprising a tarp for living space and a tent for sleeping quarters. Here, the Hilleberg Nallo 2GT shows the advantage of its wonderfully versatile vestibule.

any medical items you may need for yourself or for dealing with the potential problems you may face. The contents of this kit are the essential tools of life support and will directly relate to the level of training and experience of its owner. Ensure that it is thoroughly protected from moisture, is easily recognisable, and everyone knows where it is stored.

NOTE REGARDING FIRST-AID TRAINING

While any training is better than none, when travelling in remote wilderness it is important to have received instruction that takes into account the nature of the specific medical problems you may encounter and the complications that could arise as a result of being in a remote location.

Shelter
Tarp

A tarp is an essential item of equipment that will be used in both summer and winter. It should be lightweight and large enough to be useful. When travelling in a group, we favour a tarp that is roughly 3m/10ft square. This is a good size for a party of up to four, yet it is light and packs very small. If a tarp is too large, it can be difficult to find sufficient space between trees in which to pitch camp with it, and it is more prone to catching the wind.

Opposite A nice campsite with plenty of space can be a rare thing on a canoe trip. The ground is frequently rocky, which can mean it is impossible to use conventional tent pegs. Consequently, we may need to find ingenious ways to fasten guylines, as shown here.

Tents

In summer, a mountain tent is a very satisfactory dormitory, the living space being provided by the tarp. While some prefer a tent that combines the sleeping area with the living space, we prefer to keep them separate. We both favour tents made by Hilleberg. These are incredibly well made, with attention to detail and a manufacturing quality that verges on the fanatical. Not only will such a tent withstand fierce storms but it will also provide protection from biting insects.

In winter, lightweight canvas tents that are fitted with a wood-burning stove are perfect. Once you have a wood burner in the tent you can effectively dry your clothing. Also, being much more fuel-efficient than an open fire, the wood burner requires less firewood to be found and cut. Overall, living in such a tent reduces your calorific requirement and transforms one's experience of the forest in winter.

Above The Erätoveri is a square tarp that was designed by Finnish scouts. It can be pitched in many ways, and its very light weight and great versatility win it a regular place in our outfit.

Right The Loue was originally derived from the Sami practice of carrying half of a *laavu* when travelling. It was improved by Vihe Vaellus, who constructed it from lightweight nylon fabric to improve its portability. It is intended to be used with a fire for warmth, and is suitable for summer and winter.

Bivouac bag

If you intend to sleep under a tarp in summer, a bivvy bag is essential. Choose a lightweight breathable one that is simple in design and compact to carry.

In winter, a bivvy bag is more important, particularly if you are sleeping in a shelter. It will need to be very large to accommodate clothing and warm sleeping bags. A good choice here is the Bivanorak, made by Hilleberg, which can also be used as a waterproof if necessary. In the morning, it is likely that you will find moisture has condensed and frozen in the space between your sleeping bag and the bivvy bag. This can easily be brushed off. Without the bivvy bag, this moisture would have condensed inside your sleeping bag.

Left The Hilleberg Bivanorak is an excellent bivvy bag in winter. It is very versatile and can be used as a waterproof when necessary.

Sleeping bag

Your sleeping bag is one of the most important items of your outfit. You should choose carefully, invest in quality, protect it on the trail and store it correctly between trips. We prefer to carry down sleeping bags as they are light and compress to a small volume. While any sleeping bag that becomes wet loses its insulative properties, a down bag when soaked is virtually impossible to dry in the field. For this reason, your bag needs to be carefully protected. We use a large lightweight dry bag to contain our sleeping bag. This in turn is stored in a tough dry bag, which in its turn is protected by the pack in which it is carried.

Sleeping mat

A sleeping mat provides two important components for a good night's sleep: insulation from the cold ground and comfort. Inflatable foam mats are an excellent choice, and a good one should last many years. Do ensure that you carry a puncture-repair kit. In winter, a reindeer skin is the perfect sleeping mat since the hollow nature of each hair provides incredible insulation.

Mosquito net

If you intend to travel light in the middle of summer and sleep only under a tarp, you will almost certainly require a mosquito net. This need only be small, to protect you when sleeping. Such a net can also be used inside a cabin; sometimes these seem to contain more hungry mosquitos than the forest outside…

You can also buy a group tarp that is fitted with a mosquito net at its edge. In fly season this is a wonderful thing, while at all other times it is rather cumbersome.

Packs
Hiking

For hiking, a pack should be simple, free from too many straps and fittings. It needs to be light and ideally will have capacious outside pockets so that it can be lived out of without you needing to open the main section until you pitch camp. A capacity of 55–60 litres should enable you to carry a week's supply of food in summer. If you're intending to hike for more than

Left In winter, a warm sleeping bag is absolutely essential for comfort and survival. It should be packed in a dry bag to protect it from moisture.

Top left Frost River Timber Cruiser and Timber Cruiser Jr are traditional canoe packs that make an excellent basis for a summer canoe outfit.

Top right Repairing a traditional pulk (sledge). Repair and care of equipment has always been part of northern life; the best kit is that which can be repaired.

a week, you will be better served by a pack with an external frame in which food for up to 10 days can be carried.

When hiking in winter, a larger pack with a capacity of 80–120 litres will be needed to accommodate the increased bulk of the extra insulation.

Canoeing

Blue plastic barrels have become popular for canoe packing. These are strong, can be fitted with a packing harness and are very bear-proof. However, we are traditionalists and prefer more old-fashioned, aesthetically pleasing canoe packs made from canvas and leather. We think that Frost River makes the highest-quality ones. For solo travelling, a Timber Cruiser Jr for a daypack and a Timber Cruiser for the main pack serves us well for two weeks. Longer journeys will require extra food packs, as necessary.

Winter travel

If you are travelling during the winter by dog team or snowmobile, a combination of a *komatik* (sledge) and canoe packs serve admirably. If a person is hauling a toboggan then long, narrow, zipped duffel bags are best since they sit beautifully on the sled. Label each one so that you can easily locate the individual items of your outfit.

Dry bags

Any item that must be kept dry, such as a sleeping bag and spare clothes, should be packed into roll-top dry bags. The outer pack protects the dry bag from puncture and abrasion while the dry bag keeps the contents dry. Use lightweight dry bags for individual items and heavyweight ones as pack liners. Choose large dry bags as they are easier to handle, especially with cold hands. The added advantage of dry bags is that they also increase the buoyancy of the pack.

Water

Water bottle

Water bottles are fundamental items of equipment; two 1-litre (2-pint) bottles are ideal for summer travel. In camp, a water bag with a capacity of 10 litres (2½ US gallons) that can be coupled to a gravity-fed water purifier is ideal.

Vacuum flask

In winter, an unbreakable vacuum flask replaces the water bottle. This is an important item of equipment. For the sake of hygiene, only use it to carry hot water – mix your drinks in your cup.

Water purifiers

Waterborne pathogens can spoil a trip and, at worst, cause lasting health problems. Water filtration equipment is therefore important. This should be easy to clean or back flush, since when travelling on a large river and on lake systems sediment can quickly slow the filter's flow rate. On canoe trips, a gravity-feed system is ideal, but when hiking, a small hand pump will be lighter. Some filtration systems require secondary chemical disinfection. Ensure you are familiar with the operating instructions before you set out.

Cooking outfits

Our cooking outfit is simple. We prefer equipment made from stainless steel because it is hygienic and rugged enough for hard trail use.

Stove

It may not be possible to always rely on open fires, depending upon local park regulations and fire risks. In these scenarios, a portable hike stove will be necessary.

Above left British Army water bottle and stainless-steel mug – indestructible items that go on every trip.

Above middle Native people would filter their water in this way, using cotton cloth tightly stretched over a willow hoop frame. This method works well today to pre-filter water before using more modern purification methods.

Above A camp cooking outfit for two to four people.

Opposite top The common petrol stove has become part of life in the north country. Here, it is being used to make blood soup.

advance and battery life will improve.

As it stands, such equipment gives a greater degree of security and enables us to modify plans and receive warnings about unexpected storms. It also provides the comfort of simply staying in touch with loved ones. The kit is delicate, however, and must be properly protected against the rigours of bush travel. If you are heading out into the wilderness, it is worth keeping the following in reach: satellite phone; solar charger; spare batteries.

Below Your PFD should be equipped with a rescue light, a whistle, a rescue knife and, where possible, a field dressing, waterproof matches and some electrical tape.

Firebox

In parks, which are often greatly used, it is preferable to carry a collapsible environmental fireplace or small stove to reduce your environmental impact.

Basic food supplies

Salt, pepper, sugar, flour, oil, Worcestershire sauce, tea, coffee, milk powder, potato flakes.

Communication

When we first explored remote wildernesses, the notion of communication with the outside world was but a dream. Although radio communication existed, the bulk of the equipment was prohibited to all but the military. Today, however, we can communicate with great ease using satellite-communication equipment and, as time progresses, no doubt this technology will

Safety and rescue
PFD

Your PFD is a life-saving piece of equipment. Keep emergency items (see Items Carried in the PFD on page 69) in its pockets. Never use your PFD as a seat as this will reduce its buoyancy over time. A PFD should be worn as a precaution during the autumn and spring when travelling on ice that is of suspect thickness.

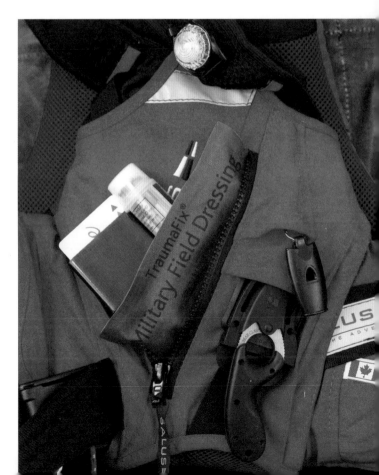

Throw bag

A throw bag with a floating rope is essential canoe-rescue equipment; ensure you have received the required training to use it correctly. Bear in mind that a throw line may also be necessary when travelling in the winter.

Ice picks

Whenever travelling on ice it is wise to wear ice picks. These are worn around your neck so that in the eventuality of ice breaking beneath you, you have the means to grip slippery ice and haul yourself out.

MODIFYING EQUIPMENT

It has been our shared experience that very few items of equipment are perfect when purchased; it is quite normal to have to modify them in some way to improve their function. For example, the metal handles of tools to be used in winter can be bound in ice-hockey tape. This provides insulation to the conductive surface, which greatly reduces conductive heat loss and prevents these items sticking to bare skin.

Above Axes wrapped with electrical tape, for protection and to prevent slippage.

Left Wrapping the aluminium shaft of a snow shovel with ice-hockey on snowmachine tape provides insulation.

Outfit for a canoe expedition in summer

Items carried on the body

- Whistle
- Ferrocerium rod
- Tweezers
- Microlite
- Miniature compass
- Main compass
- Knife
- Folding saw
- Small first-aid pouch
- Head net
- Cord
- Vaseline

Items carried in the daypack

- Tarp
- Kettle
- Brew kit
- Cord
- Sharpening kit
- Mug
- Water bottle
- Vacuum flask
- Water purifier
- Dry bag
- Warm jacket
- Waterproof
- clothing
- inReach satellite communication device
- Snare wire
- Head torch
- Spare batteries
- Insect repellent
- Sunscreen
- Bugsuit

Items carried in the PFD

- Whistle
- Light
- Storm-proof matches
- Military field dressing
- Duct tape

Items carried in the main pack

- Sleeping bag
- Therm-a-rest mat
- Spare clothes
- Dry shoes
- Warm clothing
- Tent
- Wanigan bag
- Repair kit
- Fishing kit
- Fishing rod
- Solar panel
- Cookset
- Fry pan
- Spare knife

Outfit for expeditions in winter

Items carried on the body

- Leather belt holding a knife, folding saw and hooks for gloves
- Small first-aid pouch
- Whistle
- Microlight torch
- Miniature compass
- Main compass
- Cord
- Fire stick
- Pullover mitt made of windproof and waterproof material
- Beanie hat
- Small brush to remove snow

Items carried in the PFD

- Whistle
- Light
- Storm-proof matches
- Military field dressing
- Duct tape
- Ice picks

Items carried in the daypack

- Tarp
- Axe
- Shovel
- Kettle
- Brew kit
- Cord
- Sharpening kit
- Mug (kåsa)
- Vacuum flask
- Warm fur cap
- Leather mittens with wool inner liners
- Sleeping bag
- Therm-a-rest mat
- Satellite communication device
- Snare wire
- Head torch
- Spare batteries
- Candle

Items carried in the main pack

- Sleeping bag
- Therm-a-rest mat
- Arctic overboots
- Axe
- Shovel
- Extra insoles
- Warm clothing
- Tent
- Wanigan bag
- Repair kit
- Candle
- Winter fishing kit
- Cookset
- Fry pan
- Spare knife

Items carried on the snowmobile

- Rescue rope with karabiner hooks
- Ice picks
- Tent
- Stove
- Winter fishing kit
- Ice drill
- Candle
- Signalling tools
- Skis or snowshoes

Cold Injury

'… FROM LATE OCTOBER until early March these northern regions sink into a negative heat balance: More energy is lost to the atmosphere and outer space than the solar energy gained. The farther north, the greater the deficit. It is, to say the least, disconcerting to be a warm-blooded creature trying to exist in a world that operates on a net energy loss for over a third of the year. No wonder northerners have a complex psychological response to winter!'

J DAVID HENRY *Canadas's Boreal Forest*

'Travelling at 50 below is all
right, so long as it's all right.'
TRADITIONAL SAYING FROM ALASKA

Previous pages In extreme cold,
travellers in the boreal forest must
have more than just a knowledge
of how to make fire; it is vitally
important to understand, recognise
and know how to prevent
cold injuries.

Opposite One of the characteristics
of the northern environment in
winter is the rapid and dramatic
fluctuations in ambient temperature
that can occur. These can catch you
out if you are unable to recognise
signs that the temperature is falling.

If you have ever made an excursion in the boreal summer, it isn't long before you wonder how it might be to do the same in the boreal winter. Well, open the door of a domestic freezer: you will find that the temperature inside is -18°C (0°F). It seems impossible that one can live at those temperatures, let alone sleep out and travel long distances, yet for seasoned winter wanderers -18°C (0°F) would be a fairly comfortable temperature.

For more than 20 years we have taught students how to live and travel in the boreal winter. By consulting our records we can see that one year the temperature was an uncommonly warm 6°C (43°F) in the day and -10°C (14°F) at night; the average low temperature has been -25°C (-13°F); and the coldest temperature we have recorded was -55°C (-67°F). As these figures highlight, a wide fluctuation of temperature is not uncommon in the north – indeed, rapid changes can occur in only a few hours and have caught out many unwary or exhausted travellers.

Travelling in winter temperatures is of course challenging, but does actually bring many advantages. The fact that lakes, rivers, swamps and muskeg (peatland) freeze solid makes progress much easier, although we must have a means to move on snow and certainly must always remain cautious when travelling on ice. For us, the clean, insect-devoid winter has been by far the most frequent background to our friendship; we have spent many winters exploring our interest, experimenting with ancient skills and talking at length to the native inhabitants of the taiga.

People often ask us with astonishment, 'Why camp in the winter?' That is a strange question indeed, for when you have learned to enjoy the winter it becomes the season to look forward to. Apart from the breathtaking beauty of the frosted landscape, travelling in the cold months brings validity to all of the summer journeys, since now we are able to fully understand the mechanisms of the boreal environment – how small trees are contorted under the weight of snow, the way small mammals shelter in tunnels under the snow.

Safety in the cold environment

To travel safely and enjoy winter in the boreal forest requires a good understanding of the effects of cold and a strategy to deal with it. If our physiology is any guide, it would seem certain that the human species evolved in the tropics, for we are most able to function in the temperature range of 28–34°C (82–93°F). Our bodies are also better able to lose heat than to gain or generate it. In fact, with the exception of very hot and humid climates, we are constantly losing heat to our environment. For life to be possible, we need to maintain a body temperature of 37°C (98°F), ±1.5°C (2.7°F). Venturing into the boreal forest in winter therefore requires us to create a portable tropical microclimate. We achieve this with our clothing, shelter and sleeping bag.

HOW COLD IS IT?

Outside the teaching environment we do not normally carry a thermometer with us, but with experience it is possible to approximately gauge the temperature by observing the environment:

-15°C (5°F)	Snow starts to sound like polystyrene packaging.
-30°C (-22°F)	The needles on spruce trees are frosted.
-40°C (-40°F)	Eyelashes frost while working.
-45°C (-49°F)	Dry spruce fires billow smoke.
-50°C (-58°F)	Snow sounds like porcelain; boiling water thrown into the air vaporises.

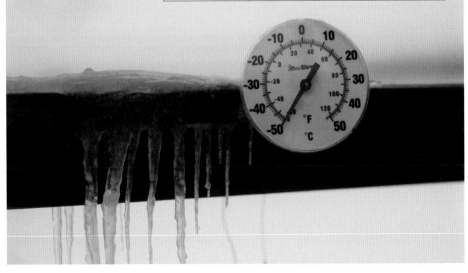

How we lose heat

We lose heat to the environment by four key processes. Understanding these enables us to make informed choices about clothing, guides our design of shelter, aids our decision-making, and is vital when treating a casualty suffering with a cold injury. The processes are:

Heat lost by radiation

Radiant heat loss is warmth lost in the form of electromagnetic waves that travel at the speed of light. Mostly in the infrared wavelength, radiant heat loss is invisible, rather mysterious and little understood. We lose heat by this process constantly, particularly to nearby cold, solid objects. Although unaffected by the ambient temperature, in extreme cold of ≤ -30°C (-22°F) radiant heat loss is a very significant contribution to the cooling of our body; at these temperatures it is sometimes possible to feel this loss of warmth to nearby objects.

We are also able to gain heat through radiation, the most obvious sources being the sun or our fire.

This reinforces the vital importance of being able to construct and light a large, efficient, warming fire (and, by extension, the necessity of carrying an axe to achieve this) and, very significantly, of stopping the construction process soon enough so that we don't become too cold.

Choice of shelter design in these circumstances is also vitally important. For example, a shelter dug into snow under a spruce tree may provide a convenient roof and shelter from the wind, but it will be cold since we will constantly lose radiant heat to the trunk of the tree

itself. From experience, we know that at -50°C (-58°F) the tree trunk in such a shelter is a noticeably cold presence, even when a fire is burning. In this scenario, a bed built between two fires or a lean-to of light brushwood is a warmer option.

Despite continuing research and many experiments with reflective materials, there is currently no clothing that provides any practical means of preventing heat loss by radiation.

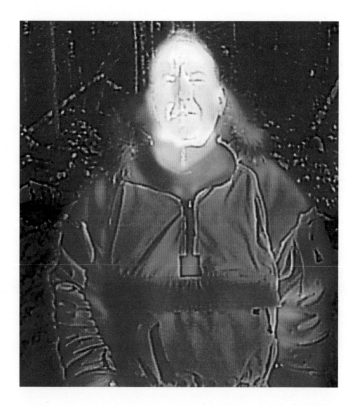

Heat lost by convection

Heat is lost by convection whenever a fluid that has a lower temperature than our body passes across our skin. We warm the fluid and it carries that heat away and is replaced by more cool fluid. The heat lost by convection depends upon the temperature difference between the fluid and the skin and the speed at which the fluid is flowing. The faster the fluid moves, the more pronounced the cooling effect.

Air is the fluid to which we have the most constant exposure. It only requires a small amount of heat to warm air, which is why it is a good insulator. We harness this quality in our thermal clothing, which functions by trapping many tiny pockets of air around our body. That said, even when standing still on the calmest day there will be a movement of air within our clothing as warm air rises and is replaced with cooler air. However, the real problem comes if we are working in wind or moving on skis, or by dog sledge or snowmobile. In these situations we need to ensure that we are wearing well-designed

Left This infrared image shows how dramatic the loss of heat is from an unprotected head and neck area in conditions of -21°C (-6°F).

windproof clothing. Without this important layer the wind will constantly force warm air out of our clothing and replace it with cold air.

The cooling effect of air convection is called windchill. As a general rule, as the wind speed doubles, the chilling effect increases fourfold.

Water is the other common fluid we encounter regularly in the northern environment. Immersion in water in winter has the most serious consequences, as it requires far more heat to warm water than air (see the table below). Indeed, heating a given volume of water requires more than 3,000 times the amount of heat than is needed for the equivalent volume of air. This greatly increases the danger of heat loss should we fall into moving water or if we are thrashing around in water. Coupled to this, we also lose significant heat to water by conduction (below). The message should be clear: stay out of the water and stay dry.

ISOBARIC VOLUMETRIC HEAT CAPACITY

Substance	Isobaric volumetric heat capacity MJ/m³K
Air (sea level, dry, 0°C/32°F)	0.001297
Water (25°C/77°F)	4.1796
Ethanol	1.925

Heat lost by conduction

Conduction is the transfer of heat from our body to an object with which we are in direct contact. The conductivity of the substance that the object is made from will determine the rate of conductive heat loss. For example, air is a very poor conductor of heat compared to water, which conducts heat 24 times more efficiently. This is the reason that our insulation layers dramatically lose their effectiveness when they become soaked by perspiration or other sources of moisture,

Above Simply placing some spruce boughs beneath your feet provides significant insulation and reduces heat loss by conduction.

such as when snow falls down our neck, as often occurs when gathering firewood if we forget to raise our anorak hood before swinging the axe.

Just standing around, we inevitably lose heat by conduction to the ground. To reduce this, we place spruce boughs on the ground in our camp area. Certain items of our equipment, such as an aluminium snow shovel, can be very cold to handle. As you can see from the table below, aluminium conducts heat nearly 100 times faster than ice. This means that the danger of a cold injury to your hands greatly increases when handling such an item. To reduce conduction a little, we tape the handle of the metal tools we use with ice-hockey tape.

Heat lost by evaporation

Evaporative heat loss occurs directly from our skin through perspiration or respiration and from our clothing when it is damp or wet. Perspiration in the winter environment must therefore be carefully managed. The greatest risk is from over-heating and sweating into our insulation layers, which then later fail to provide the necessary insulation. We can manage perspiration by adjusting our layers of clothing to suit our activity level and by physically venting moist air from our clothing when we are working hard. To do this, we pull open our clothing layers at the neck and move so as to pump out the hot, moist air. Generally, we try to remain a little cool while exerting ourselves to minimise excess production of perspiration. If we know that we are going to become sweaty we kindle a fire in advance, so that as soon as our work is complete we can strip off wet layers and dry them by the fire.

About two-thirds of the heat we lose from the skin is lost by perspiration, and the remaining third is lost in respiration. In extreme cold, this proportion may be even higher. To maintain efficient respiration our body humidifies the air we inhale to 100 per cent humidity. In the super-dry cold of the boreal winter this process strips our body of both warmth and moisture. Heat-exchange

THERMAL CONDUCTIVITY

Material	Thermal conductivity W/(mK)	Material	Thermal conductivity W/(mK)
Air	0.024	Water	0.58
Feathers	0.034	Glass	1.05
Polystyrene, expanded styrofoam	0.03	Ice	2.18
		Solid rock	2.0–7.0
Cotton	0.04	Stainless steel	16
Snow (temp <0°C/32°F)	0.05–0.25	Titanium	22
Wool felt	0.07	Carbon steel	43
Softwoods (fir, pine etc)	0.12	Cast iron	55
Leather (dry)	0.14	Brass	109
Rubber	0.13	Aluminium	205
Charcoal	0.2	Copper	401

face masks (see Outfit and Clothing chapter) greatly reduce this loss of heat and moisture and can help to prevent cold-induced asthma.

If our clothing becomes wet, in a cold breeze the resulting loss of heat by evaporation can be very severe. For this reason it is important to brush off snow from clothing before entering warm spaces. Always wear a snow-proof outer layer over your insulation layers.

Whenever we notice moisture steaming from our clothing we equate that with a loss of heat and take it as a signal to have a warm drink and, if possible, to change into dry clothes and dry the damp ones by the fire or in a heated tent.

It takes experience to manage evaporative heat loss. Some items of clothing are particularly well suited to high-activity levels – most notably Brynje string vests. Their net construction allows excess moisture to escape freely from the skin as a vapour while maintaining a warm regulated cushion of air next to the skin.

Liquid fuel at low temperatures

In the north, liquid fuel poses a real danger. Due to its combustible nature it must be stored at a safe distance from any naked flames. This almost certainly means that the fuel will be exposed to the ambient temperature. As you can see from the Freezing and Melting Point table (right), liquid fuel does not freeze at the temperatures we are likely to encounter. Instead, for example, if a can of gasoline has been sitting exposed to -20°C (-4°F) conditions, the fuel will be the same temperature.

It must never be handled with bare hands. Any spill is likely to cause an instant cold injury, worsened by the evaporation of the volatile fuel and the fact that most fuels also have a relatively high volumetric heat capacity.

FREEZING AND MELTING POINT

Fluid	Freezing and Melting Point °C/°F
Fresh water	0°C/32°F
Sea water and IV fluid	-2°C/28°F
Urine	≤ -5°C/23°F
Diesel	-10°C/14°F (gel point)
Antifreeze	-13°C/8.6°F
Alcohol (80 proof)	-27°C/-17°F
Motor oil 10W30	-30°C/-22°F
Kerosene	-40°C/-40°F
Gasoline	< -40°C/-40°F
Avgas 100LL	-58°C/-72°F
Methylated spirit	-114°C/-173°F
Butane	-140°C/-220°F
Propane	-188°C/-306°F

Alcohol at low temperatures

Alcohol poses a range of dangers to northern travellers. The first and by far the greatest danger is caused by intoxication. Under the influence of alcohol it is difficult to attend to the many considerations required for safety in the cold environment, and operating any machinery is potentially lethal. Every year there are many alcohol-related driving accidents, particularly involving snowmobiles. These range from cold injuries and collisions to drowning from driving on to thin ice or open water.

Alcohol consumption is also implicated in hypothermia. It has long been argued that the resulting vasodilation that accompanies alcohol consumption, familiar in the typical drinker's rosy face, causes rapid heat loss. However, in tests this effect seems to be overridden by the body's defensive mechanism of vasoconstriction. Whatever the case, inebriation does bring about a feeling of warmth and a dangerous loss of sensation to cold, which can result in failure to recognise the onset of hypothermia, an underestimation of conditions and associated poor decision making. Alcohol also increases dehydration, with further detrimental impact in cases of hypothermia.

Although we may be familiar with the notion of a Swiss St Bernard alpine-rescue dog with a brandy barrel attached to its collar to revive the avalanche victims it rescues, the reality is rather different. In extreme cold, alcohol should never be given to someone who is exhausted. The combined effect of alcohol and

TO STAY WARM, EMPLOY THE COLD PRINCIPLE:

C **Clean** clothing maintains its insulative properties better than dirty clothing.

O **Overheating** should be avoided as it produces discomfort and perspiration.

L **Layers** are the most adaptable way to dress; keep them loose and long.

D **Dry** means warm; avoid becoming wet in the snow, rain or through sweating.

exhaustion can impair liver function, resulting in a profound drop in blood sugar, failure of the body to shiver, and a rapid cooling of the core temperature. Also, just like fuel, alcohol has a very low freezing point -27°C (-17°F) for 80 proof spirits. Drinking this super-cooled liquid can result in frost burns to the lips and tongue. Worse still, a deep swig of super-cooled alcohol can prove fatal if it reaches the oesophagus at the back of the throat.

Clearly, then, good sense, caution and moderation need to be exercised when carrying alcohol in the north. And for the record: St Bernards do locate avalanche victims in Switzerland, but wisely they do *not* bring them brandy.

How we are affected by the cold

Runny nose

Every breath we take in the cold environment needs to be warmed. To achieve this, our body circulates more blood to our nostrils. The by-product of this is excess production of nasal mucus.

Manual dexterity

The critical air temperature for good manual dexterity is 12°C (54°F); for touch sensitivity it is 8°C (46°F). Hence the necessity for good handwear.

Vasoconstriction

When we begin to lose heat from our core (vital organs), our body reduces circulation to our extremities to maintain a viable core temperature. This results in pale skin, a loss of sensation and dexterity, and cold fingers and toes.

Urination

Exposure to cold causes vasoconstriction, which reduces blood flow to the skin's surface. This reduces overall blood volume. The body responds by reducing the body's fluid volume by urination.

Dehydration

Increased urination and the necessity to humidify the freeze-dried air we are breathing contribute to dehydration. Also, we tend to feel reluctant to drink frequently in the cold.

Shivering

As we become cold our body responds with the shivering reflex, which generates warmth by muscle spasms. Gentle shivering, such as that experienced while drying off after a swim, is of little concern. Severe, uncontrollable shivering is a sign of hypothermia that must not be ignored.

Acclimatisation to cold

Travelling with Inuit in the extreme north beyond the northern boundary of the forest has taught us several things about dealing with the cold. The first is that beyond the safety provided by abundant firewood they are highly dependent upon their clothing, and consequently are masters of tailoring clothing perfectly adapted to the extreme conditions of their homeland. But the most interesting thing we discovered is just how well adapted they are to the conditions. They can cope with the most astonishing cold, using their bare hands to do finer tasks than we can and for long periods, without gloves. We have watched with astonishment as men pull in fishing nets from under the ice, untangling freezing fish from the mesh with incredible dexterity. When they stop, and you would expect them to seek mitts for cold fingers, they just smile and strike a match to a cigarette.

The reason for this ability is that over many generations they have adapted to the cold climate. Tests have shown that they have warmer skin, and at temperatures of -20°C (-4°F) or colder they experience periodic flushes of cold-induced vasodilation, which supplies their extremities with warmth.

We cannot replicate this level of adaptation, which is commonly found among the First Nations of the north. However, prolonged and repeated exposure to the cold and the effects of vasoconstriction does translate into a less-pronounced cold acclimatisation. In short, the longer and more often we travel in the winter, the better we adapt to the cold.

' …The trouble with him was that he was without imagination. He was quick and alert in the things of life, but only in the things, and not in the significances. Fifty degrees below zero meant eighty-odd degrees of frost. Such fact impressed him as being cold and uncomfortable, and that was all. It did not lead him to meditate upon his frailty as a creature of temperature, and upon man's frailty in general, able only to live within certain narrow limits of heat and cold; and from there on it did not lead him to the conjectural field of immortality and man's place in the universe. Fifty degrees below zero stood for a bite of frost that hurt and that must be guarded against by the use of mittens, ear-flaps, warm moccasins, and thick socks. Fifty degrees below zero was to him just precisely fifty degrees below zero. That there should be anything more to it than that was a thought that never entered his head.'
JACK LONDON *To Build A Fire*

Teamwork and organisation

If you watch a military ski patrol setting out, you will witness the self-discipline and teamwork that make winter travel easy. The skis will be ready to go, having been correctly stowed the previous night and the appropriate wax applied early so that all is prepared for departure. At the time appointed, each member of the party will be standing by, correctly clothed and equipped, and will don their skis and depart without any waiting around for a straggler still searching for items of clothing. After five minutes of gentle skiing, with bodies warming to the journey, motherships can be removed and the party picks up the pace.

At rest halts, each man checks his neighbour for any signs of frostnip. Humour powers the team banter – a good sign of party morale and, if perhaps a voice is absent, an early warning that a team-member is struggling in some way. Like a loon on a lake, all appears smooth and graceful – the hard work hidden beneath the surface.

Winter travel demands the highest degree of organisation and teamwork. In fact, without close cooperation winter travel becomes dangerous. With many layers of clothing and several pairs of gloves to manage and keep dry, personal administration has to be of the highest order. Each member of a party needs to be constantly thinking ahead, arranging their equipment in their mind. It takes time to don winter layers, and it is incumbent upon each individual to allow sufficient time

for this to prevent other members of a party having to wait around in the cold.

When camping in the snow, it is all too easy to lose items of equipment carelessly placed on a sleeping mat or spruce boughs. It is important to develop the habit of always carefully putting away items after they have been used. Small, lightweight nylon stuff sacks can be very useful here. These can in turn be stowed in a larger storage bag with a zip closure.

When camping in company in a tent, sleeping space can be crowded, which increases the potential for items to be lost. With many layers of clothing it is inevitable that we all become clumsier. This requires everyone to be tolerant of and to care for each other. For example, if you see a drying mitt accidentally dislodged from its place on a drying rack as another member exits a cabin with a pack on, simply pick it up and replace it where it was. This simple act can prevent frostbitten fingers and even save a life.

It takes time to develop a good winter camping routine: be patient and practise.

Hygiene

One of the greatest boreal misconceptions is that bacterial infections are not an issue due to the effect of the extreme cold. This is not so. As we have already discussed, we survive in the north in the tropical microclimate provided by our clothing and shelter. This warm, moist environment provides the perfect breeding ground in which bacteria can multiply. Washing was so important to many northern populations that they employed saunas to meet their hygiene needs. On the trail, a wash with a washcloth, soap and hot water is important. We usually bathe in the evening rather than in the morning. By so doing we preserve the natural oils in our skin that help to protect us from cold injury.

If a member of our party has an open wound, it should be kept clean to reduce the chances of infection and they should refrain from cooking duties until the wound has healed. Any tools used in gralloching (disembowelling), butchering, filleting or that have had any other contact with raw meat should be cleaned before being returned to the sheath.

Injury in the cold environment

Despite what many people think, frostbite and hypothermia are not common events in the north. Certainly, no one should assume that such injuries are inevitable when travelling in remote regions. We have both been doing so in the winter for many years and neither one of us has sustained a serious cold injury. There is no secret to how to avoid such injuries: all that is required is that you understand cold, how cold injuries occur, and consciously and consistently act to prevent them. In a perverse way, heat injuries such as burns are far more common in this environment.

Hypothermia

This is the greatest threat to our health at any season, but most particularly during the winter.

The normal core temperature of a healthy human being is 37°C (98°F) with a fluctuation range of ±1.5°C (2.7°F) for men and ± 1.2°C (2.1°F) for women. When a subject's core temperature drops below this they experience cold stress and eventually hypothermia, a condition that gradually worsens and, if unchecked, will result in death.

The falling core temperature triggers a range of physiological responses with progressively more serious consequences and associated complexity of treatment. For the convenience of diagnosis and to guide the medical response to the condition, hypothermia is divided into three stages:

MILD HYPOTHERMIA   Occurs when the core temperature drops to 35–32°C (96–89.6°F).

MODERATE HYPOTHERMIA   Occurs when the core temperature drops to 32–28°C (89.6–82.4°F).

SEVERE HYPOTHERMIA   Occurs when the core temperature drops below 28°C (82.4°F). At 25°C (77°F), spontaneous ventricular fibrillation (heart fluttering) and cardiac arrest may occur. An unconscious casualty of hypothermia cannot, however, be pronounced dead until the body has returned to a normal temperature, as there have been miraculous cases recorded of people regaining consciousness.

Detecting the onset of hypothermia

In its first stages, hypothermia is relatively easy to treat. Indeed, a determined individual may be able to correct the condition alone. However, as their condition deteriorates they become progressively more helpless. Early diagnosis of hypothermia in its mild stage is therefore critical in remote wilderness. Unfortunately, while mild hypothermia is easy to treat it is notoriously difficult to recognise, often taking wilderness travellers by surprise.

Given that it is not normal to routinely carry a thermometer with which to diagnose hypothermia, we must be very alert to any physical signs that can indicate its onset. (Even medical experts can have difficulty accurately measuring the core temperature of a hypothermic casualty.)

Factors that increase the risk of hypothermia

Experience has taught us that the single most important factor in detecting the onset of hypothermia is being aware that the potential for it occuring exists or has increased. This is not as simple as recognising that it is cold, wet and windy; there are other significant factors that can predispose a member of an expedition to becoming hypothermic.

NO ONE IS IMMUNE TO HYPOTHERMIA. There are many circumstances in which it may strike:

For young, healthy soldiers, hypothermia is frequently associated with them trying to do the impossible. Determination to achieve their objective, coupled with a willingness to push themselves to the limit, can lead them to ignore the growing danger posed by worsening conditions. But we are all mortal and there comes a point when the weather becomes the greatest enemy. As Finland so ably demonstrated during the Winter War 1939–1940, the army that best handles bad weather has the tactical advantage.

For civilian adventurers, hunters and those who love fishing, fitness levels may not be ideal and they may be managing medical conditions that under normal circumstances are not an issue but that can change the dynamic of health when influenced by cold stress.

Wind, wet and cold are the classic environmental conditions that lead to hypothermia. Each is dangerous in its own right, but as they combine the risk of hypothermia increases exponentially. It is obvious that we need to ensure that our clothing and equipment is suitable to afford us the necessary protection from these elements. However, there are also internal conditions that can greatly increase our risk of hypothermia and all too often hasten the chilling of our core temperature:

DEHYDRATION Without adequate hydration, our body cannot function efficiently in cold weather.

EXHAUSTION/LACK OF FOOD Exhaustion occurs when we have burned the energy in our body. This is a very significant factor in hypothermia.

INJURY/FATIGUE Injuries greatly increase the risk of hypothermia, as does fatigue; continuous exertion

reduces even the fittest person's ability to resist cold stress. Rest is not a luxury: it is an important component of a safe and successful expedition.

Other factors that can predispose hypothermia

It is important that expedition members make the team leader aware of any medical conditions that could impair their performance in the cold. Expedition leaders should also be aware that every human is unique – we each cope with cold stress differently. Do not assume, therefore, that everyone in your party is feeling the same as you. Pay great attention to the needs of the coldest team member, for it is far preferable to function as a healthy team than as one with a casualty to care for. These are some of the things that need to be taken into account:

• Age is a very significant factor in hypothermia. The young, teenagers and older members of a team will be the most at risk.
• Previous victims of hypothermia are more prone to future cold injury.
• Health and medical conditions, such as diabetes, disfunction of the central nervous system, circulatory issues or shock following a trauma all have a bearing.
• Sobriety level must be considered. Alcohol and drugs can greatly complicate our physiological response to cold and increase our risk from hypothermia.

When working in extreme cold, all of these considerations must be taken seriously and we should always maintain a reserve of energy to allow us to respond to misfortune such as falling into water.

Behavioural symptoms of hypothermia

The earliest indications that someone is becoming hypothermic are very subtle and difficult to spot, and can vary enormously between individuals. A party leader must stay alert to uncharacteristic changes in mood, behaviour and emotion, including:

OVER-COMPENSATION A committed team member may not want to let down their teammates and could attempt to compensate for their condition; this over-compensation may be exhibited as exaggerated behaviour, or sudden short-lived bursts of activity.

INCREASED SELF-CONCERN When a party member becomes uncharacteristically irritated by events, particularly at delays and rest stops.

THE 'INVISIBLE MAN' Perhaps most alarmingly, some people simply become withdrawn. They become 'invisible', may even lag behind a party and become separated from the group in poor visibility. This indication is rarely mentioned in literature on hypothermia but from field experience we know this to be one of the most common early indications.

THE 'UMBLES' As a person cools we may see progressive deterioration in their motor functions, frequently referred to as the 'Umbles'. The stages of this are the patient:

- Mumbles
- Grumbles
- Fumbles
- Stumbles
- Tumbles

SHIVERING At 34°C (93.2°F), a mildly hypothermic casualty begins to shiver uncontrollably. This is an involuntary response by the body to raise the core temperature through muscular activity. The shivering reflex, however, may be reduced by: alcohol, drugs, low blood pressure, high altitude or even dehydration. Uncontrollable shivering must never be ignored. In the wilderness this is a warning threshold that should not be passed. Failure to take action now may prove disastrous.

Symptoms of moderate and severe hypothermia

Shivering usually ceases at around 32°C (89.6°F). When the casualty's core temperature begins to fall below this it becomes increasingly difficult to halt, as they progressively lose the ability to re-warm themselves. You can expect to see any existing symptoms worsen, although because individuals respond differently to cold it is difficult to specify with any accuracy at precisely which temperature any particular symptom will occur.

Casualties with a core temperature below 32°C (89.6°F) frequently exhibit the following:

'Uncontrollable shivering must never be ignored.'

Below Woodlore
Arctic students
practise wrapping a
hypothermic casualty
in order to prevent
further heat loss.

• Confusion.

• They may slur their speech and stagger drunkenly.

• They may fail to manage their clothing correctly
and lose important items such as gloves, further
exacerbating their cooling.

• They may become unresponsive to questioning
and even to pain stimulus.

• They may have urinated in their clothing.

Eventually they will collapse and, usually, at 30°C (86°F)
they become unconscious. They are now at severe risk
of cardiac arrest. As they cool further, vital signs become
weaker and by the time their temperature reaches
28°C (82.4°F) it may be difficult to take a pulse or detect
breathing in the casualty. However, as stated earlier,
they may be alive. Even in cardiac arrest, casualties have
survived for prolonged periods due to the protective
cooling of the brain. A casualty of hypothermia can only
be pronounced dead by a doctor after the body has been
re-warmed to >32°C (89.6°F) or above and when further
resuscitation attempts have proven fruitless.

Treatment of hypothermia in the wilderness

Hypothermia develops relatively slowly: on land,
over hours or days; in cases of immersion, between
30 minutes and several hours, depending upon the

conditions and the nature of the casualty. As their core temperature falls, hypothermia victims become progressively more vulnerable to rough handling from a would-be helper, which can trigger ventricular fibrillation and cardiac arrest. Take some moments to organise your treatment, brief your teammates and assemble the equipment you will need so as to minimise the physical handling of the casualty. These are the steps that must be taken:

1. PREVENT FURTHER HEAT LOSS

Hypothermia results from the cooling of the body's core. For this reason, the first and most important step in the treatment of any hypothermia casualty is to prevent any further loss of body warmth. This is achieved by protecting them from heat loss by convection, conduction and evaporation. If possible, they should be placed in a shelter, on an insulating surface such as spruce boughs and sleeping mats. Ideally, any wet clothing should be removed and they should be wrapped in several sleeping bags and finally in a bivvi bag or tarp that will protect the layers of insulation from moisture. Ensure that their head and neck are well insulated. If it is not practical to remove wet clothing due to the conditions, wrap them in their clothing inside a tarp to protect the insulation layers before wrapping them in sleeping bags and a bivvi bag as before.

2. PROVIDE CARDIOVASCULAR SUPPORT

Appoint a first-aid-trained member of the party to monitor the patient and ensure that the basic A, B, C aspects of life support are being monitored and maintained.

3. PROVIDE PHYSIOLOGICAL SUPPORT

Hypothermia casualties may be dehydrated and lacking in energy. If they are able to swallow freely, provide a warm sugary drink, the aim being to administer the sugar to replace energy expended shivering. (Paramedics may have the equipment to administer oxygen, warmed to 42°C/107.6°F and humidified, and warmed IV fluids.)

Absolutely no alcohol or opiates should be administered, and no smoking should be allowed anywhere near the patient.

Re-warming a hypothermia casualty in the wilderness

Careful judgement must be made with regards to re-warming a casualty in the wilderness. Re-warmed too quickly or in the wrong way, a casualty can die by sudden death resulting from ventricular fibrillation. The problem arises from 'afterdrop', a term that refers to the continued cooling of the body core that occurs for many hours after a casualty has been removed from the cold environment. Moderate and severe hypothermia casualties are usually depleted of body fluids. When placed in a warm environment the extremities vasodilate, allowing warm blood to flood to the periphery of the body. This can cause a drop in blood pressure, complicated by blood cooled at the periphery returning and further cooling the heart.

A similar situation arises when such casualties are winched from water. Once the water pressure exerted on the lower limbs and torso is no longer present, blood again floods away from the heart with similar consequences. Unwittingly, rescuers can effect the same result by massaging and manipulating the limbs of a victim.

It is always easier and preferable to re-warm a hypothermic casualty from the inside. This requires early detection of the problem, at a stage when they are still able to generate their own heat internally. This process can be supported by providing energy-rich foods or liquids. Do not allow the casualty to eat cold food or to try to melt snow in their mouth for a drink.

MILD HYPOTHERMIA

Mild hypothermic casualties who are just beginning to shiver may be able to generate sufficient warmth just by walking to the safety of a cabin or warmed tent as long as the activity is only light. First, however, they must be protected from further heat loss. Look for the root cause of their condition: do they have wet clothing etc? Try to rectify this situation, provide them with additional layers of insulation and, if they can swallow freely, an energy-rich sugary drink. Maintain a watch over them while they re-warm in a dry sleeping bag or two.

A casualty who is shivering uncontrollably should be wrapped as described earlier. They can also be provided with a mechanism for re-warming, such as a hot-water bottle wrapped in a beanie hat or a chemical heat pack in a spare sock. Care must be taken to avoid causing any burns to the casualty. Place warm items under the armpits where heat exchange is efficient. Another person can be placed in the sleeping bag with the casualty, although care must be exercised here not to increase heat loss by convection from the warm wrap. Also, the donor must be in excellent physical condition or they run the risk of becoming hypothermic also. If sledging, a sledge dog can be brushed of moisture and used as a source of warmth.

MODERATE AND SEVERE HYPOTHERMIA

At these advanced stages the risk of ventricular fibrillation is greatly increased. Casualties are usually unconscious and become very difficult to treat in the field. All of the above can be applied where the patient exhibits signs of life. Extraction by rescue services is vitally important. The patient must be kept horizontal and handled with even greater care. Never allow them to sit up until properly re-warmed.

If no signs of life can be found, check again for at least one minute for very faint vital signs. If no pulse or breathing can be detected, provide emergency breathing for three minutes, which may stimulate respiration. If breathing and pulse remain absent, CPR becomes the first-aid priority.

Freezing-cold injury: frostbite

Frostbite injury is usually very localised, occurring in the tips of fingers and toes, the nose or ears, over cheekbones and, in the case of hypothermic casualties, the genitalia. These areas of the body are vulnerable because they lack large heat-producing muscles, are frequently exposed to the cold or, as with feet, are in constant contact with a cold surface and are greatly affected by vasoconstriction. When snowmobiling we encounter white frostnips on ear tips, cheeks, nose or chin. These can be dealt with by cupping a warm hand above them. The cornea can be frostbitten if travelling fast at a low temperature, highlighting the importance of goggles.

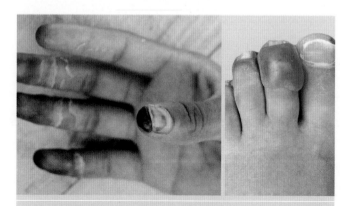

WHEN DEALING WITH FROSTBITE WE:

- **Never rub** the frozen area with snow.
- **Never rub** or massage the frozen area.
- **Never cut** away any frozen tissue.

Circumstances frequently associated with frostbite

HYPOTHERMIA Not surprisingly, hypothermia and its associated vasoconstriction is a major cause of frostbite, particularly when the casualty has been immobile for some time, for example when a passenger on a snowmobile or standing still while ice-fishing.

RESTRICTIVE CLOTHING If boots are too tight the resulting reduction in circulation frequently results in frostbite. Novices often wear too many socks in a bid to ensure they have warm feet, actually achieving the opposite result. The same holds true for tight cuffs and gloves.

HANDLING METAL WITH BARE HANDS Metal is a wonderful conductor of heat and handling it with bare hands can result in a frost injury in just a few minutes. This is particularly the case when handling brass camera bodies (see Thermal Conductivity table on page 77).

SPILLING LIQUID FUEL ON TO EXPOSED SKIN As described above, super-cooled fuels such as gasoline and methylated spirit will cause instantaneous frost injury if spilled on to bare hands.

DEHYDRATION This can play a significant role, causing a reduced supply of oxygen and fuel to muscles at the extremities.

Left The aftermath of frostbite, demonstrating the importance of not allowing the injury to occur in the first place. Blisters should not be burst and are usually an indication that there is a good chance of recovery.

Predisposition to frostbite

The greatest risk occurs among: those previously injured with frostbite; climbers at high altitude where frostbite is associated with hypoxia; smokers (nicotine causes vasoconstriction); people with the blood group O; and people from warmer latitudes.

> 'Prevention is better
> than cure.'

Symptoms of frostbite

In the worst conditions, frostbite can occur very quickly and, because when tissue freezes we lose sensation, we may not realise that we have frostbite. Fortunately, in most cases this loss of sensation is preceded by symptoms that provide us with an early warning. We should never disregard these symptoms.

When the skin surface reaches 10°C (50°F) it reddens due to a surplus of oxygen that results from the reduction in metabolism in the now-cool tissues. At this stage the affected area feels painful. This tells us to act to prevent further chilling and can be thought of as 'good pain' that must not be ignored.

If we fail to respond, at a skin temperature of 7°C (44.6°F) the pain abates and becomes numbness. This is the final warning to respond as freezing is about to begin.

As freezing occurs there is a loss of sensation. This is frequently mistaken for an improvement. As freezing continues, the depth and scale of the frost injury also increases.

Preventing frostbite

Severe frost injury can usually be prevented by early treatment. The greatest enemy is apathy; we can only re-warm the affected part by taking active steps to rectify the situation.

COLDNESS When your feet or hands begin to feel cold you should move them: wiggle your toes in your boots, your fingers in your gloves. Wave your feet and arms around vigorously to increase circulation. Jog 50m (55 yards) back and forth to generate more general body warmth. Take a warm drink from your flask and consider whether you need more clothing layers, mitts or overboots.

PAIN When localised pain is detected it is important to act immediately. Seek help from your buddy, find some shelter and examine the area in question.

If your fingertips are affected, your buddy can cup them in his or her warm hands until the pain ceases. If you have been handling metal you may have some very localised areas of frostnip, which show as small, waxy white spots. These should disappear in two or three minutes.

If your feet are affected, find an insulated place to sit down, put on your mothership jacket, brush any snow from your boot and remove it. Do not put your boot on to the ground as any moisture trapped in it will freeze, and there is normally always some moisture trapped in footwear. Instead, tuck the boot under your jacket. Your buddy should don their jacket. Your foot can now be examined and placed under your buddy's armpit for re-warming.

Follow up these treatments with a warm sugary drink and try to rectify the cause of the frostbite: loosen your boot when you put it back on, change into dry socks – do whatever is required.

NUMBNESS When you feel numbness in your toes or fingers you must act quickly. Assuming there is no freezing, the situation is still salvageable by the process outlined above. Once feeling has been restored, if you are near to a warm cabin or tent, go in and warm up your whole body, put on dry clothing, look for the cause of the problem and rest. If you are returning to the cold, ensure that you have identified the problem and taken steps to prevent it. The area affected will be more prone to freezing and will consequently need extra insulation.

Dealing with frostbite

As tissues freeze we lose the sensation of pain and numbness. Once again, though, a swift response is always preferable so that the frostbite is arrested at its superficial stage.

SUPERFICIAL FROSTBITE This is the initial stage of freezing. It is characterised by localised hard white spots on the area of skin, which can be moved in relation to the layers beneath. It is possible to move the skin over joints.

In most cases, superficial frostbite will respond to the treatment described above for numbness, although it may need the warmth from several teammates'

armpits to achieve this. However, once warm, the casualty should keep the affected area well protected from cold as these tissues will now be extremely vulnerable to further frost injury. Further frosting is highly damaging. Ideally, this casualty should remain in a warm environment, which may require their evacuation from the wilderness.

If after 15 minutes the frostbitten part cannot be warmed, the casualty should be evacuated to warm shelter where they can be for cared better. Here, with dry clothing and warm drinks, the situation may be found to improve. However, if the superficial frostbite is extensive the affected person should ideally be evacuated to a hospital. Whether they should be evacuated to a hospital or whether the frostbite should be re-warmed in the field requires a judgement call, depending on the severity of the frostbite and the overall situation.

DEEP FROSTBITE This type of frostbite penetrates into the tissues beneath the skin. The frostbitten area is hard and white, like frozen meat. The skin cannot now be moved independently of either the tissues beneath or over joints.

Deep frostbite cannot be treated on the spot. The affected part should be protected to prevent the frostbite spreading. Provide the casualty with extra clothing and a hot sugary drink and keep them under observation to ensure that they do not become hypothermic.

In a crisis, the casualty can walk on frozen feet but if they thaw they will immediately become a stretcher casualty. Thawed tissue is highly susceptible to further freezing, which would greatly complicate the injury.

Recent research indicates that less damage results from frostbite that is rapidly re-warmed in warm water rather than slowly re-warmed in warm air. Ideally, it should be thawed quickly under medical supervision. This will require the casualty to be evacuated to hospital as soon as possible. Under medical supervision, the affected part can be thawed quickly in a water bath kept at 37–39°C (98.6–102.2°F), the pain of this treatment can be managed, and infection can be prevented.

Re-warming in the field

This is exceptionally difficult and should be avoided if at all possible. This is because, once re-warmed, the victim is a stretcher casualty.

If re-warming in the field is the best option, any constricting items such as rings must be removed. The affected area will then need to be submerged in a large volume of water at 37–39°C (98.6–102.2°F). This water must be maintained at this temperature, which is difficult as the frozen limb cools the water in the same way that adding ice would. To keep the water at the correct temperature, the limb will need to be removed while fresh hot water is added and mixed. Never heat the water bath directly. Stir the water during the bath.

The pain of re-warming may be severe, but it can be managed with painkillers such as aspirin. To manage this situation usually requires a team of people with a coordinated plan. Once you embark on it you must see it through to the end. Re-warming is normally achieved in less than an hour, after which time the pain usually passes.

After re-warming

Once thawed, any frostbite injury – superficial or deep – must be carefully managed. Remember to treat the casualty as a whole: do not just focus on the affected area. Reassure them and keep them warm and well nourished. Nicotine causes vasoconstriction so smoking should be avoided as it will interfere with the healing process.

The affected area should be elevated and protected from contact that could cause irritation or injury. Sterile absorbent dressings should be placed between toes or fingers to absorb fluid. Arrange a frame to keep insulation layers from coming into contact with the affected area. Blisters may develop over all or part of the affected area – these are a good sign and should be left intact to prevent infection. Evacuation to hospital will be required at the soonest opportunity. Protect the injury from infection with gentle swabbing with disinfected lukewarm water mixed with disinfectant soap. An expedition medic might also consider management of infection with broad-spectrum antibiotics.

Non-freezing cold injury: trench foot

Trench foot is an injury usually experienced by soldiers in combat conditions that prohibit proper foot care. However, it can also be experienced by novices who are lacking the correct footwear or training while on extended wilderness trips.

Trench foot results from prolonged exposure by the feet to wet and cold, and can easily be prevented by wearing dry socks and drying footwear properly. For example, when canoeing in bad weather feet may be cold and wet all day but they can be restored at the day's end by washing, gentle massage, thorough drying, changing into dry socks and sleeping warmly.

Symptoms of trench foot

Symptoms can vary from tingling or a prickly sensation to numbness and pain. Sleep is often disrupted by these sensations and it is usually severely painful when first standing on feet in the morning. As the condition develops, feet swell and become red in colour. Blisters may also appear. Swelling can make it difficult to take off and put on boots, which is why it is not uncommon for those suffering with trench foot to leave their boots on. This can lead to the death of tissue and gangrene.

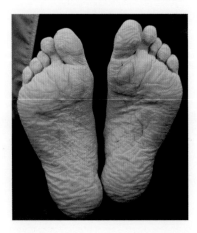

Minor trench foot that only involves skin reddening and some swelling can be treated by an improved footcare regime as described above, by elevating the feet to reduce swelling, and by keeping the patient warm. More serious trench foot will require hospital treatment and normally is associated with lasting neural damage.

Victims of trench foot tend to exhibit lasting increased sensitivity to cold injury.

Carbon-monoxide poisoning

Carbon monoxide (CO) is a poisonous gas produced when carbon compounds are burned without a sufficient supply of oxygen. Being both colourless and odourless, it is a particularly dangerous gas that acts to reduce our ability to absorb oxygen. It can be encountered when using any stove inside a tent or shelter with inadequate ventilation.

Symptoms of CO poisoning

The signs of CO poisoning are a headache, tirednesss, loss of concentration, nausea and difficulty breathing. Unchecked, the headache can become more intense and be accompanied by a feeling of general weakness, collapse and the loss of consciousness. Victims of CO poisoning frequently fall asleep under its influence and are therefore unable to help themselves. They may be identified by very red skin.

Prevention

Whenever a stove is used in a confined space, tent, shelter or cabin, there must be a good supply of air to ensure complete combustion. Some cabins may be fitted with CO alarms; these should be tested to ensure they are in working order. Generally, it is wise to be suspicious of the air supply to cabin stoves, which may

Left Feet that have been damp and cold for prolonged periods can develop trench foot. Relatively easy to prevent with proper footcare, it is a problem most often encountered by soldiers in combat when time is at a premium.

have been left unattended for long periods. Make sure there is a good supply of air: better a chilly draught of fresh air than a deadly one of warm, poisonous gas. Also, always maintain the necessary ventilation. If there is a risk of snowfall obstructing a vent then a watch system should be established to prevent this from occurring.

Treatment
Remove the casualty immediately to fresh air. Manage the airway, paying attention to the possibility that they may have vomited. If necessary, provide artificial respiration, keep the patient warm and seek medical help.

Snow blindness
This results from exposure to the bright ultraviolet rays in sunlight. In a snowy landscape these rays are reflected to a much higher degree than normal. Prevention of snowblindness is simple: wear a cap to shade the eyes and UV-protective sunglasses or snow goggles. If these are not available, the native solution of improvised goggles made from slits cut into bark or of carved wooden goggles can be used.

Symptoms occur several hours after exposure and include itching irritation and a feeling of having grit in the eyes. Treatment is to protect the eyes from further exposure to UV, if necessary covering them with a bandanna or scarf. The condition usually disappears after a couple of days.

Right In bright sunlight, the snowy landscape reflects harmful UV rays. This can lead to severe sunburn, frequently in unexpected places, such as underneath the chin and nose.

Burns
There are many factors that contribute to a higher-than-normal incidence of burns when travelling in winter. Fortunately, these are usually minor burns, but they are of course best avoided. In winter, we operate in close proximity to open fires and wood-burning stoves. Wearing many layers of clothing contributes to clumsiness and insulates us from heat as well as cold. Consequently, we may blunder into a fire or brush against a hot stove without knowing. We also lose sensation from our hands due to the effects of vasoconstriction. For this reason it is easy to pick up a fry pan or kettle without realising that it is too hot to handle until we have already become injured. Clumsiness is prevented by concentration and, when handling anything that may be hot, always using work gloves or our mitts for protection. In the tent, we usually suspend a pair of work gloves close to the stove.

Sunburn
Despite low temperatures, on bright days the ultraviolet rays bouncing off snow surfaces can cause unexpected sunburn, particularly to places that you would not expect to be affected in the summer, such as the underside of the nose, chin, lips and ears. Prevention is to use sunscreen or to cover up, as you would expect.

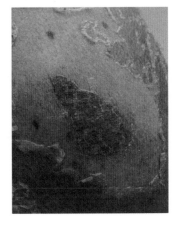

A CAUTIONARY TALE

February 1988

My ordinary job was OC of one ranger squadron, but at this specific moment I was going through a training sequence as 2iC of a ranger battalion and, as such, one of my tasks was to plan and prepare for the battalion's exfiltration from behind enemy lines to territory controlled by own forces. This was a two-week exercise and the preparations for exfiltration were to commence at the start of week two. So I left our base area with a reconnaissance party of three: myself and two troopers – despatch riders on snowmobiles. It was between 25 and 30 degrees below zero and clear skies.

I figured we needed multiple crossings over one of the major creeks in the area. The idea was to identify suitable fords and drill holes in the ice in accordance with a specific pattern in order to determine the status and thickness of the ice. In one shallow ford I drilled right in to the sandy bottom of the creek and ruined the edges of the drill – the ice in the creek was at least 70cm (27½in) thick. I figured the ice was at least as thick everywhere, but I soon got to change my mind.

At one potential crossing on a pond, like a beaver's pond but man-made, the snowdrift had created walls, almost like a tunnel, and if we lay down on our belly and crawled out to the edge we could see the surface of the ice below. My idea was initially to make a track over the snowdrift, down on the ice and up again on the other side, but I feared that the steep banks and the snowdrift would be too difficult to negotiate with the snowmobiles – though maybe with the other, heavier, oversnow vehicles (Hägglunds Bv 202). But I needed to check the ice anyway, but now my drill was ruined, so I decided to use an axe instead. I told the troopers to take cover in the treeline about a hundred metres away and start a campfire, make a brew and take something to eat.

Dressed in a snow camouflage suit over my warm jacket and uniform, with webbing and gun on top of everything and with an axe in my hand, I slid through the snow, down the bank of the creek and down on the ice surface.

There was almost no ice, less than a centimeter, and I fell straight through. A split second later I found myself standing on the floor of the creek with a clear memory of seeing the hole in the ice as a circle of daylight over my head and nothing else. My clothes were full of air and even though I was weighed down by my webkit and had my assault rifle slung over my back, I popped up like a cork.

I tried to get hold of the edge of the ice but it was too mushy and just slush. I felt how my legs were swept away by the current and I feared that the water would carry me away under the ice so that I would drown, just metres away from where I plunged though the ice, but under ice and snow. I literally fought for my life and after what felt like an eternity, during which time I was swept under the ice and managed to fight myself up again several times, I saw one of the trooper's faces over the edge of the snow. He realised immediately the situation and reached for me, the snow crumbled under him and he almost joined me in the water. But, finally, risking his own life,

he managed to get hold of me. However, soaked in water, and with snow and ice disintegrating under him, he could not pull me to safety, but called out for his partner, who came and assessed the situation. The first trooper secured me while the second rushed off to get one of the snowmobiles in position and threw down the towing line to me. With a joint effort the troopers tied a lasso, a loop, and somehow got it under my arms and managed to tow me out of the water to safe ground by the force of the snowmobile – an Ockelbo 8000 – a real workhorse.

I still remember when I stumbled in upright position, safe but soaking wet from top to toe and inside out and with a high risk of becoming hypothermic if we did not take the right decisions.

One of the troopers looked at me and said with a smile in the corner of his mouth, 'Well sir, would you like to change socks? Or should we just hit it?' We hit it, and I decided to ride on the sleigh after one of the snowmobiles instead of being towed standing on my skis, just to save time.

It was late in the afternoon and daylight started to fade and the temperature fell another few degrees, so I reckon it was colder than 30 degrees, below zero, and we had about an hour to our relatively safe base where we had warm tents. Aborting the exercise and going to the town and barracks was not an option. We had about a forty-minute ride to the camp and we stopped every few minutes so that I could get off the sleigh and run a few laps around the snowmobiles, waving my arms and stomping my feet to keep the temperature and circulation working. The ride took almost an hour and a half due to the many stops.

When we reached the safety of our camp I could not speak, nor could I use my hands and I did not feel my feet, but after changing my clothes to dry ones and quite a few cups of coffee, my spirit returned. I did not get any injuries due to the cold, no white toes and fingers, no blisters and so on, but when the temperature in my hands and feet returned the pain was terrible, mostly in the feet.

My full recovery took less than 24 hours, after which I had a nightly rendezvouz with

the CO of the regiment, who just wanted to check in on me and give the final orders for exfiltration…

When the exfiltration started everyone in the unit was on their skis, along the routes and crossings I had prepared. Suddenly one 'surprise training sequence' was activated by the exercise director – a passage through a chemical-contaminated area, in this case tear gas. Everything worked fine – protective measures were taken, clothing adjusted, specially equipped reconnaissance parties were organised and set off in advance of the units – only one thing failed: my own gasmask was frozen. I had it attached to my webbing when I was in the water and now it was useless, the filter was completely solid and the consequences of that were quite obvious; there is no dignity in crying and vomiting due to tear gas. Finally, the umpires counted me as a casualty and I was taken out of the final moments of the exercise.

By Peter Gustavsson

Basic Forest Skills

'AT ONE OF THESE CAMPSITES Ed discovered the spot where some lone traveller had camped in the previous spring. The campfire had been built small and neatly laid out in an open space among the white poplars. Across the fire the woodsman had placed a stout poplar pole, pointed at one end and thrust under a spruce root, so that the other notched end angled upward and could hold the bale of a pail or pot. Ed kindled his own campfire there, hung his tea pail on the pole, and studied the layout closely, learning a bit of woodcraft, which, with variations, he would employ ever after.'

AL KARRAS *Face the North Wind*

Previous pages The forest can seem
a forbidding place, but to those with
a few basic skills it is a great provider.

Opposite Forest life demands adaptability and the
application of a versatile skill set. Here, a Finnish
Erätoveri tarp is pitched to capture and reflect the
warmth from the campfire — a wonderful way
in which to sleep out in the early autumn.

Modern life can create great confusion and we can forget that humanity is an integral component in the natural world. Undoubtedly, we humans still have an important role to fulfil within the ecosystem of the boreal forest. When we travel in remote parts of the woods we have the opportunity to explore this relationship with nature. The first thing to understand about travel in this environment is that the forest can be your friend; it can supply you with almost everything you need for life if you learn where and how to look. The second thing is that you can be a friend to the forest; if you consider carefully the consequences of your actions, you can learn to harvest resources without causing any harm, sometimes even assisting the natural process of forest growth. Put another way, if we take care of the forest it will take care of us. All across the boreal forest the First Nations understood this and it was a guiding principle as they utilised resources to make their lives possible. Sensitive in this way to their impact on the habitat, their woodcraft enabled them to manufacture whatever they needed, relying upon their ingenuity and only the simplest tool kit. The range of things they made is truly astonishing.

Today, as we travel, we follow this same concept and learn to rely in a far smaller way upon the forest for some of our support. In so doing we obviously derive material benefit but, more importantly, we expand our knowledge of the forest and start to recognise its component parts for the allies in life that they are. In this way we begin to see the forest as our home, something to cherish and to protect.

'Har du glömt att skogen är ditt hem?'
'Have you forgotten that the forest is your home?'
BO SETTERLIND, *Swedish writer and poet*

At a purely practical level, these basic skills open the doors to a more traditional style of forest travel. They are the foundation upon which a higher level of forest bushcraft can be built

How to pitch a tarp

One of the greatest advances in forest travel is the availability of lightweight tarps. Stretched tightly between trees, they provide shelter from rain and a comfortable living space. Quickly pitching one requires the ability to manage cordage and tension cords.

How to pitch a tarp > **Hanking cord**

Hanking cord will prevent tangles from forming and facilitate easy tarp-pitching in bad weather. All cords should be protected from unravelling: those used for a tarp by having their ends heat-welded, while offcuts can be knotted as illustrated.

1 Begin hanking as shown here.

2 Keeping your hand firmly splayed open, continue hanking in a figure-eight pattern.

3 Complete the hank by wrapping it tightly with the last length of cord.

4 On the penultimate wrap, trap your thumb and pass a finishing loop through the space created. Pull the loop tight.

5 The hanked cord should not unravel. It can be undone by pulling on either end.

How to pitch a tarp > **The Evenk hitch**

1 The Evenk reindeer-herders in Siberia employ a range of quick-tie, easy-to-release knots that are ideal for use in cold weather. We use this hitch to attach a line we intend to tension firmly. Begin by taking a turn around the tree.

2 Take a turn around your fingers, maintaining a gentle pull to prevent the line from slipping off your fingers.

3 Rotate your left hand under the main line, without allowing the cord wrapped around your fingers to slip off.

4 Pinch the cord end between your index and middle fingers, then withdraw your fingers from the wrapped loop.

5 In this way you should pull a loop of the cord end through as shown. Pull the loop snug and secure.

6 Tighten the formed knot against the tree. This is a secure beginning, which can easily be released by pulling on the cord end.

1 Having secured one end of the tarp main line (see previous pages), it's time to tension the opposite end. To do this, form a small loop in the cord 60–100cm (24–40in) away from the second tree.

2 Using the free end of the cord, pass a bight of cord through the loop.

6 Maintaining the tension, take the end of the cord back around the tree.

7 Wrap the end of the cord around the main line, gaining a little more tension.

8 To tie off, pass a loop around and under the last wrap.

3 Pulling this snug will form a slip loop, as shown.

4 Without allowing the loop to collapse, pass the end of the cord around the second tree and push the end through the slip loop.

5 Pulling on the end of the cord will now gain the advantage of the loop to provide considerable tension.

9 (*Left*) Maintaining the tension by preventing any slippage at this point, complete the knot by passing a second loop through the first and pulling it tight.

10 (*Right*) The completed knot should look like this. It can be easily released by pulling on its free end when it is time to break camp.

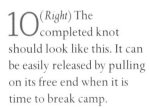

How to use a knife

The knife is the most fundamental tool for forest living – essential for safety and survival as well as craft and daily work – so much so that it is inconceivable to be without one when travelling in the forest. It must, however, be kept sharp and handled with care to prevent injury. With experience it becomes an extension of your hand, enabling the swift achievement of simple tasks or the manufacture of beautiful objects.

PASSING SAFELY

In forest life we employ a knife with a single edge, which is kept razor-sharp for safe, efficient use. Generally we never lend our knife. There is an old saying, ' Lend a knife, lose a friend', which refers to the possibility of the knife being returned damaged in some way. There will, however, inevitably be times when a sharp knife must be handed to someone else, in which case the safe way to do so is in the manner depicted here.

How to use a knife > **How to sharpen a knife**

Sharpening a knife at home is easy, with access to a work bench and large sharpening stones. In the field, we try to achieve similar results with smaller pocket stones and no bench. To do so, wearing safety gloves, take a sapling 80cm (32in) long and the same width or just a little narrower than the stone you are using.

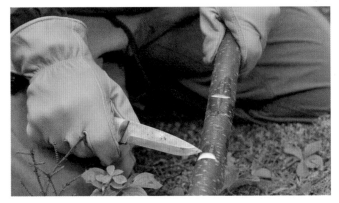

1 Place the stone one-third of the way along the length of the stick. Cut two notches about 1.25cm (½in) deep either side of the stone, so the distance between them is exactly the same as the length of the stone.

2 Cut out the wood between these notches to form a depression.

3 Smooth the wood flat using a dull knife.

4 Fit the stone into the resulting gap. You should have to push the stone so that it fits very snugly.

5 Depending upon the type of stone you are using, add water or the recommended lubricant.

6 Using a backwards-and-forwards action, sharpen both sides of the blade as necessary. If you have a combination stone, repeat the process with the fine side of the stone.

1 The forward grip is the main way in which we hold a knife. It is a very secure grasp, which provides great control of the blade and facilitates the application of great power to cuts.

2 The reverse grip is also secure but is employed less commonly since the edge is facing the user, posing a safety risk. This grip is mostly used when cutting a tensioned cord held by another person, the inherent hazard faced solely by the person wielding the knife.

3 When making a powerful cut, the free hand always grasps the wood behind the knife, with the cut being made away from the body.

4 The chest lever grip provides control of the knife angle while the power comes from the expansion of the chest. This results in a safe and very powerful, well-controlled cut.

5 The forward reinforced grip can be used to carry out fine work with great control and precision. It involves the forward grip, reinforced by the thumb of the hand holding the work piece.

6 For the reverse reinforced grip, the cut is made towards the body, the force and length of the cut being generated entirely by the fingers of the supporting hand.

Opposite Carving the tools and utensils of the trail is a traditional forest pastime that has its origins in the impoverished past of frontier communities. Today it can bring great joy to modern travellers and bushcraft enthusiasts.

How to use a knife > **Cuts**

1 The simplest way to cut a stick to length is with many small cuts made around its circumference so as to narrow the thickness.

2 The stick can now easily be broken by hand. Although not elegant, it represents an important principle. When using a knife, control is achieved by the use of many small cuts rather than one big one. Control = Safety.

3 The shaving cut relies upon the hand to control the cutting angle while the power is generated using either the back and a straight arm or, once the cutter is more experienced, the arm muscles. The cut is best when a thin shaving is removed, and astonishing control can be achieved once it is mastered.

7 Making three clean cuts is the efficient way to create a point.

8 Cutting a sapling is best done by first tensioning the wood fibres.

9 Angle the cut steeply into the sapling. There is a natural tendency to make this cut at too shallow an angle.

4 Pointing requires a power cut. Force is applied to the work piece with the point of the blade slightly raised to allow for a slicing action. This cut will require a safe follow-through.

5 As the energy releases from this cut, the completion is very swift, reiterating the need for a safe area for the follow-through.

6 The cut is repeated twice more to create a point.

10 (Left) Cut with power and follow through. Done correctly, one cut will be all that is needed.

11 (Right) The combination of a sharp blade and good technique epitomises the skills of bushcraft.

How to use a knife > **With baton**

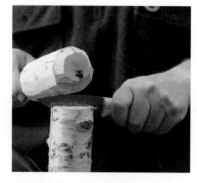

1 If you have no saw or axe with you, a strong full-tang knife can be put to tasks requiring power with the aid of a baton. Never risk breaking the blade; many small cuts will achieve the task without risk of injury or damage to your blade. If your knife has a narrow-tang design, the use of a baton is not recommended.

2 Wood can be split with the use of a baton or, as we prefer, the split can be established with the knife.

3 The split should then be completed with the use of a wedge – a more efficient and intelligent method than using the knife alone.

How to use a knife > **Draw knife**

1 The small knife can be transformed into an incredibly useful draw knife.

2 To hold the work piece, create a vice with a split sapling and a windlass for tightening the vice.

3 By grasping the knife tip in a split stick you create a draw knife.

How to use a knife > **Notch-cutting**

1 To cut a hooked notch, begin by making two crossed stop cuts.

2 Cut upwards to the cuts to form the notch.

3 (*Left*) Carefully tidy up the tip of the notch cut.

4 (*Above*) The completed notch cut in profile. Simple and efficient, this cut has many applications.

How to use an axe

> How to sharpen an axe

Below Where possible, sharpen the axe supported on the ground and held as shown here.

1 A small file is the prime axe-sharpening tool. When it is needed, fit it with a handle cut from a piece of firewood. An oversized handle such as this will greatly reduce the risk of an accident while sharpening the axe head.

5 Filing can be the only method of sharpening, but if you have a stone with you for knife-sharpening, some modern steels will respond very favourably to honing.

2 Elevate the blade edge to a convenient sharpening angle by wedging it with a small stone or piece of wood.

3 Sharpen by filing towards the edge. Never drag the file backwards as this will dull the file.

4 Always sharpen to maintain the overall cutting angle. If you just concentrate on the very edge, the axe will change in performance as the edge angle becomes increasingly obtuse.

6 The stone is used in a similar way to the file, although with a circular action.

7 Again, hone all of the angle, not just the very edge.

8 Test the edge with your thumb pad for sharpness. Clean the edge after sharpening it.

How to use an axe

> Splitting down small firewood

1 This is the safest way to split down small firewood. Hold the axe and firewood together and drop them on to a splitting surface.

2 No force should be necessary; the weight of the axe coupled with its momentum will complete the task.

> Splitting wood for a stove

Above When splitting wood for a stove, saw the wood into suitable lengths that are, where possible, free from knots. Stand with your heels in line with the face of the log. Split the log using a swift follow-through cut. This method requires no chopping block and is particularly useful when splitting on snow.

> Hewing and truncating wood

Above When hewing and truncating wood, keep your supporting hand well outside the arc of the cut. If cutting an angle, cut vertically and angle the wood rather than the axe. This is far safer than making an angled cut, which is prone to glancing and inaccuracy.

> Classic splitting

Below Classic splitting on a chopping block is achieved with a flick of the wrist timed to coincide with the edge striking the log. The axe recoils from the log, does not contact the chopping block and the splitting force does its work. This skilful technique places less stress on both the axe and the person splitting. **Note:** with a short cutting block it is safer to work kneeling down.

How to use an axe > **Limbing**

1 (*Left*) Small branches can be trimmed away with one swift cut. Always ensure that the trunk is between the cutter and the axe, and that toes are well out of the way.

2 (*Right*) Thicker limbs will require a different approach. Begin with a normal limbing stroke.

3 Next, cut at 90 degrees to the first cut.

4 Now the limb has been reduced in thickness and should be prepared with a platform of foliage for the third cut.

5 Complete the cut using a normal follow-through limbing stroke at the narrowed point of the branch.

It is sometimes necessary to truncate a felled or wind-blown tree. This is best achieved with a full-size axe rather than the smaller trail axe we usually carry. However, sometimes we must make do with the tools we have.

1, 2, 3 Chopping through a thick log is usually carried out standing atop the log to be cut.

4, 5 We favour ambidextrous changing grip when changing the direction of cut. This places even strain on the muscles used and is better for the back than a back-winding backhand stroke with a forehand grip.

6 Cut the notch so that it is at least as wide as the log is thick. With a correctly set-up axe, the chips will fly.

7, 8 Use the weight of the axe to do the work, use your strength to guide the accuracy of the cut. When you have cut halfway through the log, turn around and cut in the same way from the reverse side.

How to use a saw

The saw is the least-regarded cutting tool, yet it has much to recommend it: it is the easiest cutting tool to learn to use; it can be employed safely even in poor light; and, moreover, the saw provides a clean, tidy cut, which is very advantageous when firewood is to be cut and split to fit a wood-burning stove.

1 Place your arm through the saw bow when establishing a cut. This is so that there is no possibility of the blade jumping out of the cut and lacerating the back of the supporting hand.

2 Once the cut is established and is deeper than the blade is thick, a thumb can be placed over the cut to prevent the saw blade from jumping out.

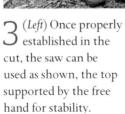

3 (*Left*) Once properly established in the cut, the saw can be used as shown, the top supported by the free hand for stability.

4 (*Above*) Small-diameter wood for a stove can be cut to convenient lengths in the manner portrayed.

How to suspend a cooking pot

Suspending a pot for cooking is a task that we may have to perform more than once each day, and there is something elegantly symbolic about this absolutely practical skill. Inevitably, we shall need several techniques at our disposal to suit a wide variety of circumstances.

Below Illustrations from the height of the fur trade depict billycans swung from tripods of canoe paddles. This was because, perhaps due to the heavy traffic of the fur-company canoe brigades, the campsites at this time had become denuded of convenient alternative materials. Without doubt, this method is a risky proposition that could harm the paddles, though it does demonstrate the adaptability and improvisational skills of the voyagers.

How to suspend a cooking pot > **Green-wood tripod**

Above For a speedy lunchtime brew, a pot can be elevated atop three thumb-thick sticks of green (living) wood and a quick, hot fire of feathers and splints kindled beneath. Done correctly, the pot boils before the green sticks burn.

How to suspend a cooking pot > **Support-stick method**

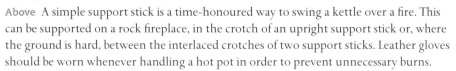

Above A simple support stick is a time-honoured way to swing a kettle over a fire. This can be supported on a rock fireplace, in the crotch of an upright support stick or, where the ground is hard, between the interlaced crotches of two support sticks. Leather gloves should be worn whenever handling a hot pot in order to prevent unnecessary burns.

How to suspend a cooking pot > **The collapsible pot hanger**

Any straight stick can be used to support a kettle, even dead wood, since using a pot hanger means the stick is sufficiently high and far enough away from the fire that it won't burn. A hook can be fashioned to fit conveniently inside a kettle and carried for many seasons.

1 The collapsible pot hanger can be carried for continual use, and can be fashioned to conveniently fit inside a kettle. To make one, locate two similarly sized crotched hardwood sticks.

2 Clean off the bark from the sticks and tidy up their shape.

3 Carve in the locking catch as shown and fashion a locking cross peg, as shown.

4 When fitted together, the pot hanger has two opposing hooks.

How to suspend a cooking pot > **The tripod**

An ancient method of hanging a pot, the tripod is perfect for use on rocky ground or in deep snow. Begin with three long spires. These can be of green wood or dead wood so long as it retains its strength.

1 Tie the three sticks at chest height with a withe and a clove hitch. Form the withe from a branch with a suitable crotch for use as a hook.

2 Splay the tripod out and loop the hook end of the withe over the apex of the tripod to lock it tight.

3 The pot can now be suspended at various heights by raising or lowering the tripod.

4 (*Left*) In windy conditions, a fourth spire can be added on the windward side and a windbreak fashioned from a suitable piece of fabric.

5 (*Below*) To cook for larger groups, the tripod can be enlarged with a ridgepole and bipod arrangement, as shown. From this, multiple pots can be suspended over a longer fire.

How to tie knots

Our outdoors lives are bound in fibres, threads, strings, cords, lines and ropes. They unite us with our outfit, keep our canoe fast to the shore, and in times of danger we fasten our lives to them. Knowing how to tie knots to serve a wide variety of tasks is the most fundamental knowledge in bushcraft.

How to tie knots > **Overhand knot**

1 The overhand knot is where knot-tying begins. A simple, elegant knot, it can be used to stop cord unravelling or as a way to prevent a lace pulling through an eyelet. It is also the genesis of a range of other useful knots. This picture shows how it looks when it is open, to reveal its formation.

2 This is how it looks when it is closed, as it is when in use.

> **Honda knot**

1 Two overhand knots comprise the beginning of the honda knot used by cowboys to form the loop in the end of their lariats.

2 Tighten the end knot.

3 Pass the tightened knot through the knot that remains open.

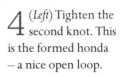

4 (*Left*) Tighten the second knot. This is the formed honda – a nice open loop.

5 (*Right*) Pass the free end through the loop. Here we have an improvised lasso or knot for an emergency snare.

How to tie knots > **Fisherman's eye**

1 The fisherman's eye is a simple knot that can be used to fashion a loop in the end of a cord. Begin with an overhand knot with a loop on one side.

2 Tie an overhand knot in the free end, encompassing the main part of the cord.

3 Carefully tightened, a strong loop is now formed, which requires little cord.

How to tie knots > **Fisherman's knot**

1 The fisherman's knot is a simple method of joining two cords of the same diameter. Tie an overhand knot in the end of each cord, encompassing the opposing cord.

2 Tightened, each overhand knot jams against its neighbour.

How to tie knots > **Double fisherman's knot**

1 The double fisherman's knot is vastly superior to the single fisherman's knot and is only a little more complicated, involving tying two fisherman's knots, as shown.

2 Tightened, the double fisherman's knot is very secure and is well suited to more serious usage, such as rescue situations for making strops, prussik loops and joining ropes.

How to tie knots > **Figure-eight bend**

1 The figure-eight bend is used to join cords or tapes of the same diameter. Tie one figure-eight knot at the end of one cord, then simply follow it back with the end of the opposing rope.

2 The figure of eight loop is an important knot for safety and rescue. It is this knot that is most often used to secure a rope to a harness, belay or karabiner.

How to tie knots > **Clove hitch**

> **Slippery clove hitch**

1 The clove hitch is a simple beginning for many lashings, and is secure and easy to undo. Form two loops and cross them.

2 Pass the spar through the loops and pull tight.

3 The clove hitch can be made into a quick-release 'slippery clove hitch' by forming it with a loop, as here.

How to tie knots > **Round turn and two half hitches**

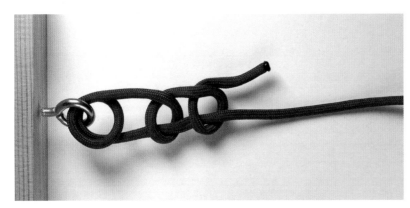

1 The round turn and two half hitches is a secure means of securing a line and can be tied while under load. Passing the end through the hook or around the post twice takes the strain while you form the knot, while the half hitches lock the end.

2 Pull tight to complete the knot.

How to tie knots > **Constrictor hitch**

1 (*Left*) The constrictor hitch is a modified clove hitch. It binds down upon itself, making it resistant to working or vibrating loose, particularly when soft cord is used to bind to hard surfaces or hard cord to soft materials. This method of tying enables the hitch to be passed over the end of the post. First, form a loop.

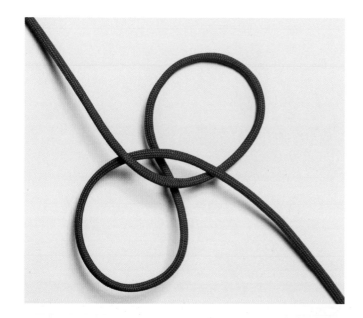

2 (*Right*) Reach under the bottom end and twist the loop again into the figure-eight shape.

3 Bring the ends together and pass the post through the loop.

4 Turn the hitch around to see how it binds down upon itself.

How to tie knots > **Bowline**

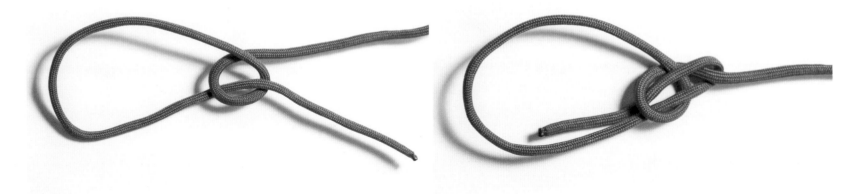

Above The bowline can be quickly tied. It has been used for safety and rescue, often used to secure a person to the end of a rope, as the loop will not slip closed, tightening on the person secured within it.

How to tie knots > **Timber hitch**

1 The timber hitch is a quickly tied hitch that relies upon friction and loading to remain fast. Form it as shown here.

2 Tightened, it can be used to begin lashings and was once used to haul logs by horse.

How to tie knots > **Sheet bend**

1 The sheet bend is a strong knot frequently used to attach ropes of differing diameters to an eyelet or to attach a line to the corner of a cloth sheet, sail or tarp. It is a simple knot to form, as shown here.

2 Pull tight to complete the knot.

How to tie knots > **Slippery sheet bend**

1 The slippery sheet bend is an exceptional knot for joining extensions to tarp guy lines. It is formed in the same way as the sheet bend, except with a release loop.

2 As its name suggests, this knot is a quick-release version of the sheet bend. To release it, simply pull on the short end.

How to tie knots > **Double sheet bend**

> **Sheet bend for hauling**

1 The double sheet bend is more secure than the single sheet bend, incorporating an extra loop, as shown.

2 Tightened, this bend is also resistant to flapping in the wind.

1 The single sheet bend can be modified to facilitate hauling of a heavy line over a branch with a light line. The end is tucked back down as shown to present a more streamlined knot that is less prone to snagging.

How to tie knots > **Slippery adjustable knot**

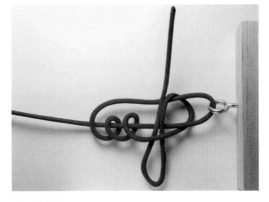

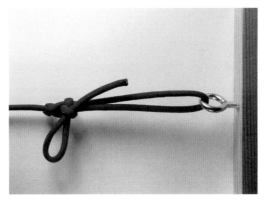

1 The slippery adjustable knot is a quick-release knot that we use to form adjustable guy lines. The initial turns will provide a non-slip purchase on the main line.

2 Build in a release loop.

3 Tighten to secure. When using slippery cords, extra turns may be needed.

How to tie knots > **Half blood knot**

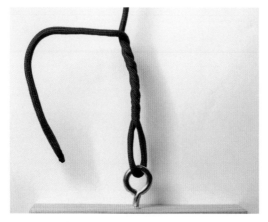  

1 The half blood knot is our most frequently used fishing knot. It is tied by first creating six turns around the main line.

2 The end is then passed through the eye formed by the twisting.

3 It must be carefully tightened. When using monofilament line, wet the line prior to tightening.

How to tie knots > **Vice versa knot**

  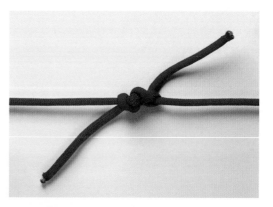

1 The vice versa knot is excellent for joining the ends of elastic shock cord, particularly when repairing shock cord inside tent poles.

2 It is a very simple knot that is not as complicated as it first appears.

3 Tighten the knot well to prevent it becoming loose.

How to make a withe

Withes were once very widely employed in the boreal forest. They are formed from flexible branches of conifer and hardwood trees, which are twisted to loosen the fibres and increase their suppleness. They are immensely strong and can be tied securely; the woodsman's alternative to wire.

1 Begin by choosing a young shoot or branch. In winter, birch is a reliable choice. Remove all the side shoots, being careful not to cut into the main stem.

2 Twist the shoot from its tip, gradually working down to the shoot's base. Hold the shoot so that it provides leverage in the twisting.

3 Do not over-twist the fibres or they will break; just twist sufficiently to loosen them. Once twisted, cut the shoot cleanly at its base.

How to make a spoon

One of the great joys of forest travel is the abundance of available wood. From this, we can fashion many of the tools we need for life. This sort of craftwork has long been central to forest life. More than just a practical skill, spoon-carving requires strength and hand-eye coordination, and involves the use of the axe for roughing out and fine shaping. It also develops knife skills, with straight, inside, outside, concave and convex cuts all being employed, and teaches an understanding of the grain structure of wood. With practice, very beautiful objects can be fashioned and carving becomes a satisfying form of self-expression.

The basic spoon shape

1 Choose a piece of green wood with a suitable spoon-like bend. Slit it into two halves.
2 Using your axe, remove the bark and square off the wood.
3 Rough out the spoon's outline.
4 Rough out the spoon's profile.
5 Aim to achieve symmetry early in the roughing stage.
6 Alternate your shaping between the outline and the profile, working always on the dimension that least resembles the finished spoon.

7 With most of the shaping completed with the axe, switch to using a knife for the final shaping and fine detail.

8 Holding up the spoon to the sky will create a silhouette view that makes it easier to detect poor symmetry.

9 Carve clean cuts; try to avoid hesitant, furry carving.

10 Do not overwork the neck of the spoon. All cuts here must be carefully considered.

11 Try to carve slowly and with maximum control, holding both knife and spoon firmly.

12 Final cuts should be very clean to negate the need for sanding. If necessary, resharpen your knife before you do any final tidying.

13 The bowl of the spoon is best carved with a spoon knife or crooked knife. The final shaping is to blend in the edge to the hollowed bowl.

14 The finished spoon. Once dry, the wood can be sanded, decorated and oiled with non-toxic drying oil, such as walnut oil.

Shaping the spoon

How to dry clothing

Inevitably, our boots and clothing will at some point become soaked, or we will wash our clothes, or rinse them out after a long, hot day's travel. Drying clothes can be difficult in bad weather or when rest time is short, occasions when having drying skills will make an especially big difference to your overall comfort.

Below Improvised pegs made early in a trip can be carried throughout a journey and discarded at the end. These simple tools make drying clothes on a line far more efficient.

Right In bad weather, clothes can be dried on an improvised frame constructed from willow shoots placed over a bed of embers. Turn the clothes frequently, maintaining close supervision. Do not place the frame over a fire with flames or the clothes will scorch and burn.

Left and right The humble clothes peg makes drying clothes on a line far more efficient. It provides security and the possibility of properly opening up clothes to dry after a hard day's paddling.

How to dry clothing > **Boots**

Above At the end of a day canoeing with wet feet, even fast-drying footwear should be hung in sunlight.

Above An old beer can fitted with a tea-light candle can speed boot-drying by creating a warming updraft, although care must be exercised not to overheat the boot. If necessary, reduce the wick's length.

Above This is the old way to dry boots. Opened up to allow moist air to escape from their insides, the boots are suspended high in warm air but well away from the harmful heat of the fire, which can crack leather.

USING NEWSPAPER TO DRY BOOTS

When it is available, newspaper can be stuffed into wet boots to blot up excess moisture. In days gone by, oats and other dried grains were sometimes used for this purpose.

Remove insoles, open up the lacing and place boots in sunlight where there is a breeze. After an hour, remove the paper and change it if possible, or simply leave the boots in a warm, dry location.

Navigation

'WHEN I WAS A BOY my father was my compass,
I followed him. But now I am older I am the compass.'

SERGEI FOFONOFF *Skolt Sami, Finland*

Even for experienced boreal travellers, the vastness of the northern forest is difficult to comprehend. Without a man-made structure of any size to provide a contrast, the expansive evergreen canopy rolls onwards to the horizon in all directions. If we could see out the whole time it would feel like traversing an arboreus ocean, but such open vistas are rare. At best, lake travel by canoe provides some sense of scale; on the scant occasions when we are able to elevate our point of view in a floatplane, we gain little more in terms of perspective. Floatplanes fly at relatively low altitude, from where all that can be seen is the forest and lakes rolling on seemingly endlessly, like a great sleeping giant.

Navigation in any forest environment is challenging; the lack of visibility hinders our ability to read the landscape. In many ways the process is akin to navigating at night or in fog. With progress obstructed by vegetation, rocky ground or swamps it is very easy to lose one's sense of direction and become turned-around. In winter, travel is somewhat easier in the forest as many summer obstacles such as lakes and swamps, can be traversed on skis, snowshoes or by snowmobile. That said, with snow covering the ground and the presence of ice, it takes experienced eyes to differentiate between river, swamp and lake. Extra care must be taken to watch the terrain, as the topographic survey maps we depend upon for route-finding do not record exactly where ice forms thinly or remains open during the winter.

Local knowledge is always essential. In preparation for travelling in the forest, we always seek native advice and mark up our maps accordingly. Indigenous people largely navigate by their knowledge of the ground, gleaned by travelling over it since childhood. From experience, they not only know where there are dangers but can also point out places where it is easy to become confused and the key landmarks that will keep a person on the right course.

One of the saddest tales of boreal exploration is fatefully bound to a navigational error. On 15 July 1903, Leonidas Hubbard led a small expedition into a region of

Above It's important to understand how other professional navigators work in the boreal forest. Floatplane pilots, for instance, prefer to use the names of lakes rather than grid references.

Opposite Dense forest is a challenging environment to navigate through at the best of times, but when it is covered in snow the whole process becomes even more taxing.

Previous pages The vastness of the unpopulated regions of the boreal forest means that it is possible to become lost for many months. Navigation is a critical skill in order to be able to explore this beautiful forest.

Labrador, which at that time was uncharted. Mistaking the Susan Brook for the Naskaupi River he took his party on, even when the river they were travelling clearly failed to match the description given by local inhabitants. He was not the first or the last navigator to push on regardless of better judgement, but for him, failure to identify the correct river would have fatal consequences. On 15 September, after months of arduous travel and with their supplies all but consumed, the exhausted party turned back. The return journey is one of the epic tragedies of northern exploration. Eventually, despite his determination to reach home, Hubbard, unable to go further, perished from the combined effects of starvation, exhaustion and cold, on or around 19 October. The expedition remains a salutary reminder to all wilderness navigators of the importance of good navigation and of the role that sound judgement must play in the process of route-finding.

Today, navigation is easier than ever before. We have excellent topographical maps and many fancy navigational tools. Hand-held devices can receive signals from satellites that enable us to locate our position on the Earth's surface to within a few centimetres. There is little excuse to be lost, you might say. Yet, despite these advances, people do still lose their way. We are constantly surprised by how many travellers have only a cursory understanding of navigation, or no skill at all. But make no mistake: navigation is the most vital and fundamental skill for safe wilderness travel. It is also a highly enjoyable and rewarding process.

Above Canoeists study maps one morning prior to departure. Every member of a party should be engaged in the navigation process – aware of where they have been, where they are and where they are going. Anticipation is the secret to good navigation.

Right A map and a compass are the woodman's friends, keys that unlock the wonders to be found in wild country.

Out On The Land

Below

1 The parallel red lines inside the compass housing are called orienting lines.

2 The compass needle's red end points to magnetic north.

3 Here, the orange orienting arrow is aligned with the compass needle. The black needle is a specialised feature for measuring the angle of a slope.

Right

A magnifying glass built into the compass base is a real advantage when you are reading fine detail.

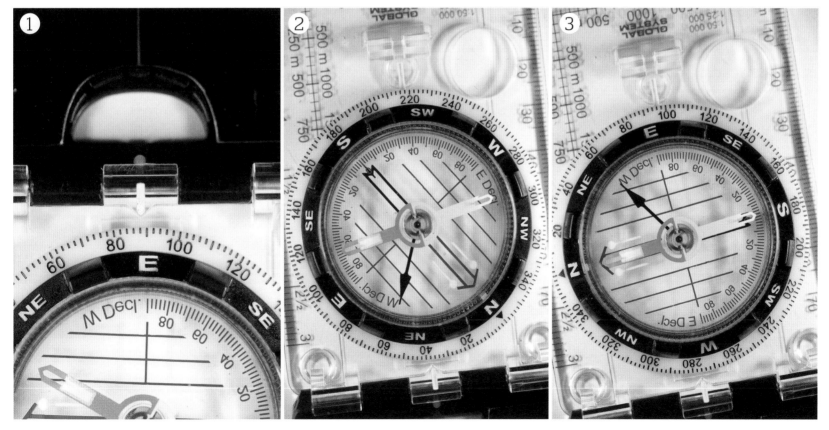

How to be a good navigator

No doubt there will be further technological advances in navigation equipment. For us, however, the elegantly simple map and compass are still the master tools, being quick to use, requiring no battery power and encouraging an expansive view of the landscape.

Of the two tools, the more important is the compass, for with this ancient wonder you can create a map. At dusk, in the long shadows of the forest, the compass needle is indeed our best friend, providing a bearing that will return us to our campsite, our outfit and our grub.

So important is this tool that we carry two. One, small, is always around our neck with other essential tools; the other, in our top pocket, is our main compass for navigation, our personal key to unlocking the wilderness.

Navigation, though, is not just about gadgets. Being a competent navigator requires attention to detail, and the ability to think ahead, remember landscapes and features, and adapt to changing conditions. The following scenario illustrates the case in point. After travelling by canoe at a steady pace all day, we round a point into driving wind and find that, mysteriously, the landscape has become larger than the map suggests it should be. We can't have overshot the campsite we are heading to, but surely we should have reached it by now. Yes, it is windy, but we are paddling hard and fast, aren't we? Despite these misgivings, we need to trust our navigational skills – we seem to be in the wrong place simply because we have misjudged the strength of the wind and just how much it has slowed our pace.

Below left A miniature compass carried around the neck at all times can prove incredibly useful.

Below middle Illuminated, having been charged with light from a flash light, the base plate can easily be read in darkness.

Below Any small compass can be held in this way during use, the point at which the index fingers meet being used as a reference marker.

A competent navigator must remain mindful of the constantly changing circumstances of travel, wind, current, fatigue, injury and so forth. There can also be places where a high concentration of magnetic iron ore can interfere with your otherwise reliable compass. Such spots are not uncommon in the boreal landscape but are only rarely marked on topographic maps. Once again, local knowledge is the key, and it is especially important to make enquiries if you know the area to have been a centre of mining operations. When traversing this sort of terrain, a satellite-navigation device is a real help, although natural signs of direction can equally be called on to provide a check on direction.

Above A good navigator is always looking for indications of direction in the landscape. Wood-ant nests are usually found on the south side of tree trunks.

Left The compass shows the tree is north of the ants' nest.

Right In the boreal forest, pine-tree branches reach out most horizontally to the south side of the tree.

Deep in the forest we may have to navigate by dead reckoning, travelling on compass bearings and counting our paces to establish the distance covered. This is a reliable method of navigation but requires much practice to master.

Navigation is a subject that truly embodies the notion of the journey being more important than the destination, requiring us to break down any journey into multiple small legs and move from one waypoint to another. Particularly when travelling in winter, when the warmth at the journey's end may call to chilling limbs, it is important to remain focused on one leg of the journey at a time. It is all too easy to become blinded by desire to reach the destination and to make a costly mistake, such as driving a snowmobile over a precipice that is hard to see when hidden by deep snow and difficult to spot on a snow-covered map.

For this reason, we always study our maps carefully before and during our journeys, visualising our route for the coming day, noting hazards, places of interest, potential campsites and key waypoints. We also record information on the map, such as details of the portage trails, rapids and campsites, for future use. To date there is no digital alternative to this process; most satellite-navigation devices with a map display provide only an unsatisfactory keyhole perspective of the landscape.

Below left To take a bearing from a map, line up two points that you wish to travel between, with the direction-of-travel arrow, or in this case the compass mirror, pointing in the direction in which you intend to travel.

Below right Turn the compass housing so that the orienting arrow is pointing to the north of the map and the orienting lines are exactly parallel to the grid lines that run north–south.

In short, the good navigator is always thinking ahead, pays attention to the landscape and relies on many sources for direction, including natural indications. For example, as a competent navigator flies into a lake in a floatplane he can look out at the trees below and by their shadow and the time of day establish the direction in which the plane is flying. For he knows that at local noon the sun will be due south of his position, and that every hour the sun moves 15 degrees across the sky. Looking at his watch, he sees that the time is just on 10am. The sun will therefore be 30 degrees east of due south and consequently the shadows below will be 30 degrees west of north. With this simple information he can establish a rough bearing for the direction in which his plane is flying.

Knowing how to navigate with a map, compass and watch is therefore the most fundamental skill for wilderness travel. Our main navigation compass is a baseplate model. This incorporates a compass needle with a protractor for measuring the angles we use in navigation and to transfer those angles – known as bearings – from the land to the map or the map to the land.

Bearings

Bearings are simply angles measured from a north/south line technically called a meridian. On your map, each of the vertical grid lines is a meridian from which we can measure our bearings. On the land, our compass needle provides a meridian.

How to use a compass

1 To take a bearing that will enable you to travel from point A to point B using a map and a compass, position the compass on the map so that the edge is along the desired line of travel.

2 Turn the dial until the meridian/orienting lines on the transparent bottom are parallel with the north/south grid lines/meridian map lines. The north orienting arrow always points north on the map. Now the magnetic declination can be added or subtracted as necessary.

3 Remove the compass from the map (holding it at chest height and arm's length) and, without changing the dial setting, turn the compass and the alignment of your entire body until the magnetic needle is parallel with the north/south lines and the red magnetic arrow end is pointing in the same direction as the north orienting arrow.

Note: It is important to hold the compass at chest height, an arm's length away from your body. This is to avoid possible interference from metal (a knife or an axe you may be carrying), or magnetic disturbances. If the compass is too close to interference it will not give an accurate reading and the arrows will spin. The same will happen if two compasses are too close together.

How to take a bearing from a map

1 Make an estimation of the angle you are about to measure. For example, is it less than 90 degrees and greater than 45 degrees? If when you use your compass you achieve a reading outside these parameters then you should check to see if you have made a mistake. It is good practice to get into the habit of thinking one step ahead in order to identify errors early on.

2 Place the edge of the compass baseplate so that it connects the points you wish to navigate between and the direction of travel arrow is pointing in the direction in which you will be travelling.

3 Rotate the bezel until the orienting/meridian lines in the housing are parallel to a north/south grid line, with the orienting arrow pointing to north on your map.

4 You can now read the bearing from the index mark.

How to follow a bearing

1 To employ this bearing, keep the compass in front of you with the direction of travel arrow pointing straight ahead.

2 Now turn your whole body until the north end of the compass needle is aligned with the north end of the orienting arrow. Look ahead for an object in the landscape.

3 Travel to that object and repeat this process using a new object/waypoint, and repeat until you reach your destination. Do not travel while watching your compass.

Note: When walking, we turn our map to north and hold the map with our thumb positioned to where we are located on the map. This makes it easier to find the position while following the direction of travel.

Above left When navigating, keep your compass lined up as shown, using your thumb to keep it steady so that it's easy to orient the map to the land features.

Above right Sighting along the bearing indicated by the compass. Hold the compass with your arm outstretched for the greatest accuracy.

How to take a bearing on land

1 Hold the compass at chest height, an arm's length away from your body. Look for a fixed point in the distance to head to and use the compass mirror to simultaneously view the target and the compass capsule.

2 Keeping the compass in front of you with the direction of travel arrow pointing ahead, rotate your body until you are facing your destination or the feature you wish to take a bearing to.

3 Make a rough estimate of the bearing from magnetic north, as indicated by your compass needle.

4 Now measure the angle accurately by rotating the bezel until the north end of the orienting arrow is aligned with the north end of your compass needle. Check this is within the parameter of your estimated bearing. Any large difference may indicate you have made a mistake.

5 To use this bearing on the map, place the edge of your compass baseplate on your position on the map and rotate the whole compass around this point, like the hand of a watch, until the orienting lines/meridian lines align with the north/south grid lines, with the orienting arrow pointing to the north of your map. The object you have taken a bearing on should be found along the edge of your compass.

Magnetic declination

There is only one slight complication when using a compass, but it is very easy to deal with. Strange as it may seem, more than one north is used in navigation. These are:

Magnetic north This is the north that our compass needle points to. All the bearings we take using our compass needle in the forest use this north. To differentiate them from other bearings, they are called 'magnetic bearings'.

Grid north This is a north of convenience chosen by cartographers to facilitate map-making. All the bearings we take from our topographic survey map use this north. To differentiate them from other bearings, they are called 'grid bearings'.

True north This is the celestial north we call true north. When we look into the night sky in the boreal forest we can locate Polaris, the North Star. This, to all practical purposes, indicates true north. To differentiate bearings taken using this north from other bearings, they are called 'true bearings'.

Above The North Star can be located in the sky using the Plough, or as here the large W-shaped constellation Cassiopeia. To use Cassiopeia we use only the left V in the W; imagine a base line connecting the widest stars in this part of the constellation, now picture a line passing from the remaining star through the mid point of our imaginary base line and continuing onwards across the sky. This line will lead to the bright North Star Polaris, which can be used as a guide to true North.

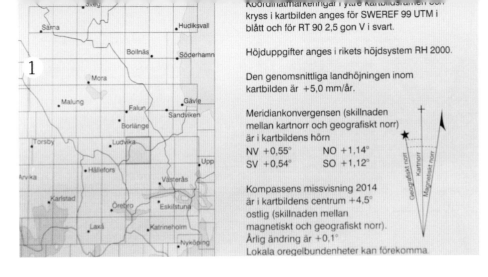

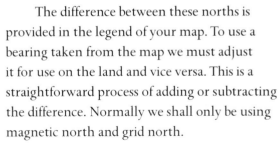

The difference between these norths is provided in the legend of your map. To use a bearing taken from the map we must adjust it for use on the land and vice versa. This is a straightforward process of adding or subtracting the difference. Normally we shall only be using magnetic north and grid north.

The difference between magnetic north and grid north is called by several names: grid magnetic angle (GMA), magnetic declination or sometimes magnetic variation. We shall use the term 'declination', as this will be found marked on your compass as 'Decl.'.

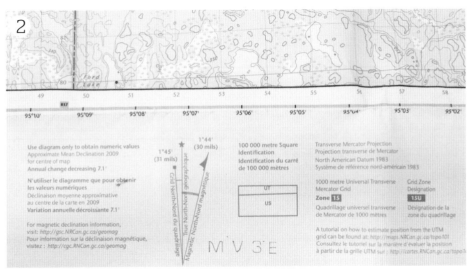

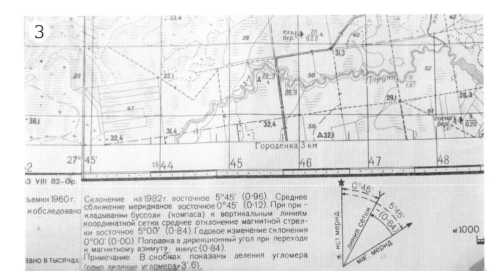

Left Here are examples of how magnetic declination is indicated on three different maps. It is important to be able to locate this information on maps that are unfamiliar to you.

1 Swedish.
2 Canadian.
3 Estonian.

How to calculate declination Consider if you will whether a bearing taken from your map needs to be enlarged or reduced for use with your compass if magnetic north is east or west of grid north.

Mag N West

When magnetic north is east of grid north:
GRID to MAG subtract Decl.
MAG to GRID add Decl.

Mag N East

When magnetic north (MAG) is west of grid north (GRID):
GRID to MAG add Decl.
MAG to GRID subtract Decl.

In some parts of the boreal forest the declination will be so small – perhaps 1–2 degrees – as to be practically insignificant for all but surveyors' needs. In other parts, however, it can be so great as 20 degrees, in which case it is impossible to navigate without making

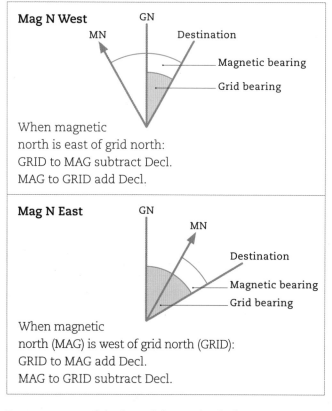

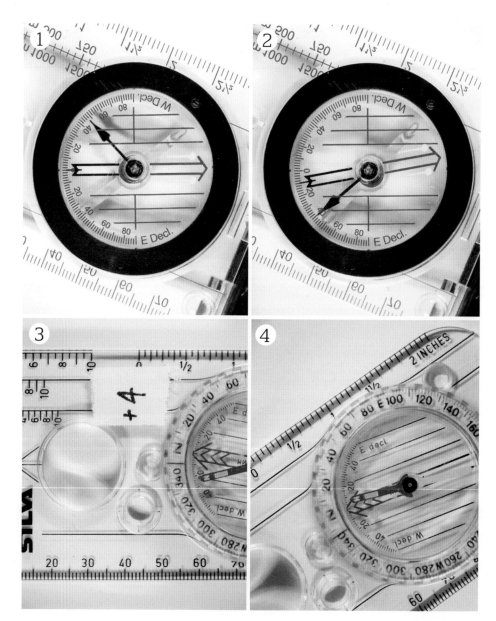

Opposite
1 Reading from
its underside, it is
possible to see how
this compass can be
adjusted for magnetic
declination. This is
achieved by turning
the small screw with a
special tool attached to
the compass lanyard.
2 Here the compass
has been adjusted for
a declination of 10
degrees east.
3 An old-fashioned way
to adjust for magnetic
declination was to
mark your compass
with the adjustment
from grid to magnetic.
This could be adjusted
by using simple
mathematics.
4 An alternative and
not always easy-to-read
method is to align the
needle on an internal
declination scale. Here
the needle indicates
7 degrees east.

Right When measuring
a magnetic bearing,
take the utmost care
to maximise accuracy.

the appropriate adjustment. As a principle of best practice we always adjust for declination.

The Earth's magnetic field is a mysterious force that swirls around our planet and changes each year. This means that, unless our map is very recently surveyed, we have to work out the declination appropriate to the date on which we are travelling.

Once again our map legend is the key.

Once established, adjust your compass if it has a Decl. adjustment device or mark the Decl. on your baseplate. Do not assume that each map sheet has the same Decl. – very often this varies from sheet to sheet. We write the current Decl. on the map sheet in preparation for departure.

PUTTING IT ALL INTO PRACTICE

Here is an example of how to calculate a bearing in a certain scenario:

Magnetic Decl.: 20 degrees W

Bearing from camp to island with good fishing:

Estimated bearing: >360 degrees and <45 degrees
Measured bearing from map with compass:
38 degrees GRID

Therefore, the compass must be set to 58 degrees MAG

Decl. is 6 degrees E

Bearing taken in the field of direction of logging road:

Estimated bearing: >225 degrees and <270 degrees
Bearing measured with compass: 267 degrees MAG

Therefore, to locate this on the map the compass must be set to 273 degrees GRID

Resection

If you are not certain of your location but can identify two or more features in the landscape that can be found on your map, you can accurately establish your position by resection. This simply involves taking bearings from the identifiable features. Where these cross will be roughly your position, allowing for the accuracy achievable with map and compass. Three bearings will usually indicate your location as a triangle, in which case assume that you are located at the intersection nearest to any hazard, such as a cliff, and navigate accordingly and with due diligence.

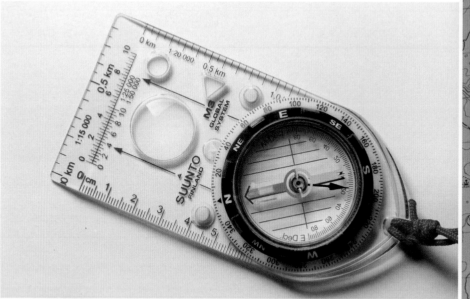

Back/reciprocal bearing

To find your way back in the same direction of travel, simply turn the compass dial so that the magnetic north arrow is positioned over the orienting red arrow. This will read an opposite bearing of your direction of travel.

Having navigated on a bearing, you may wish to return to your point of origin. To do this, we employ a reciprocal or back bearing. This is your original bearing plus 180 degrees. The easiest method does not involve any addition; simply use your compass with the original heading still set and read the south end of the needle instead of the north end.

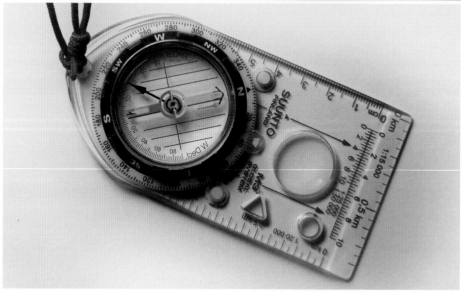

Aiming off

Although our compass provides a high degree of accuracy in our navigation, the practical realities of field navigation mean that some inaccuracies will always

Left Various compasses are available, either with or without mirrors. Mirrored ones are usually used by the more advanced navigator. Ones without a mirror have the advantage of being easier to hold in your hand when you are aligning your body position to point to the direction of travel.

Some compasses are divided into different numbers of degrees; we recommend 360 degrees, as this is generally the most widely used convention in navigation.

Dead reckoning

We employ dead reckoning when we are navigating in poor-visibility conditions or dense forest in which it is impossible to see out, using visible features to establish our location. Dead reckoning requires us to record our bearings and our progress in distance travelled. Ideally, we will use a game trail or Indian trail and simply record the distance between major changes in the trail's direction. This can be plotted directly on to our map or recorded in our notebook and plotted later during a rest break.

How to measure the bearing of river bends, track bends and shoreline angles

To establish our location on a river, shore or logging road we can take the bearings of a bend in that location and search on the map for a place on the particular feature that shows corresponding bearings. It is extremely rare to find two points with the same bearings in close proximity. However, if in any doubt repeat the exercise with a second bend or search for some other identifiable feature for corroboration.

Opposite top
A compass set to travel on a bearing of 34 degrees.

Opposite bottom
The back bearing to return to your starting point is most easily achieved by reading the compass with the south end of the needle rather than the north end.

creep in. If, for example, we are searching for a campsite on the far shore of a lake, rather than taking a bearing directly to the campsite we will choose instead to aim off deliberately to a favourable side. The reason for this is simple: should we aim directly to the campsite and miss it, we will have difficulty knowing whether it lies to our left or right. By deliberately aiming off, we know which way to turn when we hit the lakeshore and simply use that as a handrail that leads us to the campsite. By aiming off to the upwind side, we will also have the wind favourably behind us as we search for the campsite.

Opposite top left
Romer navigation
tools greatly assist
the navigator when
reading the scales on
a map since they help
give an accurate grid
reference to the user.

Opposite top right
A tally counter greatly
improves accuracy
when you are
counting paces.

Opposite bottom
Stop regularly at way-
points, such as a swamp
area or a lake, and confirm
you are on the right track.
   If an area is difficult to
walk in, we sometimes
count our steps (every

left foot; 60 steps is
usually 100m), although
it depends of course on
the terrain and the weight
of equipment carried.
   For safety, we also look
at our watches to see our
starting time. If we veer

off our course and it is
difficult to see exactly
where we are, we can
measure our distance
using our timepiece.
Normally we walk 3km/
hour in difficult terrain.

Other measurements and navigational techniques

How to establish distance travelled on land

Modern topographic maps use metric scales, the grid providing a convenient means of establishing km distances at a glance. Consequently, we never use miles as a means of determining distance.

How to estimate speed of travel

Speed is the relationship between time and distance. In open country, this is an excellent means of establishing distance travelled. To facilitate this process we affix a laminated time and distance chart to the cover of our compass. By timing our progress with a watch between two points a known distance apart, we can establish our speed. This can then be used to predict our movement across the terrain.

How to estimate speed of travel by canoe

When travelling by canoe there are many variables, including whether we are: solo or tandem; heavily laden or lightly loaded; experiencing a head or tail wind; have the current for or against us; are experienced and efficient paddlers rather than novices; and the number of portage trails and how well maintained they are. For all of these reasons and more, establishing a practical judgement of speed of travel requires a constant awareness of progress. We normally base our initial estimation on 4km/hour over flat water, plus 30 minutes per portage of less than 1km. This is just a base line used for initial planning and will need to be tweaked constantly throughout the journey. If in doubt, underestimate your speed when planning – all too often enthusiasm results in the setting of overly ambitious goals.

How to pace dense woodland

In dense trees, counting paces is a very reliable means of establishing distance travelled. In open country, it is normal to record paced 100m legs, having first established how many of our paces take us 100m. This will vary according to whether or not we are carrying a heavy rucksack. However, in dense forest it is better to count 10m legs, particularly where the terrain is steep. To this end, establish how many paces it takes to travel 10m. A full pace is the distance measured between steps taken with the same foot. For example, 10m may be seven steps

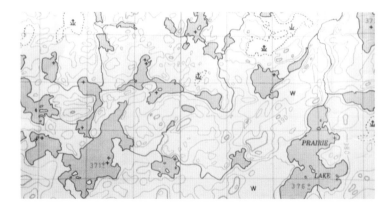

recorded with your left foot. This must be established
by practice beforehand.

We record these paces with a tally counter. Simply
adding a zero to the reading will give a reading in metres
travelled. For greater accuracy, several members of a
party should record their paced distance and the average
should be taken. In steep terrain, pacing is less reliable. To
compensate for this, switch to recording estimated 10m
horizontal distances. To do so, look ahead for a tree that
is horizontally 10m ahead and add a click to your tally
counter when you reach it. With practice, this becomes
a straightforward and surprisingly accurate process.

Transit point

Two islands align to create a transit that places us
accurately on our bearing or handrail.

Handrail

In navigational terminology, a handrail is a feature in
the landscape that can easily be followed to a destination
or waypoint. For example, a shoreline can be used as an
effective handrail.

NAVIGATIONAL PRE-FLIGHT CHECKS

Opposite left
Take into account any obstacles that may be encountered; the detour should not affect your position. We always check the map again when navigating around obstacles. Not making regular checks with your map and compass could result in you wandering off your chosen path. It is also all too easy to navigate around an obstacle and then continue without observing the correct position on the map, which will eventually result in a different bearing.

Opposite
When reading the map, it is a good idea to stop and make regular checks against your map, your compass and the terrain to determine your correct position.

When going on an expedition in the boreal forest, your destination may be a particular lake that may or may not be marked on your map. It is therefore important to check and, if necessary, write the name of the lake or lakes on your map prior to departure.

Good preparations are vital for safe travel. These should include sitting down before you leave with both the outfitter and the pilot who will be dropping you off at your destination, to ensure you are all familiar with the plans of the expedition. Floatplane pilots navigate using the names of lakes and will usually ask for the drop-off or pick-up points to be on a certain area of the targeted lake, such as its north, south, east or west corner.

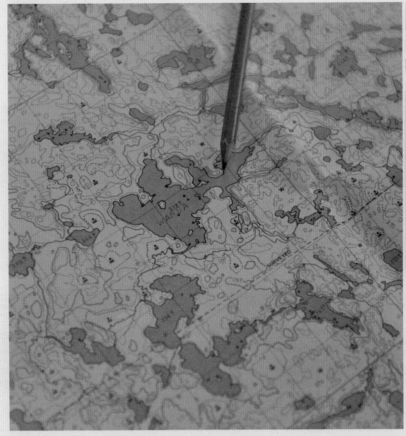

Left When working with floatplanes, it is a good idea to write the names of lakes on your map prior to departure as these may well be absent in the mapping.

Above These are some of the tools we carry to facilitate marking up our maps. All paper maps need to be well protected in good-quality map cases.

Fire

'I CALLED TO THE MAN but received no response,
and going closer found that he was frozen to death.
The mail was in the sled under him. Between his teeth
was a match and between his knees was a box where he
had tried to scratch the match when his hands had frozen.

WILLIAM 'BILLY' MITCHELL *The Opening of Alaska 1901-1903*

Opposite page Symbolising humanity, providing comfort and warmth, and boosting morale at difficult times, the campfire is the focus for life in the wilderness. For this reason, being able to make fire is the most fundamental skill for wilderness travel.

Right Today, the Sirius patrol in Greenland leaves matches sticking out of a box so that a hypothermic person can obtain one, even if they then have to hold it between their teeth to strike it.

In the frigid chill of the boreal forest one quickly learns that warmth is a tangible thing, a commodity often more important to our survival than shelter, food or water. Despite great advances in materials and the equipment we carry, the ability to kindle a fire, swiftly and without fail, remains the most fundamental skill of life support in the boreal forest.

A fire is our single most versatile tool, destroying harmful micro-organisms in food and water, transforming materials we shape, drying clothes and providing life-saving warmth. But more than all this, it also provides a focus for our community – a place where we can gather and share ideas, experiences and wisdom. The cheery glow from a campfire is the very symbol of humanity itself.

In the boreal forest, there are many highly combustible materials to be found – the north woods are a living 'tinderbox', one of the easiest places on earth to start a fire. As if to prove the point, lightning storms spark off a multitude of forest fires each year. Yet despite its incendiary nature there are countless accounts of people struggling to light a fire here or, worse still, failing altogether.

Perhaps the most insidious problem is that posed by the cold itself. Hypothermia results in a classic problem: the rapid loss of manual dexterity caused by vasoconstriction as the body desperately tries to reserve warmth in its core. Under these circumstances the simplest tasks become incredibly difficult and minor technical errors, such as failing to collect enough tinder or not striking a match correctly, can prove fatal. This has even claimed the lives of hypothermic travellers who had managed to find their way to shelter, and even a cabin with a stove, but who were so chilled that they could not open a simple cardboard matchbox to light the stove.

Clearly then, even in the north woods, fire-lighting can prove to be difficult. The importance of training and practice cannot be overemphasised. Once the skills have been learned, we advocate their honing by practice under the most adverse conditions.

To make a fire you are going to need: **tinder**, a **source of ignition**, **kindling** and **fuel**. You will need to know where and how to light your fire, what design of fire to build, how to maintain the fire and, when you have finished with it, how to extinguish it.

Previous pages A warming fire can make the difference between life and death in the frigid cold of the boreal forest in winter.

Tinder

The most important step in fire-lighting is producing a reliable flame. This is not as simple as striking a match or cigarette lighter, for while these admittedly do produce a flame, it is a fragile one that is easily extinguished by a gust of wind. To be considered a reliable flame it needs to be larger, stronger, more constant and less vulnerable to inclement weather.

Tinder is critically important to combustion, linking our source of ignition to the kindling. It can come in many guises; generally we are looking for a mass of thin, dry, fibrous or shaved fuel that will ignite easily, but the term can equally be applied to materials that combust due to their chemical composition. We therefore define tinder as any material that can be easily ignited with a match or with sparks. Igniting a mass of tinder is the soundest beginning when kindling a fire in wet and windy weather, so knowing where to find a reliable type in the boreal forest in wet or dry, summer or winter, is essential fire-lighting knowledge.

There is only one universally available tinder – shavings from the core of standing dead wood – but that is only accessible if you have a knife, so you may require other options. Not only do you need to know what these are, but since each type of tinder has its own characteristics, you should develop a broad knowledge of all the kinds.

On expeditions, it is not unusual to pack artificial tinder in the form of a chemical fuel tablet, fire-starter or newspaper soaked in paraffin wax. With time and experience, however, this will be unnecessary since your familiarity and skill with natural tinders will enable you to rely totally on the forest for your needs.

Opposite top
Cattail seed down
is excellent tinder,
particularly for friction
fire-lighting methods.

Opposite middle
Thistle down is good
tinder that works very
well with sparks from a
ferrocerium rod.

Opposite bottom
Fireweed seed down has
long been used as tinder
with a traditional flint
and steel.

be located everywhere in the forest, even in the worst
weather. The core of this is perfectly dry and can be shaved
into tinder. Ideally, search for vertical dead wood, which
has not yet started to rot. This can be sawn into 40cm (16in)
sections between knots and then split into splints that can
be shaved down to provide a mass of easily ignited shavings.

Any sharp knife can be used to feather wood, but
those with the flat bevel edge found so commonly on
Scandinavian knives are best for the task. The reason
for this is that the bevel provides support when carving,
making it easy to maintain the correct angle of cut.
In Siberia, the Evenk produce feathers by supporting
the knife in a steady position in front of their knee and
drawing the wood towards the edge. This particularly suits
the knives they make, which are only bevelled on one side.

When first learning to feather wood, support the far
end of the splint on a log and shave downwards, keeping
your arm locked straight. This will encourage you to use
your back muscles to provide the power and your hand
to control the all-important cutting angle. Carve slowly,
and do not cut in too deeply – shave up a long, thin curl of
wood. With experience, you will be able to judge the angle
needed and shave feathers without the need to lock your
arm. Your speed will also improve alongside your efficiency.

Feather sticks

The concept of shaving wood to produce tinder is
simple, sound and important. While many consider
birch bark to be the ubiquitous tinder of the boreal
forest, there are actually large regions where this cannot
be easily found. By contrast, standing dead wood can

Below The fuzz
stick described in
many woodcraft
manuals does work,
but it is slow and
awkward to carve.

Shaving clusters These are the easiest and most
quickly made type of tinder as the wood used does
not necessarily even have to be sawn or split. They are
produced by carving handfuls of shavings that are left
attached to the main wood by deepening the cut of each

Left top
The shaving cluster is the most commonly used method of shaving wood for fire-lighting.

Left middle
A shaving cluster produced in a cabin from thick firewood.

Left bottom
Using shaving clusters is one of the best ways to ignite a wood-burning stove.

shaving at its end. These are then shaved off intact as a cluster with a final deeper cut. If you take the time to split out a decent splint, shaving clusters can be very quickly produced in quantity. This method is particularly effective when lighting a fire in a cabin as they are easily made from firewood and, being compact in size, can be arranged inside the stove without difficulty.

True feather sticks

The true feather stick differs from the shaving cluster in that it retains a wooden stem that functions as kindling and facilitates easy handling for fire-lighting. It is possible to shave an intense mass of shavings on the feather stick by radiating the shavings through 180 degrees around one side of the stick.

Starter feather stick

A starter feather stick can be ignited with sparks or other improvised sources of ignition. To make a starter feather stick, pick your best feather stick – one that has a mass of fine feathers. Behind the last shaving, use the edge of your knife as a

Opposite left Fat pine is resin-saturated wood found in old pine stumps. This makes the best shaving clusters or feather sticks for fire-lighting.

Opposite right Pine knots hold a lot of resin and can be knocked out of decaying pine logs. They produce good light when burned on the fire.

Right The true feather stick is made with a splint that has been split from larger stock. The stem of the feather stick should ignite from the flame produced by the shavings.

Far right The starter feather stick has terminal shavings that are so fine they can be ignited with sparks. This method is particularly useful in country devoid of birch bark.

scraper to produce a mass of very fine cotton-wool-like shavings. These can be easily ignited with a spark from a ferrocerium rod. To do this, try to produce one large spark so that it falls into the centre of the mass of tiny scrapings. All being well, the scrapings will light and in turn ignite the shavings.

In practice, we use shaving clusters and feather sticks interchangeably as circumstances dictate. Perhaps of greater importance is the fact that in bad weather these are our 'go-to' methods for fire-starting in the boreal forest.

Fat pine Old pine stumps frequently become impregnated with pine resin. When this happens, the wood develops a strong smell of turpentine. Fat pine can be split out from the stump and then into splints to make a really classic fire-starter that can be simply ignited with a match or lighter, although it is at its best when carved into a feather stick. Fat pine burns hot and long.

A FIRE IN TERRIBLE WEATHER

Caught on the lake by a clap of thunder and flash of lightning, we raced for the protection of the nearest island. As we hauled our canoes ashore the heavens opened and the thick black clouds conspired above to rob us of the last hour of daylight. Illuminated in brief but frequent flashes of lightning, the island was dank and dismal, with no clear space, no campsite – just a spiky, impenetrable tangle of trees that had been blown down the previous winter. Is there any feeling worse than that, standing soaking in the heaviest rain in darkness, with only slippery logs for a footing? At times like this it can be difficult to think and even to talk, with voices drowned out by the drumming rain. But the answer is always the same: light a fire.

I cannot honestly say a spot was chosen for the fire, more that one was nominated, each place being as wet as the next. Nevertheless, the tarp was strung over it and we set to. In the clean air of this wilderness, all the small branches that might normally have been considered for fire-lighting were festooned with now-soaking lichen. There was no point even trying to light snap wood. Instead, out came the saw and a dead standing tree was selected and cut into knot-free sections. We had to work very carefully, for the darkness, wetness and slippery conditions did nothing to promote safety. In fact, when placed in a stressful situation such as this, even the skilful become clumsy, can break tools and are prone to accidents. Eventually though, with a tickle from the axe, the damp, unpromising outer wood popped open to reveal its perfectly dry heartwood.

Huddled under the tarp, we worked as a team shaving out a pile of feather sticks and, pulling out some birch bark from a pocket, ignited the blaze. The rest of the sawn sections provided the fuel, and in minutes a cheery glow illuminated the tarp like a Chinese lantern. We now had a home in the wild – humanity had established another temporary outpost in the dark forest. On went the kettle and, while it heated, up went the tent. Now it was time for a meal and to dry out and joke beside the fire before sleep. Therein lies the power of fire.

Barks

There are several barks that make the most wonderful tinders: birch, juniper, cedar and cinquefoil. The most important of these by far is birch bark, which also has many uses beyond just fire-making. In Sweden, the cultural importance of birch bark is reflected in the fact that it is called *näver*, a special word for a particularly important bark.

Birch bark Although not found everywhere in the boreal forest, birch trees are extremely widespread. A pioneer species, they are able to grow in open areas without shade and thereby establish the more shady forest conditions that are ideal for the growth of other tree species. The bark of the birch tree has a cell structure that causes the bark to split naturally as it grows, peeling away in papery strips and sheets. This has many remarkable properties; principal among them from a fire-lighting perspective is the fact that it contains an oil that is both highly flammable and resistant to water. Because of this, birch bark will ignite when wet, even if it has been submerged in water. Little wonder, then, that it is normal to always carry a few strips of birch bark in one's pocket and pack when travelling.

It is not necessary to harm the tree in order to collect birch bark – you simply harvest the strips that peel naturally from the living tree or cut the bark free from fallen dead ones.

A strip of birch bark can be used as a spill to light fine kindling. When it is ignited, birch bark tends to curl

up, making it difficult to handle and sometimes causing it to extinguish itself. To prevent this, fold a strip of bark into a loop or small concertina-like fan and ignite the end with a match or lighter. As it burns, note the dense black smoke from the sputtering flame, which indicates the oil content. This spill will burn with a strong flame that is larger and more reliable than that of the original match and can then be used to ignite fine kindling.

Birch bark can also be ignited with sparks from a ferrocerium rod. To do this, take a piece of bark 10cm (4in) long and 5cm (2in) wide and scrape the light exterior surface of the bark to produce a mass of fine shavings. These will ignite with a single large spark. Have thin strips of bark ready to enlarge the initial flame. As the flame establishes itself in the bark strips, ensure that it has a plentiful supply of air and is not smothered when you first introduce your kindling.

Birch bark can also be used as a tinder bundle for friction fire-lighting or igniting smouldering fungus tinder. However, it needs special handling as it spits hot oil, making it virtually impossible to hold in a conventional way. To overcome this problem, roll a tight, dense mass of thin strips and scrapings inside a small roll of birch bark to create a tube 3–4cm (1¼–1½in) in diameter and 12.5–15cm (5–6in) long. Introduce your

glowing ember into the tinder at one end of the tube and blow on it, as though you are attempting to blow the ember through the tube. The tube of bark will protect you as the tinder spits, and it will also concentrate your breath better, inspiring the coal to flame.

Juniper bark, cedar bark, inner poplar bark, cinquefoil bark
Juniper bark sheds naturally from the trunk of the tree and is delicate and papery. Cedar bark peels from its tree as a flaky, more woody,

Far left top Decaying hardwood logs will sometimes reveal papery fibres of inner bark.

Far left bottom Bark fibres can easily be collected and dried for use as tinder by any fire-lighting means.

Left The outer bark of cinquefoil can be used as good tinder, although it is fiddly to collect.

Lichen

Lichen are in many cases a sign of very clean air, so it should come as no surprise that they abound in the boreal forest. There are several lichens that grow like beards and festoon the branches of trees, particularly pine trees. These wool-like lichens can be used as a source of tinder. The most commonly used beard lichen belong to the following genera: *Bryoria*, *Alectoria* and, to a lesser extent, *Usnea*.

On rare occasions, lichen can be found dry enough for use without preparation. More usually, though, they will hold moisture and will have to be dried in the pocket before they can be ignited with sparks from a ferrocerium rod or used as a tinder bundle. Once ignited, lichen tinder burns fast and fiercely so compact the lichen into a dense ball and have your fine kindling ready for immediate ignition.

Top left Cedar bark is really effective tinder that can be used for all methods of fire-lighting. Its dark hue predisposes it for ignition with condensed sunlight.

Top right Juniper bark, here buffed into a tinder bundle, is top-rate tinder that can even work when slightly damp.

Right Beard lichens must be dried for use as a tinder, but catch well with sparks.

fibrous bark. The inside of poplar bark can be gathered in quantity from beneath the outer bark of a dead and partially decayed tree. Cinquefoil is a low shrub, the bark of which peels in thin papery strips from the stem. If the bark is damp, suspend it in a drying breeze or dry it in a pocket for later use.

All of these barks can be buffed between your hands to loosen and separate their fibres into a soft, fluffy bundle of filaments, at which point they can be ignited with sparks from a ferrocerium rod or used as a tinder bundle with fungi ignited by traditional flint and steel or with any ember produced by friction.

Fungi

Historically, fungi have long been used as tinder for fire-lighting, and some are even prepared and sold commercially. Tinder from fungus is normally used sparingly to enlarge a spark, the resulting ember subsequently needing to be combined with a more fibrous tinder for ignition. However, if used extravagantly, a mass of fungus tinder will glow well enough to ignite fine kindling. Many fungi found in the boreal forest can be used for tinder but the most important ones are:

• The hoof fungus (*Fomes fomentarius*), predominantly found on dead and decaying birch, maple and poplar.
• The willow bracket (*Phellinus igniarius*), predominantly found on dead and decaying willow, birch and aspen.
• The razorstrop fungus (*Piptoporus betulinus*), found on dead and living birch.
• Chaga (*Inonotus obliquus*), predominantly found on birch but also elm and alder.

The hoof fungus (*Fomes fomentarius*) This is so well regarded for fire-lighting that it is also known as the tinder fungus. It is found growing on dead and decaying hardwood trees in boreal latitudes, mostly on birch trees. A very pale grey colour, it derives its common name from its shape, which resembles a horse's hoof. At first inspection it seems an unlikely candidate for tinder, as it comprises a hard outer cuticle and an underside of densely packed spore tubes. The secret lies in the trama layer of hyphal tissue that is found above

Left Chaga fungus erupts from beneath the bark of dead birch trees. It is wonderful fire tinder, often referred to as 'touchwood'.

Opposite
The hoof fungus was used commercially to produce tinder called amadou. It is the layer of fibres just beneath the grey outer cuticle of the 'hoof' that are used for tinder.

the spore tubes and beneath the cuticle.

Before the ready availability of friction matches, a tinder called amadou was prepared from this fungus. The making of this involved the removal of the spongy trama layer, which was pounded and rolled into leather-like sheets that were subsequently treated with saltpetre to improve their ability to catch a spark from a flint and steel. Interestingly, a whole industry sprang up around this process, with the fungal leather being used to fashion all manner of items, even hats.

The poor man's equivalent of amadou was made by cutting away the cuticle and slicing thin strips of the trama, which were then massaged until soft, sometimes with the addition of soft hardwood ash. Although not as easy to use as its commercial counterpart, this home-made amadou was effective, especially once a charred edge was achieved.

In order to learn the best way to use this fungus, however, we need to study the method employed in prehistory, before the availability of steel to generate

sparks. At this time, sparks were generated using flint scratched against the interior of a broken iron-pyrite nodule. This action produces a small quantity of very dull red sparks, which consequently require the very finest tinder for ignition. This was made in a very simple way: the trama layer was scraped with the edge of a flint blade to produce a very fine cotton-wool-like mass of hyphal fibres. These were sometimes contained in a freshwater mussel shell for fire-lighting.

Tantalising evidence for this process has been found in the remains discovered in Neolithic burial sites. At Star Carr, an upper Paleolithic site in the UK, two large *Fomes fomentarius* fruit bodies were found discarded after the top trama layer had been prised away. It is our belief that the cuticle would have been deliberately left intact, as it is not necessary to cut it away, to help protect the trama from moisture and for ease of transportation. Perhaps future archaeology will shed more light on this process.

The willow bracket (*Phellinus igniarius*)
This can be used in the same way as the hoof fungus.

The razorstrop fungus (*Piptoporus betulinus*)
Very different in form, this erupts from under the bark of birch trees, and the fruit body forms smooth white brackets with a very rounded edge and a light-brown top. The pore layer is very thin, the fruit body largely comprising a rubbery hyphal tissue.

Historically, it has had many uses, one of which is reflected in its name, which is derived from the practice of cutting a slice from a large fruit body, which was then dried and sanded flat before being glued to a wooden board and treated with honing paste. This was then used as a strop for cut-throat razors. When dry, this fungus is highly absorbent and was used as a styptic for wounds and even as blotting paper. Treated with saltpetre, long strips were used as slow fuses in the early blasting industry, although this proved to be a highly dangerous and unreliable technique. For tinder, the dried fruit body can simply be scraped with the edge of a knife to produce a fine tinder powder that takes a spark very readily.

Chaga (*Inonotus obliquus*) Also called touch wood and, among the Cree, *pesogan* or *passogan*, this erupts from its host tree as a woody black canker with a deeply fissured crust. Beneath this, the woody fruit body has a golden-brown, crumbly, cork-like appearance. For use, chaga needs to be thoroughly dry, when it will very readily accept a spark and can be blown into a hot, long-lasting ember.

Firedogs

Firedogs are the cold remains of the firewood found once a fire has gone out, and can be an excellent tinder for fire-lighting. Left unattended, a star-shaped fire will usually burn out. This is because as firewood burns away from the heart of the fire, the glowing ends of the logs can no longer support each other and eventually the ember base cools. Normally in the morning, the camper awakes to find the star-shaped fire cool, with a central dome of ash and with the charred ends of the logs separated around the outside. On close inspection, you will discover that the logs closest to the ground usually burn furthest. This results in these logs being protected from the rain by the protruding longer ends of the logs above.

Above left Old fire embers called firedogs can be ignited with sparks. This is a very good way to reignite a fire in the morning.

Above right To create fire, you need to bring three glowing firedogs together and blow on them as shown, to increase their warmth and produce flames.

Left Amadou burns as a small ember.

The charred undersides of the log ends are normally fissured and show a very light-grey ash. These can often be reignited with the application of a spark or small flame. Once glowing, other similar log ends can be brought together so that the glow passes between them. If there are three glowing and touching embers it should be possible to blow on them to inspire a flame. This is a quick and efficient way of reigniting a campfire, sometimes from logs that have lain cold for months, and is our favourite method of relighting a dying fire in the morning.

Decaying wood

It is not unusual to encounter fallen trees so consumed by the action of fungi that they can be crumbled to a powder between your hands. If dry, this punky wood can be used as tinder. In some cases the decayed wood may be capable of accepting a spark in a similar way to chaga. In all cases, the wood may be used to enlarge an ember. Decayng wood that is dark in colour in particular will readily catch when used in conjunction with condensed sunlight.

Cotton wool

Cotton wool is an excellent tinder that can usually be found in our outfit within our first-aid supplies. In a crisis, when a fire must be made without fail, consider pulling apart a field dressing or a tampon and using it for tinder. When training young adults for their first wilderness expedition, we normally start with this

method. It is not as fancy or as clever as those methods described above but it works really well.

Protect the cotton wool from rain and tease it apart into a large, fine mass. Ideally, add fuel to the cotton wool – this can be any combustible fluid or grease you may be carrying, such as friar's balsam, petroleum jelly (an excellent substance to carry since it can be used to prevent skin abrasion when hiking), hand gel, cooking oil, butter, rum – consider what you normally carry and do some experiments to see what burns. Adding fuel in this way will create a fire-starter with great longevity. Strike a spark into the edge of the cotton-wool bundle and away you go.

Right Cotton wool impregnated with petroleum jelly can be carried in a small plastic bag and kept in the pocket in case of emergency – it makes excellent emergency tinder. Simply tear open the plastic bag and spark on the teased cotton wool. The bag will ignite too.

Fuel tablets

Military stoves usually employ solid-fuel tablets. These can be excellent emergency fire-starters that can be ignited with sparks.

Trioxane This comes individually foil-wrapped. It ignites instantly from a spark from a ferrocerium rod.

Hexamine and meta fuel tablets These do not ignite instantly, unlike Trioxane. To ignite them with sparks, scrape or slice the edge to create some powder. This ignites immediately with a good spark from a ferrocerium rod. In windy weather, this is a more reliable ignition method than using a cigarette lighter or match.

Candles

It is comforting that in a technological age the humble candle still shines in the wilderness. It has many uses, from waxing skis in wet weather to lighting a snow cave. As a source of tinder it is excellent; a candle flame, while still fragile, is more reliable than that of the short-lived match. Moreover, it can be ignited with sparks from a ferrocerium rod. To do this, expose 1cm (⅖in) of the wick and, using the point of your knife, unravel the fibres of the wick until they resemble cotton wool. At this point they can be ignited with a spark.

Rubber

Rubber is another excellent emergency tinder. It can be carried as a lump cut from an old motorcar tyre or as a band cut from an inner tube. Inner-tube bands of course have the added benefit of being useful for binding items together. Totally unaffected by moisture, rubber cut into a strip can be ignited with a match or lighter and will burn long and hot. Even a broken or worn-out snowmobile drive belt can be put to use if you cut strips from the smooth outer surface.

Left Dead pine needles burn fast and with a resinous intensity. They are a good aid to fire-lighting, and as such they can also present a high risk for forest fire.

Below A candle can be ignited with sparks. First fluff up the wick, then spark heavily on to it.

Right Snapwood is the finest kindling. No thicker than a matchstick, it should be dead, dry and brittle – as the name suggests.

Kindling

After tinder, the next link in the fire chain is kindling. This is the small fuel that creates a flame that is strong enough to ignite full-sized fuel. Generally, kindling ranges in thickness from matchstick to thumb-width. It should be used progressively from thin to thick. The thinnest kindling is the most important. To be certain of success when fire-starting in bad weather, ensure that you have a mass of good kindling: never shortcut this step in fire-making. Perhaps the most common mistakes made by novice fire-lighters are using too little kindling and kindling of poor quality.

Snapwood

Snapwood is the term used to describe thin dead branches that snap cleanly when broken. Although the term can be considered applicable to dead wood up to thumb-thickness in diameter, we normally only use it to describe twigs of approximately the same diameter as a matchstick, which will comprise the most important kindling. In the boreal forest there are two classic sources of snapwood. The first is the many small dead branches found low on conifers that have been shaded out by higher boughs. The other source is supplied by dead birch branches, very often found caught in living branches above the ground. Normally we do not collect snapwood from the ground as it has too high a moisture content, although in prolonged dry weather an exception can be made.

When collecting snapwood, do not break it too short: an ideal length is the same as the distance between your elbow and your outstretched fingertip – about 50–60cm (20–24in). Normally we will gather a good bundle of such dead branches, which may be finger-thick at their widest part, and break them down into snapwood, pencil-thick branches and finger-thick branches at the fire site. The easiest way to break these branches is simply to pull them apart at the crotch. Ensure you always have a bundle of the thinnest snapwood that is at least 15cm (6in) in diameter when compressed.

Splitwood

A first-rate kindling, we normally resort to splitwood when the weather is bad or when lighting a wood-burning stove. Look for straight, dead, standing wood that is not yet rotten. The more vertical the wood, the drier it will be. To find standing dead wood, search in thickets where overcrowding has caused some trees to be shaded out by their neighbours or look for swampy ground, which is always a good source for dead wood. Cut out a straight section of wood between knots and split it down into finger-thick splints. Depending on the tinder you have available, these can be used as they are or several can be feathered as necessary.

Sources of ignition
The humble match

In 1826, John Walker, a British chemist, invented the friction match and changed the world. Never before in history had fire been so instantly accessible. Later, his invention was made safer by the brilliant work of two Swedish chemists, Gustaf Erik Pasch and Edvard Lundström, and the 'safety match' was born.

Today, more than 500 billion matches are struck every year. Although they have their detractors, the fact is they remain a reliable and expedient way to make fire, which is why we like them. It is worth considering that many of our most famous explorers depended utterly on matches for their life support.

> 'A match factory gave us all the safety matches we wanted. They were packed so securely that we could quite well have towed the cases after us in the sea all the way and found the matches perfectly dry on arrival.'
> ROALD AMUNDSEN *The South Pole*

Matches, when carefully stored, can remain perfectly active and ready for use for decades. Few other fire-starting devices are so reliable and so cheap. They do, however, have two drawbacks: they are damaged by exposure to moisture and, as we will explain, they need to be struck correctly.

Keeping matches dry With all matches, it is critical to protect them from moisture. Many ways of doing this

Left The humble match remains an important fire-lighting tool; so long as it is dry it will remain ready to use for decades and relies upon no moving parts.

Below Before the availability of modern match safes, native people improvised using birch bark or antler to make a container.

Types of match There are numerous different types of matches available, many of which are designed to combat moisture and strong wind. Mostly ordinary matches will suffice for everyday fire-starting, but it is well worth packing a supply of more hi-tech ones for very bad weather. Always test any unfamiliar brand of match you are considering taking with you into the backcountry. Some makes are more reliable than others.

STRIKE-ANYWHERE MATCHES
Strike-anywhere matches are the most self-contained type of match and are designed to be struck against any rough surface. This is our favourite type, as only the match needs to be protected from moisture.

Above Amundsen used an ice pack-bag the same as this one to transport his matches to the South Pole.

Right Old-fashioned match safes still function well, if properly maintained. They are nearly always designed for use with strike-anywhere matches.

have been suggested, from encasing them in candle wax to painting each individual match with varnish. These methods work, but how truly practical they are is highly questionable given the quantity of matches that will be used. We prefer to rely instead upon a well-designed container or 'match safe'.

A good match safe should in the first instance protect the matches from moisture resulting from immersion in water, but also from perspiration when carried in a pocket on a hot day. It must be easily opened with cold hands, should be designed for attachment to your person with a lanyard and, lastly, it should be designed so that the matches are difficult to spill when in use.

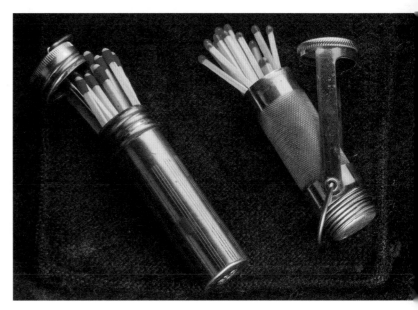

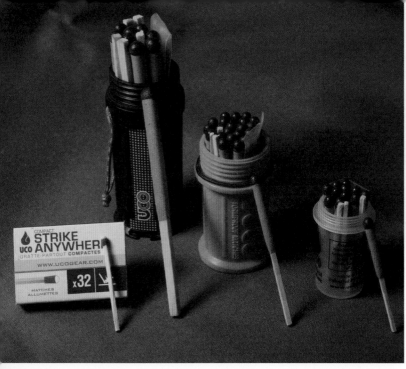

SAFETY MATCHES

Safety matches ignite when the head is struck against the chemical surface of a striker. The necessity for this chemical combination of match head and striker ensures that matches cannot ignite by rubbing against each other in the matchbox. It should be remembered that the striker will necessarily be exposed to potential damage every time it is used and that without the striker the matches are useless. To use these matches, both matches and striker must be protected from moisture.

WATERPROOF SAFETY MATCHES

These are just safety matches with a waterproof coating on the head. The striker is not protected and tends to wear faster due to extra friction caused by the waterproof coating on the matches.

STORM-PROOF MATCHES

Storm-proof or lifeboat matches are each individually lacquered for protection from moisture. They are also constructed with a much larger head than a normal match, which burns intensely and for much longer. Strong wind and rain will not extinguish these matches. The concept is to use this intense ignition period to light your fire, as a stable flame from the matchstick is not achieved until the head has finished burning fiercely. To make the best use of them they should therefore be used to ignite a tinder bundle.

PAPER MATCHES

Paper safety matches come in the form of a small booklet. They are short and difficult to work with outdoors, especially with cold hands. Being made of paper, they are very prone to becoming damp. Consider also that the matches are exposed to the elements each time the book is opened and a match is torn out for lighting. Their only advantage is their compact size and form, which can make them easy to tuck away in well-protected dry spaces. This is our least favourite type of match.

Above The paper match is cheap, but it's the least reliable type of match for wilderness use.

Left Today, there are many different types of matches available for wilderness travel, along with first-rate match safes. UCO produces a very good range of matches.

LONG-BURN AND LARGE STORM-PROOF MATCHES
Long-burn matches have a longer matchstick. As the name suggests, they will burn for considerably longer than a small conventional match. This is advantageous, although it is more difficult to find a match safe in which they will fit. They are mostly available as safety matches, although occasionally they can be found as the strike-anywhere type.

Recently, giant storm-proof safety matches have become available, although this is not a new idea and matches such as these were produced in the past. They provide greater certainty in fire-starting and they are perhaps the ideal emergency fire-starter, but definitely overkill for everyday fire-lighting.

How to strike a match It may come as a surprise that there is a wrong and a right way to strike a match. When our hands are very cold, we lose manual dexterity and can easily fail to light a match, breaking every one in the box one after another. Indeed, there are many accounts of travellers found frozen with a pile of broken matches before them and a fire that was never lit. The wrong way to strike a match is the one that is most seen: with the thumb pressing on the middle part of the matchstick as pressure is applied to the weakest part.

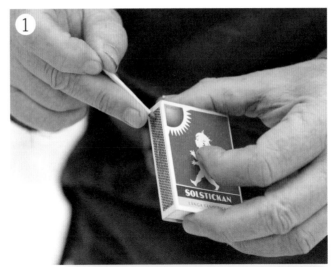

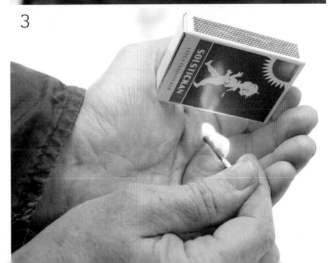

1 To strike a match correctly, grasp the end of the match between your thumb and index finger. Use your middle finger to support the match head.

2 Strike the match against the angled striker so that the force is applied to the end of the match, not its side. As soon as the head begins to combust, immediately remove your supporting middle finger.

3 Without dropping the matchbox, cup the match between your hands to protect it from breezes until the flame is fully formed. Now, still cupping the flame, move both hands to the fire and introduce the flame to your tinder. Once this catches, withdraw your hands and immediately put the matchbox away safely. Never retain the extinguished match – add it to the fire as fuel.

Ferrocerium rod

In 1903, Carl Auer von Welsbach patented a metallic compound called ferrocerium. Its name derived from the original material, which comprised 30 per cent iron and 70 per cent cerium. Originally manufactured to provide the spark in cigarette lighters, this alloy of metals first started to be used as a survival fire-lighting tool when it was included in military survival kits in the 1950s.

The original ferrocerium rods were short, of small diameter and difficult to scrape sparks from. Since then there has been a revolution in their popularity. Today, it is possible to purchase thicker, longer rods that produce excellent sparks easily, although the buyer must beware

Above
a The ferrocerium rod is the most reliable wilderness fire-lighting tool.
b An old ferrocerium rod that has been allowed to decay in a damp jacket.

Right
1 Military fuel tablets such as Hexamine and Trioxane can easily be ignited with sparks from a ferrocerium rod.
2 Trioxane requires no special preparation, igniting immediately with large sparks.

Below
1 Hexamine is best shaved on one corner to produce fine powder.
2 Sparks directed on to these fine shavings will ignite the Hexamine more quickly than using a lighter would, even in strong wind.

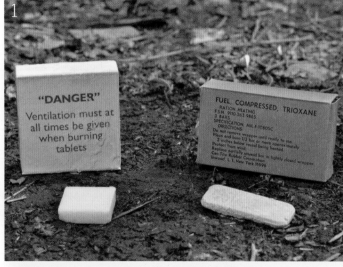

of poor copies. In recent years, we have encountered an increasing number of fake rods, which, until used, are indistinguishable from the real tool. When employed, they snap or fail to give sparks at all. Like everything in your outfit, any fire-starter you intend to carry into the wilderness must be tested prior to departure.

The 1,650°C (3,000°F) sparks emitted by a good ferrocerium rod will ignite the widest range of tinders and they are unaffected by immersion in water. In addition to this, it has great longevity, the average rod being easily capable of igniting thousands of fires. The only drawback is that when left in a damp coat pocket they can decay, eventually eroding to a powder. In practice, though, we have found that a rod that is in regular use rarely suffers in this way. We carry the rod in one of two ways: either attached to our belt by nylon cord and carried in our trouser pocket, or around our neck on nylon cord.

To produce sparks, the rod must be scraped with a tool that is harder than the rod itself. We rely entirely on the back of our knives to do this. When using a ferrocerium rod, learn to produce one large spark rather than the more easily generated shower of small sparks. The large spark will be essential for igniting more stubborn tinders, such as a starter feather stick.

Magnesium fire-starter

The magnesium fire-starter also had its origins in military survival kits. It comprises a ferrocerium rod of modest size attached to the edge of a solid block of magnesium. To use this fire-starter you shave off

Left A magnesium fire-starter consists of a block of magnesium and a ferrocerium rod or sparking insert.

Above
1 Scrape fine shavings from the magnesium side of the fire-starter.
2 Ignited with sparks from the sparking insert, the magnesium burns at an incredibly high temperature.
3 The magnesium burns very swiftly, so it is important to have kindling immediately to hand.

scrapings of magnesium from the edge of the block. When you have produced a small pile they can be ignited with sparks from the rod. Although a little fiddly, this works extremely well. The magnesium shavings burn at a temperature of 3,000°C (5,432°F). At this temperature, raindrops falling on the burning magnesium become fuel as the water is split into its component parts: hydrogen and oxygen. We do not think these fire-starters are ideal for everyday use – they were intended to be, and remain, an excellent emergency fire-starter, and including one in an emergency kit on an expedition is a first-rate choice.

The lighter

While lighters are undeniably convenient, they have many moving parts, which flies in the face of the old bush principle of KISS [Keep It Simple, Stupid]. Despite

Left
1 You can use the back of a knife and a ferrocerium rod to make fire with one hand.
2 Pull back on the ferrocerium rod so that the sparks fall beneath the blade on to birch-bark scrapings.
3 The shavings should ignite at the first attempt. This fire-lighting method should be practised in advance in preparation for the day, should it come, when you are injured and need to use it for real.

Far left The Zippo lighter. These should only be used for igniting tinder, not kindling.

Opposite top The traditional flint and strike-a-light set comprises: tinder pouch, flint blade, tinder (in this case amadou), and a steel striker – this one made from a file.

Opposite bottom Hold the tinder on top of the flint blade. Strike downwards with the steel so that the blade shaves sparks, which are tiny curls of steel, upwards into the tinder.

recent advances in lighter design we do not consider any lighter to be a top wilderness fire-starting tool. All too often we have seen them fail in the wet and cold.

When using a lighter, even a Zippo, use it solely for igniting tinder; do not waste your fuel in the vain hope that the lighter flame will ignite damp kindling. This mistake is something we have witnessed many times among our students. The result is usually burned fingers and the fuel being exhausted. If the fuel runs out, you may be able to light a fire with sparks from the lighter, although this will in no way match the sparks produced from a larger ferrocerium rod. If you do take one, it is a good idea to carry spare flints.

Flint and steel strike-a-light set

The traditional flint and steel strike-a-light set was probably the most widely carried method of fire-lighting prior to the invention of the match, and it remains highly reliable. The equipment can still be purchased today or even be made from scratch. While it is normal to bring tinder along with you, replacement tinder can easily be found and prepared in the bush.

The strike-a-light set usually comprises a piece of natural flint, a steel and some suitable tinder, all contained in a convenient pouch or tin. The sparks from this set are produced when tiny shavings are removed from the steel with the edge of the flint. They can be produced in either a downwards direction so that they fall on to the tinder, or in an upwards

direction so that they fly up on to the edge of the tinder. The sparks are smaller and cooler than those produced from a ferrocerium rod so need to be used in conjunction with fine tinder, such as that produced from fungi. Once the tinder is glowing it will need to be added to some other dry fibrous tinder in order to be blown into a flame. Although a little cumbersome compared to modern spark-generating apparatus, one can quickly become accustomed to using this ancient and very reliable method.

How to make a traditional firesteel

A firesteel is very easy to make from an old file. Depending upon your blacksmithing skill, you can make an elaborate one or keep it very simple. The secret lies with achieving the correct hardness in the steel. Take the old file (for this, a good-quality traditional file is required), and heat it deep in the embers of a hot fire until it is glowing cherry red. At this point, put the file into old ashes to cool. This process will have softened the steel, which can now be shaped if required. For example, you may wish to shorten the file to a more suitable length – say 8cm (3¼in) – and perhaps drill a hole into it. If the edges of the file have teeth, these can be filed off to create a smooth edge. If you have the skill and time, you can heat the metal and hammer out a fancy shaped steel. Once you are happy with your steel, heat it again until it glows cherry red, then quench it in water at a temperature of 40°C (104°F). If you have done this correctly, it should now produce sparks when

struck against a flint shard. All that remains is to make or find a suitable container for your flint and steel.

How to make a char-cloth tinder

If you do not have access to a natural source of tinder, you can make char cloth. This is done by deeply charring old cotton cloth. It must be 100 per cent cotton, perhaps an old T-shirt. The easiest method is simply to set light to a piece of cotton cloth measuring 5 x 10cm (2 x 4in). When you see it turn dark brown/black, extinguish it by smothering it with a frying pan or some other similar object.

The best way to produce char cloths in quantity, however, is to place pieces of cotton cloth into a tin with

Above
1 To make char cloth, old cotton rag is cut into pieces and placed inside a small tin.
2 The tin is heated on embers until the emanation of smoke from the hole in the lid reduces in intensity.
3 Remove the charred cloth from the tin once it is cool.

③

a tiny hole in the lid and then to heat the tin gently at the edge of the fire. As the cotton chars it will produce fumes – tar and smoke that will escape through the hole. Once the smoke ceases or slows to a trickle, close the hole with a pointed stick and allow it to cool. If done correctly, you should find a mass of black char cloth inside the tin. If there is only ash then you heated the tin too vigorously and will need to begin again, whereas if the cotton is only browned, it needs further heating.

To use this first-rate tinder, take a section 2cm² (¾in²), fold it and spark on to its edge. The spark should take immediately. Blow on to the char cloth to increase the glowing area and then add it to a bundle of fine fibrous tinder and blow to a flame.

How to light a fire

Choose a good fire site

Where you site your fire is of great importance. Try to choose a site close to your source of firewood, away from animal trails and stinging insects, and most definitely away from poison ivy. Search for ground that will provide a mineral base to your fire, such as soil or sand, a gravel bar in a river, or a rocky ledge. Where possible, site your fire close to water for convenience and so that it can be easily extinguished when necessary. Never light your fire on peaty ground or soil comprising decaying vegetation as this can ignite and burn underground, surfacing much later to start a forest fire. In many national parks you will find existing fireplaces at established campsites and you should use these when they are available. It is good practice always to leave the fireplace tidier than when you found it.

In the deep snow of winter, shovel down to the frozen ground. While some manuals suggest building a fire on a platform on top of the snow, this is a waste of effort as the fire will inevitably sink into the snow, taking its warmth with it.

Always ensure there is a space around your fire that is clear of vegetation, which might combust to a distance of 2m (6½ft). If the wind is threatening to blow sparks from your fire into the surrounding vegetation, improvise a windbreak so that your fire burns in the protected lee. This can be arranged using a small tarp wrapped around two sides of a tripod pot-hanger or by creating a small windbreak with rocks. If you feel the need to surround your fire with rocks, do not use those from waterlogged ground or rivers as the moisture expanding inside the

heated rock can cause it to explode with disastrous consequences. (Incidentally, although you will not encounter them in the boreal forest, we never surround a fire with concrete blocks or glassy rocks such as flint, for the same reason.)

Never light a fire against any rock wall or cave wall that extends overhead. There have been tragic instances when a fire has caused the rock to fracture and collapse, crushing those sheltering below.

How to light a fire with snapwood

This is the most fundamental way to light a fire in the boreal forest. It requires no cutting tools and, so long as the materials are chosen correctly and gathered in the correct size and quantity, is straightforward.

Below

1 Begin by placing the first bundle of snapwood on to the firebase.

2 Place the second bundle so that it crosses on top of the first.

3 Put tinder into the space between the crossed bundles and ignite it.

4 When flames appear above the bundles it is time to add the next thickness of fuel.

Begin by creating a suitable fire clearing and laying a platform of thumb-thick dead wood. Now search for very thin dead branches. The most important consideration is that the twigs you collect are very dry, as they will also be very brittle and snap cleanly. The species most appropriate for this method are spruce, pine and birch. Spruce and pine twigs are rich in resin and will be found on the lower part of the trunk where they have been shaded out by higher branches. Birch twigs are rich in oil and mostly found lodged up in the branches of other trees and bushes. While in very dry weather snapwood can be collected from the ground, generally it has too high a moisture content. In very bad weather, shake the water from your snapwood and treble the amount of kindling that you are using.

The snapwood you collect should be no shorter than the distance from your elbow to your fingertip and ideally an arm's length. It should be no thicker than a matchstick at the thin end and approximately pencil thick at the butt end. Collect a good-sized bundle that takes two hands to encompass. Keep all the branches pointing the same way, thick butt ends together as in a besom broom.

Break the bundle in half at the midpoint and set aside the thick ends. Divide the remaining thin ends into two bundles and cross them on top of the platform. Place some tinder/birch bark beneath the twigs and ignite. Once flames begin to appear through the fine twigs, place the bundle of thicker twig butts across the top. Now add fuel as desired.

How to light a fire with splitwood

We witnessed this elegant way of fire-starting being employed by the Evenk reindeer-herders of central Siberia. Highly proficient with their axes, the Evenk swiftly splint the kindling needed from dead dry spruce, larch or birch. It is a quick and efficient method employing dry wood, split into thin splints, with birch bark for tinder, and is an excellent way to light the fire in a wood-burning stove.

1 To begin with, clear the snow down to the ground and lay a platform of dry split sticks. In dry summer weather, the platform can sometimes be dispensed with.

2 Place two split sticks on top of the platform to form a ∧ shape that is crossed at the apex and with the opening towards the fire-lighter.

3 In the crotch of the ∧, place a handful of birch bark as tinder. If there is a breeze, arrange the fire so that the breeze is blowing into the ∧.

4 Ignite the birch bark with a match, or by whatever method is available to you.

5 Add progressive layers of split sticks across the burning birch bark supported on the ∧, each layer being laid at 90 degrees to the previous layer. With four or five layers added, the fuel size can be increased as needed.

How to light a fire with feather sticks

This is a very reliable way to start your fire. When you become fully competent at making good feather sticks it can be the quickest method of all. This having been said, it is usually considered an emergency fire-lighting method for use in the worst weather, particularly in prolonged heavy rain. In the boreal forest there are regions without much birch, in which case feather sticks are the most convenient way to start a fire.

When looking for good wood for your feather sticks, search for standing dead trees or stumps of rain-impregnated wood. In the winter it is easy to mistake frozen living wood for dead wood. To check the wood you choose is dry, carve off a thin shaving and place it on your tongue. If the wood is green it will seem moist, if dry it will be like blotting paper.

To light a feather stick fire, once again (and as always) first create a small platform of dead wood. On top of this create a ∧ of feather sticks with the feathers facing towards you. Ignite them by placing your match beneath the lowest feathers. As the feather sticks burn and flames emerge from the top of the pile, add more split wood as necessary.

Above
1 Begin by placing a feather stick on top of the firebase with the shavings facing towards you.
2 Alternate left and right to create a tower of shavings, as shown here.
3 Ignite the lowest feather stick.
4 Good feather sticks catch fire quickly, so be ready with the next layer of fuel.

Right If using fuzz sticks, this is the traditional way to ignite them.

4

How to extinguish a fire

Although a natural feature in the boreal landscape, a raging forest fire is a terrifying sight, one that can travel as fast as a racehorse. With so much combustible material around us we constantly need to be on our guard to avoid starting such a fire. This begins with choosing a campsite carefully, ideally one with an existing fireplace, or a sandbar or a rock base for the fire. Wherever possible, we do not light a fire on peaty ground for the reasons already given. If we do have to do so, the fire will need to be very carefully extinguished by dousing it with many gallons of water and by piercing the ground with a sharpened stick to allow this water to penetrate deeply. Concentrate this effort in the fire itself and extending outwards from its edge by at least 1m (3¼ ft). The most efficient way to do this is to create a chain gang of people between the fire site and the water source.

Normally, we do not light a fire on ground that will ignite and we plan to extinguish our fire so that as much firewood is burned to ash as possible beforehand. The fire embers are then spread a little to allow them to cool before they are doused with water until no smouldering can be detected and all the embers are cold and can be handled with bare hands.

Above A relay of campers pouring copious amounts of water on to a fire, which has burned on peaty ground. Never underestimate how much water is needed to extinguish a fire in this circumstance.

Fire
195

The nying fire

1 Carve a V-shaped groove along the length of both logs. It should be deepest for the first 30cm (12in) of each log.

2 Cut two notches at 90 degrees to the long grooves and place two green-wood branches into them.

3 This means that the logs can be stacked on top of each other with stability.

4 Fill the grooves tightly with shaving clusters.

5 Ignite the shaving clusters along the complete length of the log.

6 Stabilise the fire by hammering a wedge into a split in the top log and attaching a long stabilising bar.

The 3-log fire

1 Place the two base logs beside each other and fill the gap between them with many shaving clusters.
2 Ignite the shaving clusters.
3 Place the top log on top of the two base logs.

The star fire

Right This is an extremely efficient way to maintain a fire, with logs being fed in to the centre as it burns. The star fire is especially good for cooking.

The Raappanan fire

Left This fire was popularised in the 1930s by Aaro Raappanan, a Finnish Sheriff who wrote about hunting and fishing. A dry pine log is first split into three sections: two large outer slabs and a thin middle board. The thin board is split down and shaved into feathers. These are used to ignite the two slabs, which are positioned vertically.

Right The fire burns steadily and is excellent when boiling a kettle or frying food. To extinguish it simply separate the two slabs, which can then be reused when necessary.

In Finland, the long-range patrols
have a joke about shaving clusters,
depicted graphically here:

1 The Sergeant's shaving cluster.
2 The Private's shaving cluster.
3 The Officer's shaving cluster.

Summer Travel

'FOR THOSE OF YOU that travel, let this be a warning.
The large skies and stark beauty of
These northern places can move
And challenge you as gently, as insistently,
As completely as the warmest and
Most profound of lovers. It truly becomes
Possible to have a love affair with the land.
As for us, we all had a difficult time
Returning, and part of each of us
Probably never will.'

JESSE FORD *American ecologist and poet*

In the far north, the seasons are keenly felt. From the first day that the sun once again pokes its head across the horizon, there is the promise of winter's end, and of summer. The days lengthen dramatically in the higher latitudes. The hint that birds are returning to the north is heralded in March by the distinctive song of crossbills in the crowns of the pines. But if, like us, you are a canoeist, summer officially begins the moment that

Below and previous pages Only two weeks ago, this river was frozen. Now, with the rapid thaw, the boreal forest is filled with movement: the gushing of water, the swaying of fresh new leaves in the breeze, and the motion of animals emerging from hibernation. This is a lovely time to travel in the forest.

there is open water wide enough to float a canoe on.

Summer is a wonderful season in the north country, a time to feel the warmth of the sun on one's skin, to discard the parka and walk the damp emerald moss of the forest trails. At the higher latitudes, as if making up for its prolonged winter absence, the sun will not set in the midsummer. Now the weather can be sultry and oppressively hot, with no night for respite.

Of course you cannot expect an easy ride in the summer – nothing is ever easy in the north woods. Almost as soon as the sun hits the dark waters of pond and lake, the insects begin to breed. Soon, billions of mosquitoes fill the air in search of a blood meal. But the insects are themselves food, for the fish and the birds that abound in the forest in the summer, for everything has its purpose in nature.

Preparing the mind, body and spirit

When heading out into the remote forest in summer, it is easy to be too relaxed. Just as at any time of year, the wise go prepared for the worst while hoping for the best. Before climbing aboard a floatplane, everything needs to be carefully checked: equipment, food, communications, emergency procedures, navigation tools and maps. The pick-up details need to be confirmed with the outfitter, the weather forecast checked. Follow the pilot's directions carefully when loading and unloading and do not pester them while pre-flight checks are completed. Keep an eye on your map as you fly so that you know where you are when you are dropped off.

Travelling in this way, there is always a tantalising build-up in preparation. Then all of a sudden you're off, and then you're hearing the pilot's parting words, 'Alright, you take care.' And the radial engine guns and the Noorduyn Norseman is gone. Now you are in the land of your dreams, with the waves, the wind and the wolves for your friends. It is a magical moment, a time to feel really alive.

The canoe comes into its own now; with this remarkable vessel we can traverse the immense landscape, connecting the rivers and lakes by putting the canoe over our head and carrying it across the intervening land, a process called portage. Following canoe and portage trails originally established by First Nation people paddling canoes made from birch bark is a truly marvellous way to travel in the boreal forest, particularly in Canada and North America.

It is worth considering that we are journeying through landscapes full of stories: stories of spirits, stories of people. This forest remains a sacred landscape still for these communities – we are but visitors and must be sensitive and behave accordingly. If we are lucky, we may encounter ancient ochre rock art, their location clearly indicating that they were painted by people also travelling in canoes. Moments such as these join us in a kinship with those past artists, who like us were paddlers in the wild. If we are quiet and lucky we may encounter some of the animals depicted in these galleries – caribou, moose or wolf.

Opposite In some regions of the boreal forest, float-plane flights are akin to a metropolitan bus service, providing easy access to remote regions of the forest.

Right Where the canoe cannot travel on water, it can be carried overland by a process known as portage. Most portage trails were established by First Nations and have been in use for many hundreds of years.

A SUMMER'S DAY IN THE LIFE OF A BOREAL TRAVELLER

In the afternoon, the weather changes on us and lightning flashes in the sky. We beat to shore, grab the daypack, rig a tarp and put on a brew while we wait out the passing storm. We are drinking some tea as the skies blacken and the thunderbird hovers menacingly overhead. The power of this landscape is scintillating, it raises the hairs on our necks – we feel both energised and humbled by this awesome display of raw nature. Then as quick as it came, the storm passes and the sky clears. Raindrops glisten like jewels on the guy lines, the tarp comes down quickly with deft shakes to shed the rain and we pull away again in search of a good campsite.

Eventually a good spot is found and the trusty tarp goes up again, the kettle goes on and the canoe is unloaded and lifted out. Time to pitch the tent and to take a swim and wash dirty clothes before making dinner. As the sun sets, the sparks from our fire climb into the night sky like would-be stars. We laugh and swap stories before holding our breaths in silence as the aurora borealis dances above us.

Above When the wind is blowing in the right direction, a simple sail can be used to motor the canoe along. The WindPaddle sail is particularly convenient as it can be fitted to any canoe without the need for special modification.

Opposite Safely travelling solo by canoe requires a very high degree of bush knowledge and experience. It provides the most intense spiritual connection with the wild.

Far left
1 A typical canoe camp:
a tent in which to sleep,
a tarp under which to live,
and a fire over which to cook.
2 In bad weather, pitch the
tarp low to the ground.
3 An upturned canoe can be
used as a convenient table.

Left top Good friends, good
cheer and a good campfire;
the tiniest pocket of humanity
in the wilderness.

Left bottom Preparing hot
chocolate at the end of a good
day's paddle; add a tot of rum
to relax tired muscles.

Right The rising moon casts
a spell across the landscape.
The city holds no appeal at
moments like this.

Practical considerations

Summer really is the easiest time of year in which to travel in the boreal forest. We carry only a little equipment, but plenty of food. The first time you shoulder a month's supply of food you will be shocked: does food really weigh this much? Of course, as we travel its weight will diminish and we will also become stronger. The fact is, it is important to be fit enough to carry the full load for, despite summer's ease, canoe travel or long-distance hiking is arduous.

Summer attire

In the forest we always dress for comfort. In summer, sturdy quick-drying shirts and trousers that can also protect us from insect bites comprise our normal outer layer. Thin thermal undergarments and some warm mid-layers are carried in case of inclement or unseasonal weather. For emergency situations, we carry a dry bag containing warm clothes – a Buffalo Mountain Shirt and Salopettes take some beating. Waterproof clothing is very important when we are travelling in a canoe due to the fact that we experience constant exposure to the elements. Headgear is vital to shade our necks from the sun and a wide-brimmed hat will also greatly help to reduce the effects of glare.

Above A calm summer's evening at camp is a wonderful time to be fishing or swimming.

Right When flying
into the bush, always
keep an eye on the
map so that you
know where you are
and can gain proper
orientation before
coming in to land.

Below Before heading
out into the forest,
an expedition makes
ready its rations
and outfit. Careful
preparation is essential
for comfortable travel.

In summer, our footwear choice will reflect our
activity. Pac boots, comprising a rubber boot with
a leather upper, are ideal for walking in the damp
forest conditions. Because your foot cannot breathe in
these boots, however, you will have to dry your socks
carefully. Easily dried wool foot wraps (see page 54) are
consequently a perfect combination with these boots.
For canoeing, we have two choices: to try to stay dry, or
to accept that our feet will get wet. We are in the latter
camp, since facing the many challenges of a wilderness
canoe expedition — wading through flooded portage
trails, lining around rapids and dealing with many other
damp circumstances — make it virtually impossible to
stay dry. We choose water activity boots that provide

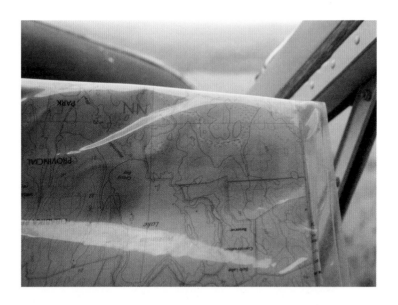

protection to the toe and ankle, drain well and dry fast. At the height of the summer these can be used with woollen socks, while at colder ends of the season neoprene divers' socks are perfect.

In camp, pac boots or moccasin boots are very comfortable. Waterproof socks can also help to dry out damp feet after a full day's canoeing. Caring for our feet is very important, as already outlined in the Cold Injury chapter, so after a day in damp boots we wash our feet carefully and massage them dry. In camp, we follow the old timers' practice of keeping our trousers tucked into our boot tops, which helps to keep ticks out and to prevent mosquito and stable-fly bites.

Below Rapids must never be taken for granted in the wilderness, where the consequences of an accident are heightened by the remoteness. Rivers must always be carefully scouted.

Coping with wildlife

When the insects are really bad, we use insect repellent
and put on an Original Bug Shirt to provide relief, along
with the gloves from our cookset. It is particularly
important to protect yourself from insects when using
cutting tools as the constant attention of the bugs can
cause dangerous distraction. We keep a head net in
our pocket for this reason. It is astonishing how much
peace a Bug Shirt or head net can provide at these times.
Fortunately, the mosquitoes do not last all summer and
in the early and late season it is possible to travel without
their unwelcome attention.

Bears are active in the forest now, fulfilling their
seasonal need to consume as many calories as possible
to sustain their long winter's sleep. They are rarely a
problem, particularly in the remote corners of little-
travelled parks. Near to popular resorts, however,
they may have picked up bad habits and become
accustomed to visiting/raiding campsites for food. For
these reasons we carry pepper spray to deter a bear
that comes too close. The most import effort, though,
must go into maintaining a clean campsite, free from
food remains or waste. All food must be stored in
zip-seal bags, dry bags or barrels to minimise attractive
scents, and kept well away from the sleeping area of
the campsite. When we travel to the very northern
edge of the boreal forest where we can encounter
polar bears, a rifle for self-defence must be carried,
ideally by a local guide who also knows the terrain and
the habits of the local bear population. Unlike other

jackets. These can be found nesting in fallen timber and easily disturbed when collecting firewood. If you do so, the first knowledge you will normally have of it is the first sting. In such circumstances, retreat immediately and swiftly. They will pursue you, but will normally abandon the chase relatively swiftly. If necessary, seek shelter in water. An allergic reaction to such stings in remote circumstances is a life-threatening emergency. Be sure you have received first-aid training covering this scenario and are carrying adrenaline or the current recommended medication for treatment.

It is easy when listing potential problems to create a negative impression of an experience. In truth, summer travel is wonderful, and precious; consider that, if lucky, we are blessed with 80 summers. There are not very many opportunities, then, to experience the wonders of the boreal forest in its most relaxed season.

'The first river you paddle runs through the rest of your life. It bubbles up in pools and eddies to remind you who you are.'
LYNN NOEL *Voyages: Canada's Heritage Rivers*

bear species, which would normally avoid humans, the polar bear can consider a human being a potential food source and stalk them accordingly. Never underestimate the stealth and intelligence of any bear.

Mosquitoes and bears aside, though, the greatest threats to our safety in the bush are to be found in more mundane forms. For example drowning, since we are constantly around water. For this reason, a PFD is mandatory when canoeing and, if you do fall in, you should never try to swim long distances across lakes as the chilling effect of cold water can prove lethal. The other hazards to be aware of are wasps or yellow

Winter Travel

'SOME PEOPLE PREFER traveling in the woods in winter, others in summer. Those who trade in furs will obviously choose the winter. So will explorers, for it is easier and cheaper to move from place to place in the winter, all the more so since one's food keeps better, that's why I my self preferred the winter.'

PAUL PROVENCHER *Last of the Coureurs de Bois*

> 'Det finns inget dåligt väder bara dåliga kläder.' ('There is no bad weather, only bad clothing'.)
> *Traditional Swedish saying*

The silence of the winter forest is a profoundly beautiful contrast to the summer. Each frosty morning fresh tracks betray the presence of fellow winter specialists, such as the long-legged lynx, the wily wolverine, the prolific hare or the regal wolf. Winter camping demands days of honest labour in the company of Whiskey Jack the grey jay, and rewards us with long nights made memorable by the magical spell of good cheer found in the glow of candles illuminating the snug of the tent, warmed by the wonderful, glowing, ticking, wood-burning stove. This is the season in which to tell stories, to share wisdom to celebrate the gift of life itself.

Special tools for winter

The snow shovel

The snow shovel is hardly a romantic tool of the north, but it is a vital one. Most folding snow shovels are designed for mountaineers, who may be digging snow holes. These shovels can be too short and too small — look for a long-handled one that can be used with a sweeping action. The handle shape is also important: a D-shaped handle is ideal as it can easily be used while wearing mitts; next best is the T grip, but avoid at all costs the ball grip as this cannot be grasped with an iced mitt.

The best snow shovel for boreal travel is the hand-made wooden snow scoop, which was used across the boreal forest by the First Nations. Although it may seem a laborious tool to make, the effort is swiftly repaid when it is put into use. A long-handled shovel of this sort enables us to move snow in volume both quickly and easily.

The ice chisel and ice auger

The means to drill through ice is an essential capability in the winter. Before the arrival of metal tools in the north, ice chisels were made with bone and antler tips. Holes were cut early in the winter when the ice was still thin and then kept open as the ice thickened. Today, we have wonderful augers capable of cutting through a metre of ice in only a few seconds. Ice chisels with metal blades are becoming a tool of the past, yet despite this they have several advantages. With no moving parts to go wrong and only a simple chisel edge to sharpen, they are versatile, very reliable and easy to maintain. The blade alone can be transported and a shaft for it made as necessary, usually being retained for the duration of the expedition. The ice chisel must be provided with a sturdy mask, as in order to cut ice the blade must be razor-sharp.

Using an ice chisel requires the cutting of a square or round hole that is wide enough to accommodate the chisel as it cuts the hole, tapering gradually down to

Previous pages Travelling by snowshoe and toboggan, once the traditional way of travelling in the north, is finding renewed interest among modern wilderness travellers. A slow and tough way to travel, it teaches us the deepest respect for the First Nations who once travelled this way.

Opposite The humble snow shovel is an overlooked piece of equipment that is essential for winter travel.

Far right When travelling with a toboggan, one should keep the load as light as possible. Historically, trappers in the north pulled only small toboggans.

Right Hand-carved wooden shovels, once common to the First Nations throughout the boreal forest, are our preferred means of moving snow.

Right middle The traditional ice chisel is easy to use and very easy to maintain.

the water. To cut with the chisel, hold it in front of you inclined between 5 degrees and 10 degrees towards you.

Ice augers cut with a drilling action. Simple manual ones are all that are necessary, although motor-powered augers have gained great popularity. Here again, the edge of the cutting blades needs to be razor-sharp. Many of these blades are curved and thus more complicated to sharpen compared to a chisel. The best edge will require the blades to be removed and sharpened. A quick field sharpening can be carried out with a carbide sharpening tool designed for the task. It is of course easy to carry spare blades, but the necessary spanner will also need to be brought along, adding more weight to the pack.

The auger requires more care in use. It is important not to lose the mask for the blades, and this must be replaced whenever the auger is not in use. When placing the auger on to the ice, do so with great care; banging it down will turn the edge and blunt the tool. Drilling will require no downward pressure if the blade is sharp.

If using a motor auger, take extra care for safety and never let go of the auger. More than once we have watched with amusement as a novice has done this, which results in the auger simply screwing itself down into the ice.

The small scrubbing brush

A small scrubbing brush kept in an outer pocket is a real advantage. It is used to brush snow from clothing, footwear and equipment, helping to preserve warmth and reduce dampness from melting snow when entering warm areas.

Moving on snow

When the snow is deep it can be next to impossible to travel and impossible to do so safely due to the incredible amount of effort that is required. Fortunately, our ancestors solved the problem of walking on snow with the invention of the ski and the snowshoe.

Skis

For the Nordic people in Norway, Sweden, Finland and Russia, skis have always been a prerequisite for traversing the forest during the winter for hunting, fishing and reindeer-herding. We know this because the oldest Nordic ski, which was found in a swamp, is over 5,000 years old.

Skis were the only transport in winter until the snowmobile became available in the 1960s. In the

beginning, skis were a necessary part of home craftwork, made for the family. Inevitably, many different kinds of wood were used, sometimes specifically for certain types of snow or for mountain or forest transports. The name ski has its origin in the Swedish word for a long piece of hewn wood, '*skida*'.

At the beginning of the 20th century, people started using skis for recreation and many ski factories were opened during that period. Initially skis were made from one piece of wood, but in the 1930s they started using wood laminates. In the 1970s, plastic made its appearance in ski manufacture. Even today, though, many people in the forest countries still use wooden skis. Items of beauty, skis made of wood can have a glide sole made of birch, hickory or plastic.

Skiing is a quiet way to travel. It does require some skill to use skis to travel both up and down slopes, but learning is both fun and rewarding and, once a basic level of skill is achieved, they save both time and energy, quickly becoming an addictive way to move on snow.

Unfortunately, the arrival of the snowmobile has greatly reduced the popularity of forest skiing. This is a great shame, because the silence and physicality of skiing is immensely more rewarding than the cold, smelly vibration of travelling by machine. We also frequently encounter people who tell us that they are a little afraid of skis, preferring the simplicity of snowshoeing. But to travel in wilderness demands a boldness of spirit. We enjoy both skiing and snowshoeing, but to us the ski is to the snowshoe as the axe is to the saw.

How to tar and wax skis

TARRING

Wooden skis need to have their base tarred, unless they have a base of plastic, in which case they only need waxing. To tar wooden skis, warm the ski base with a blowtorch or over an open ember fire in order to prevent it warping. Start heating from the middle of the ski. Brush on a thin layer of tar and warm it to cause the tar to penetrate into the pores of the wood. The surface must not be burnt; when the tar bubbles it is warm enough. Smooth out the unabsorbed tar with a brush and re-warm the area, continuing until the surface is saturated. Wipe off the excesses tar while the ski is still warm.

WAXING

In the forest, we normally don't have to wax the skis for glide and hold, unlike mountain areas. Usually we only wax when the snow is wet and sticks to the ski base. At these times we use polar wax, but if this is not available we improvise by using a candle to improve the glide.

WAXING PLASTIC SKIS

Due to their slippery nature, plastic skis have to be waxed to grip even when skiing slowly in the forest. In competitive cross-country skiing, the choice of wax can make the difference between winning or coming second. This has driven specialised research and the production of a bewildering multitude of waxes, produced for different types of snow and specific to weather conditions and temperature. This obsession for achieving the perfect balance between ski grip and ski glide has inevitably found popularity in recreational skiing. However, some of these waxes contain perfluorochemicals (PFCs) that build up in the environment and human bodies and have been implicated in potentially serious health risks, including cardiovascular disease, liver damage, hormone disruption and cancer. The wax we use is easy to handle, easy to carry and is also non-toxic.

HOW TO WAX SKIS

The ski base has a grip zone and a glide zone. The grip zone is in the middle of the ski, from your heel and forwards for 60–80cm (24–31in); the rest of the ski is the glide zone. When you place your weight on the ski the grip zone makes contact with the snow and the wax facilitates the purchase of the ski, preventing it sliding back and allowing forward motion. Grip wax is applied in two to three layers, each buffed evenly on to the ski base with a cork. Wax choice relates to air temperature measured in the shade: the colder the snow, the harder the wax.

In the mountains, choice of wax must be made carefully if any progress is to be made on the steep ground. In the forest, however, there is no need to be so obsessive. If you do not have a thermometer with you, guesstimate the temperature and put on a wax for the coldest you think it may be. If this does not grip, add a layer of wax for warmer conditions. For glide, the most commonly used wax is polar wax.

Opposite top
Excellent snowshoes made by Faber, from traditional wood and babiche. The different designs evolved to cope with different snow conditions.

Opposite bottom
Travelling by snowshoes requires little skill, but is very slow.

Snowshoes

These have been used widely wherever there is deep snow, even being fitted to the feet of horses. But without any doubt it is in the forests of the North American continent that they reached their zenith. Originally made from wood and babiche (rawhide) lacing, they were designed to suit a range of different conditions and purposes. Even the species of wood could be chosen to suit seasonal conditions: for example, yellow birch being chosen to make snowshoes in wet conditions. It was not unusual for native families to make several pairs in one season; some even crafted temporary disposable

snowshoes in the autumn when the snow level was still shallow and there was a risk of damage occurring to the lacing of fine shoes from spikes of wood just beneath the surface. In tandem with the evolution of the ski, there has also been a shift towards using modern materials for snowshoes. But just as with skis, we prefer traditional ones. In some intangible way they belong in the wilderness.

Little skill is required to walk on snowshoes, and there is no need for special footwear. It does, however, take time to develop good balance on them and some prefer to use them with ski poles. Size of snowshoe is determined by the weight of the user. Good manufacturers such as Faber Snowshoes can provide advice here. Always choose the lightest snowshoe that suits your weight. If you intend to trek on snowshoes, a longer, narrower design – like a Cree one – tends to be faster than short, wide snowshoes akin to the Montagnais design, the latter being wonderfully adapted to very deep and tight forest. This having been said, much comes down to personal choice. We like Montagnais snowshoes when travelling by snowmobile as they are easy to transport.

The snowmobile

The snowmobile is the most important means of travel in the boreal forest. These incredible machines can travel long distances at great speed, hauling heavy loads. They can be fun to drive but are sometimes very tiring to operate and constantly expose us to the effects of windchill. It also has to be said that a snowmobile can

Below left
A snowmobile set up for travelling, with reindeer-skin insulation. Note the hunting skis in case of a breakdown.

Below top In the rear compartment, a comprehensive first-aid kit.

Below bottom Under the seat, oil, replacement spark plugs, basic tools, a spare drive belt, rescue ropes and a shovel.

Above Like everything in the north, there is real skill in travelling by snowmobile. It is important to take the time to acquire this knowledge.

take us into danger on thin ice, danger from which dog teams would sometimes shy away.

Snowmobile-driving is a skill that needs to be learned. It requires good balance, concentration and the ability to discern when to drive with caution and when to drive boldly. There are many poor snowmobile drivers and relatively few good ones. Make sure you receive proper instruction in safe driving techniques. Always dress for the coldest weather, with protective goggles, helmet and mitts. Many things can go wrong on snowmobiles, such as headlights or hand-heating mechanisms that either fail or stay turned on full.

Given that a snowmobile can travel so swiftly, it is important to always travel prepared in case of

mechanical breakdown, with necessary spares, a basic tool kit, spare clothing, survival equipment and a means to walk on snow, such as snowshoes or skis. Military snowmobiles are equipped with fittings for such equipment and in some cases even feature a compartment next to the engine for using engine warmth to melt snow to produce fresh water.

How to tow a snowmobile

Mostly we travel on snow-machine trails, which consist of hard-packed snow. If the snowmobile drifts off this, it can become bogged in soft snow or overflow and will need to be towed out.

One snowmobile can tow another. To do this, first

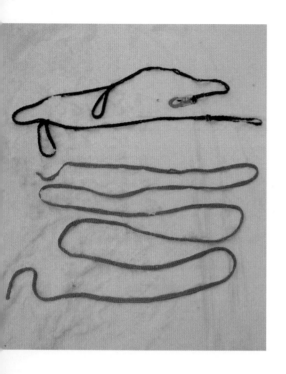

remove the drive belt from the machine to be towed. Now attach a towing strop to the ski legs – do not attach this to the bumper or ski tip. Attach the towing strop to the pulling snowmobile with a rope. This places considerable extra strain on the drive belt of the pulling snowmobile. Attached in this way, no damage should result and the unpowered machine can be steered.

How to tow a snowmobile out of soft snow or overflow

In more difficult circumstances, such as soft snow or overflow, we can still use one snowmobile to tow the other out of difficulty but a rescue track must first be created. To do this, use the still-mobile snowmobile to create a rescue track alongside the machine that is stuck.

This will require bold driving and three or four passes over the track.

Speed in rescue will prevent icing of the drivetrain on the stuck machine. The Runlock snowmobile set is perfect for this, as no knots need to be tied with cold hands and the fastenings do not jam after loading, so it is worth carrying one.

New rescue tools

Today, new tools for snowmobile rescue are available that can greatly ease the task and significantly reduce the chance of a back injury being sustained. Most notable are the Snobunje Cobra and Rattler rescue tools; these function in a similar way to a 4x4 snatch strap and make snowmobile rescue less tiring and less dangerous.

Top left A heavy-duty snowmobile towing system made by Runlock, which doesn't require the tying of any knots.

Top middle To tow a snowmobile, the drive belt should be disengaged and the towing harness attached to the main supports of the front runners, not the front grab handles.

Left Ensure that the towing line is secured to the towing hitch with a locking safety pin where required. Failing to do this, it's quite possible to lose the load being towed without noticing that it's gone.

Below In many parts of the north, people mark the snowmobile trails with subtle indicators. These aren't always easy to see in poor visibility.

Left
1 Even the most experienced snowmobile drivers will struggle in poor snow conditions.
2 In the spring, warm weather causes the snow to soften and machines to become bogged in like this.
3 It is easy to extricate yourself with help, but if you are alone you may need to resort to digging the machine out. Hence the need always to carry a shovel.

Cold starting

These days, four-stroke snowmobiles have virtually replaced the hearty two-stroke models. The old machines were less efficient and lighter than today's models but they could be pull-started in cold weather. Now, when the temperatures are very low, it may be necessary to remove the battery and store it in a warm place at night.

Warming spark plugs can help to get the snowmobile started, although this sometimes needs to be done several times. Flooding the engine with the choke when you finish driving can also help. In the very worst weather, however, you need to warm the snowmobile engine; we have even on occasion had to pitch a heated tent around the engine compartment of the snowmobile to get it warmed and going.

WHAT TO CARRY WHEN TRAVELLING BY SNOWMOBILE IN REMOTE FOREST

- Knife
- Axe
- Shovel
- Rescue rope
- Map
- Compass
- Torch
- Candle (long-life)
- Matches
- Spirit stove with fuel and utensils
- Extra emergency food
- Extra clothing, soap and towel
- Equipment for walking on snowshoes or skis
- Wind protection
- First-aid kit
- Basic toolkit
- Spare spark plugs
- Manual
- Duct tape
- Extra bulbs for lights
- Fuel tube
- Extra drive belt
- Communications equipment

Above The green hue on the frozen lake is overflow revealing itself in the tracks, left by snowmobiles. This can be a real hindrance to travel turning otherwise short trips into marathons of endurance.

Inset The snowmobile is the real workhorse of the north. Travelling in this way, using traditional camping equipment, enables rapid enjoyable movement across long distances.

Above Beautiful beard lichen. Even at the coldest temperatures, the boreal forest is inspiring.

Ice

How ice freezes

As the northern hemisphere tilts away from the warmth of the sun, the temperature cools and lakes and rivers start to lose energy to the atmosphere. As this happens, the surface of the water cools fastest, becomes more dense and then sinks, allowing warmer, less dense water beneath to rise and replace it. This cycle continues until the entire body of water reaches 4°C (39°F). Now, when the surface water cools further it becomes less dense than the surrounding water and remains at the surface, continuing to cool. Once it reaches 0°C (32°F) it freezes. This usually occurs first in the shallows at lake and river edges. The freezing then continues downwards. Unless the body of water is very shallow, there is normally water to be found beneath the ice. Where water flows through rapids and narrows, the process of freezing is disturbed and thin ice and open water can remain throughout the winter. Such places are not marked on maps but are usually well known to the local inhabitants, and can sometimes be located by the trails and presence of otters.

As the ice thickens it expands, causing buckling and cracking. On large lakes this can result in pressure ridges. In the rapids, ice can crack and tumble until lodged, freezing into a jumbled mass of broken ice sheets that are frequently interspersed with patches of open water. The ice under bridges is notoriously dangerous, as it is protected from cold by the bridge above and is therefore thinner than that found elsewhere.

Although it can seem quite solid, ice is actually an astonishingly plastic medium. Throughout the winter, following the physical laws of the universe, it will respond continuously to changing weather patterns, expanding, rising, falling or even shrinking. When the weight of snow bears down on the ice it bows and cracks, creating a pressure in the water beneath. Where cracks exist, water can then flow up on to the upper surface of the ice. If the ice is not covered by snow (glare ice), it usually freezes immediately. But where the ice is covered in snow the water is insulated and remains liquid, sometimes with a thin skin of ice. This water is sometimes visible as a light-green hue in the snow, particularly where snowmobile trails pass over it. This water is called overflow and is usually only a few centimetres deep but can, in the worst conditions, be deeper than 60cm (24in).

Overflow can be a real hindrance and needs to be negotiated with confident snowmobile-driving skills. Any machine bogged in overflow needs to be swiftly rescued or the combined effect of cold metal and water will result in the drivetrain freezing in a casing of ice, which must then be labouriously chipped away. For those on skis or snowshoes, overflow can present an even greater obstacle to travel, for as soon as the skis or snowshoes are wet they attract snow, which freezes as ice. In only a few minutes they can become loaded with 10cm (4in) of ice, which is difficult to remove and makes travel next to impossible. On skis, we can sometimes reduce the problem by candle-waxing the underside of our skis and occasionally laying down spruce branches on the ski trail to brush off the ice. But usually it is best to detour around the overflow, especially if it is deep, to avoid becoming soaked. Skis and snowshoes are easily damaged if you try to remove the accumulated ice with the back of a knife or axe. The best way to do it is to light a fire and patiently melt off the accumulation in warm air to the side of the fire.

While travel is considered to be generally easier in winter once the rivers, lakes and swamps are frozen, it must always be kept in mind that ice is treacherous by nature, difficult to predict, and constantly in a state of change. Ice is safest when it is supported by water: stay off ice that is not supported. This makes an ominous booming sound, hence its name: drum or shell ice.

If travelling on ice using motorised transport, be aware that excessive speed can generate a hydrodynamic wave capable of causing the ice to break.

Bearing strength for lake ice

New ice is stronger than old ice. On lakes, just after it freezes up ice is strongest close to the shore and thinner in the middle. Bear in mind that ice is affected by its temperature, the ambient temperature and solar-radiation levels. Ice quality is critical: consider ice that is cracked, covering fast-flowing water or opaque to be 50 per cent weaker than ice in other situations.

If you are travelling on minimum-thickness ice, keep your weight spread out and avoid moving continuously on the same track. Repeated journeys will tend to weaken the ice. Once ice has thickened it is easy to become complacent, but you should never take ice strength for granted and always observe the conditions carefully.

MINIMUM ICE THICKNESS

Load	Minimum ice thickness
1 person on skis	5cm (2in)
1 person on foot	10cm (4in)
2 persons on snowmobile	15cm (6in)

WHERE TO EXPECT THIN ICE: DANGER AREAS

 Rapids Ice is thin where water flows fast.

 Narrows Ice is thin, often open, where it passes through narrows.

 Confluence Ice is thin where rivers flow into lakes especially where marshy.

 Under bridges Ice is protected from the cold by the structure of the bridge and frequently remains thin.

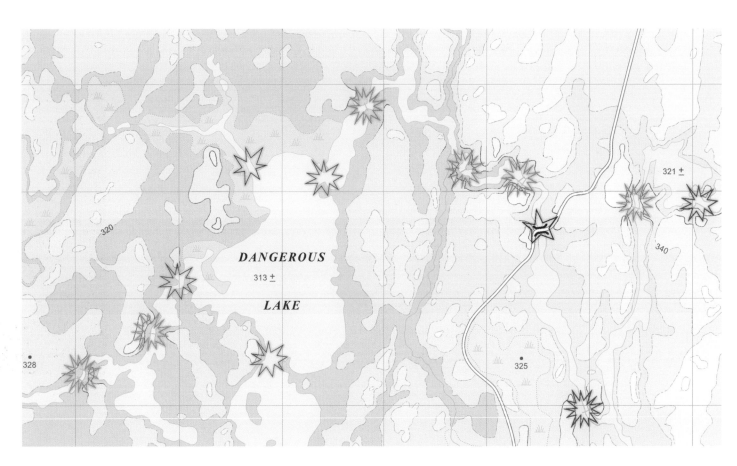

Falling through the ice: self-rescue and rescue

Should the ice break beneath you, the most dangerous response is panic caused by the shocking effect of suddenly becoming immersed in cold water. This is called 'cold shock' and we are all familiar with it: it's the reflex action that causes us to take a deep breath if we turn on a cold shower. In ice-breaking situations this effect is the biggest killer, not hypothermia.

You are more likely to survive the symptoms of cold shock when wearing a personal floatation device (PFD) or a floating overall but, unfortunately, it is not practical to always be dressed in this way. If you have no alternative but to cross ice you believe to be of suspect strength, unhitch your ski bindings so that they can be easily removed in an emergency, and take your hands from ski-pole loops. Ensure that the equipment in your pack is packed tightly in a dry bag that can act as an improvised floatation aid if necessary, and loosen the straps and unfasten the waist belt.

If you break through the ice, force yourself to control your sense of panic and try to calm your breathing, while establishing hold of the ice, preferably with ice picks carried round your neck whenever you are out on the ice. The cold shock will pass after about a minute and you will be able to think and act more clearly. Once you regain control of your breathing, stay calm: the odds are already in your favour.

Below left Ice picks like this are carried around the neck whenever travelling near thin ice. Very cheap to buy, they are one of the best insurance policies you can invest in.

Below middle Open water is not marked on maps, and poses a lethal threat to those unfamiliar with an area, particularly when travelling at night or in poor visibility. It most often occurs where there is fast-flowing water, where streams enter lakes, at narrows and under bridges.

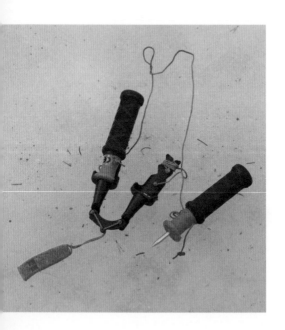

Self-rescue

Despite falling into water, you are going to survive. Free yourself from skis and poles, if possible using them to bridge the hole you have fallen through or the edge of the ice so that your weight is more widely distributed. Turn to exit in the direction you were coming from, as you know that in that direction the ice was strong enough to support your weight. Be prepared for the fact that you may have to struggle through a few more episodes of ice crumbling before you can haul yourself out. Put your arms on to the ice and flutter-kick your feet to raise the lower part of your body in the water as horizontally as possible. When you feel you have sufficient momentum, kick hard, haul yourself over the lip of the ice and roll out. This process is much easier if you have a means of gripping the ice, such as the spikes of your ski poles or ice picks. You will need to raise your determination to the task and fight your way out. On average, you have a 10-minute window of opportunity for self-rescue before cold saps your ability to help yourself.

If you are unable to get out but companions are there to help, have faith. You have on average one hour before the cold will cause you to lose consciousness. You can further help to reduce your heat loss by mostly keeping still, minimising convection to the water, only sporadically moving your legs to generate some warmth. Keep remembering the 1:10:1 theory, as illustrated right.

1:10:1

1 MINUTE:
To control your breathing

10 MINUTES:
To rescue yourself

1 HOUR:
Before you lose consciousness

How to rescue others from frozen water

Any rescue attempt that is made must not put others, including the rescuers, in danger. In some instances, providing encouragement and instruction to the victim may be all that is needed to help them self-rescue. If this isn't sufficient and time is running out, a throw line cast to the victim to pull them out is a natural first step (if the rope is long enough). They may have difficulty grasping the rope with cold hands, so you may need to ask them to wrap it around an arm a couple of times, or you could even tie a loop in the end of the rope (in almost any other rope-rescue situation this would be avoided, but these are special circumstances).

Official rescue teams will not approach this situation without a dry suit, PFD, helmet and ideally a floating rescue platform. If you have no other option and no time to wait for a recue team, a rescuer may consider approaching the victim. However, in order to do so they will need buoyancy, insulation and should be tied securely to a rescue rope so that they can be hauled back if necessary. Try to organise a means of spreading the rescuer's weight over the ice, perhaps by creating a large, light raft of saplings.

Once ashore, the victims must be treated as appropriate to the level of hypothermia (see Cold Injury chapter) they demonstrate. Do not underestimate how chilled and exhausted they may have become.

How to live in a tent in the winter

Camping out in sub-zero conditions is a skillful business that takes practice and iron-willed determination to always set camp perfectly. A tent not only provides a place in which to sleep, it is also a refuge in which to recover from the exertions of the trail, to cook, repair equipment and share the enjoyment of the expedition. In the course of our professional careers we have lived out in all manner of tents in the winter, from tiny mountain tents to Evenki chums.

Tent types and stoves

Mountain tents, while light, are far from ideal, for at low temperatures respired moisture condenses on the inside of the tent, freezes and falls on to the occupants. Consequently, it is wise to employ a bivvi bag to protect your sleeping bag from moisture. It is also extremely difficult to dry clothing in such a tent.

   The traditional tipi-shaped tents of the arctic forest had several important features. Made from many poles, it was easy to organise a drying frame inside the apex for food and clothing. Warmed by an open fire, the smoke lingered in the top two-thirds of the tent, where meat and fish could be preserved. The lowest third of the tent

Right
1 After a comfortable night at -40°C, it's great to put on snowshoes and explore the forest.
2 A tent at -40°C is uninviting until the stove and candles are lit.
3 -40°C outside, +28°C inside, a portable tropical climate that transforms the winter experience.

Left top A traditional Sami *laavu* would house a whole family, snug around an open fire. The top third of the tent was used for smoking and drying meat.

Left bottom The mountain tent is also a life-saving shelter in the north, although it comes a very poor second to a tent, heated by a wood-burning stove.

was a well-warmed smoke-free living space. A good winter tent heated by a stove, however, does not need to be so tall; a low profile means there is a reduced volume of air to heat inside. Like the tipi-shaped tent, the form of the tent should be such that you can rig a drying line or frame in the warm apex. Light-coloured tents allow for plenty of light to work by. The fabric should also be breathable yet windproof and water-repellent.

Our preference is for a tent equipped with a stove – this can be a wood-burning stove, kerosene-burning stove, wood-pellet stove or space heater. Clearly the wood-burning stove is a logical choice in the forest, in which case it should be lightweight, easily lit, easy to control and have a spark-arrestor on the chimney. If you are travelling in a group, a fire-watch system can be organised to keep the fire in. If you are alone or travelling as a pair, a fire that can burn for six hours on a single loading is highly desirable. Some stoves are equipped with water tanks, which is a real luxury. The ability to cook on the stovetop is also desirable and, at the very least, the stove should allow for the heating of a kettle. Some National Parks prohibit the cutting of firewood, in which case a wood-pellet or kerosene-fuelled stove can be used.

Whenever a stove is used in a tent, there must be plenty of ventilation to prevent carbon-monoxide poisoning problems (see Cold Injury chapter).

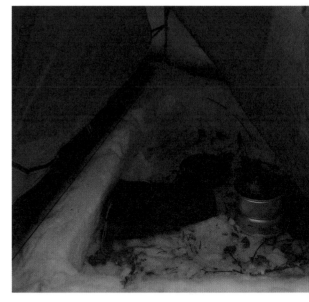

Above Inside the vestibule of a mountain tent, excavate a cold well to trap cold air. This space can also be used for cooking.

Above By comparison, the cheery glow from a wood-burning stove.

Winter Travel

235

Pitching camp

It takes time to pitch camp. Make sure that you allow for this in your schedule and, as always, practise the procedure so that the whole party understands what is required. In the frigid northern landscape, cold air flows like an invisible river, following the rivers and lakes downhill. For this reason, northern towns located on hills tend to be warmer than those in valleys. You can apply this principle when camping. Choose a raised location, perhaps a plateau above the edge of a lake. If you are using a wood-burning stove, choose a site close to a supply of fuel – deadwood is frequently found in swampy areas.

We now have two choices: to remove the snow to the ground or to mix the snow so that it will set hard. If the tent is of native design and heated by an open fire, removing the snow and laying down spruce boughs is the traditional method. If using a wood-burning stove, the snow conditions and temperature will determine the method. The advantage of hardening the snow is that it provides insulation from the ground and can be made level regardless of the ground surface. To do so, however, will require a good depth of snow – > 50cm (20in) – and ideally an ambient temperature of -15°C (5°F) or colder. To harden the snow, use your snow shovel to mix the snow all the way to the ground surface. This mixing alters the nature of the snow crystals, enabling them to sinter and freeze together. Once well mixed, tramp all over the area wearing skis

or snowshoes to compress it. Harden an area larger than the ground plan of your tent.

While the snow hardens you can unload your sledge, pulk or toboggan. Create a space around the tent to locate your equipment. Skis or snowshoes should be brushed clean of snow and stacked neatly. A latrine area can be allocated behind the tent area with a path cleared to it. Firewood can be cut and brought to the tent site. Any wood needed for the construction of the tent or to support the stove and chimney can be cut.

By the time these tasks have been completed, the snow has usually started to harden. Pitch the tent. If you are banking snow against the base of the tent walls, first place a layer of spruce boughs against the fabric to prevent it freezing to the snow. Inside the tent, dig out a cold trap inside the door. In a mountain tent this is usually the area covered by the vestibule. In a tent with a stove this is normally the region surrounding the stove. The purpose of the cold trap is to allow cold air to fall below the level at which we are sleeping. In a mountain tent a candle can be burned to warm the interior air and help to force the cold air down into the cold trap. To prevent the sleeping platform from collapsing, reinforce the rim of the cold trap with sticks laid horizontally.

Inside, the tent must be well organised. We normally create a clean area to the left side of the entrance and a dirty area to the right. The clean area is where food is stored and prepared, and where a sleeping-bag stuff sack filled with fresh, clean snow can be kept as a source for melting into water. The dirty area is for the refuse sack, firewood or the fuel line to the stove. In a safe place where everyone can reach it, a knife is stored for cutting open the fabric of the tent to make an escape route should the tent catch fire. In preparation for such a scenario, it is always worth storing emergency clothing outside your winter shelter. There are stories of people being found frozen and naked, having escaped a cabin fire only to discover with dismay that the fire had consumed their clothing.

Place some reindeer skins on the floor of the tent for insulation. If these are not available, a layer of spruce boughs will suffice. If only birch is on hand then this can also be used. Flatten springy boughs by lightly chopping them with a knife so that they compress well. Over these, roll out your sleeping mat.

As the stove warms, we normally put on a pot of snow to melt. If you have aluminium cooking pots, do not pack them tightly with snow; instead, add a little snow at a time to prevent the pan from burning through. While the snow melts, we organise our equipment, stack the firewood neatly and make a couple of candle-holders. Once the snow has melted we add some dried meat to make a simple boullion. By now the tent itself is beginning to heat up, forcing us out of our warm clothing, all of which is hung up to dry, liners separated from gloves and boots. We change into dry clothing and use our overboots as tent boots. At this stage of the proceedings, the jokes have usually started and the evening progresses.

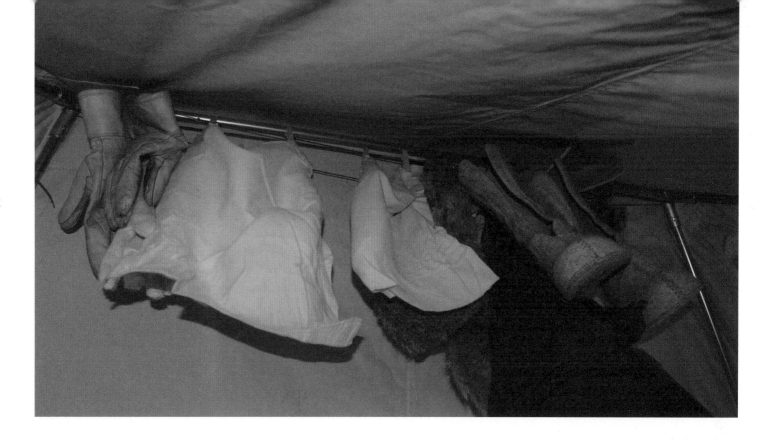

Right The apex of the tent is the hottest place, where we dry our clothing. This is the most significant advantage of camping with a tent with a wood-burning stove.

Taking watch

If we are camping as a pair we draw lots for early or late shift. Late shift keeps the fire burning till late into the evening and prepares feathers to light the fire in the morning. Early shift awakes and relights the stove and puts the coffee on in the morning.

If there are several of you camping together, a fire sentry can be organised. This is the best way to sleep in the north. Each person takes a turn through the night to keep the fire burning and warm. The fire sentry can also rotate clothes that are drying to speed the process, ensure that nothing falls on to the stove and use the time to wash and shave, write up their journal, sharpen their knife, repair equipment and so forth. The sentry awakens their replacement with a warm drink and only turns in once the new sentry is out of their sleeping bag. This is to ensure that if, by accident, the sentry dozes off, they will be woken by the cold in time to re-warm the stove before it goes out. The last sentry can wake the party at the appointed time with a hot drink and breakfast already cooking.

Food in the Wild

'ON THE FRONTIER eating a meal is not the ceremonial affair of politely restrained appetite and dainty selection seen in the best hotels and restaurants, but an honest-to-God shovelling in of fuel at a stopping-place, to enable the machinery to complete its journey, or its task. There the food supply is the most important consideration, and starvation is not merely going hungry for a few days, but becomes a fatal proposition. Civilization will not let you starve; the wilderness will, and glad of the opportunity.'

GREY OWL *Men of the Last Frontier*

Previous pages
Fruit bannock
baking by the fire
epitomises the
simple food we rely
on in the wilderness.

Right Our wanigan comprises
leather pouches containing basic food
ingredients, which are transported in a
lightweight dry bag, and simple cooking
utensils of stainless steel and mostly
hand-carved implements. Keep it simple
– it's easy to carry too many gadgets.

It takes a few days, but there comes a point in
every trip when the catering becomes simpler – when a
kettle filled with tea, a smoky bannock baked beside the
fire and some fresh pike are enough. No need now for
fancy ingredients or time wasted in food preparation.
With this acceptance comes a tuning of the spirit to
the life of the trail, of aspirations in harmony with the
bounty of the forest. From this point onwards, fresh
harvested berries or edible mushrooms are elevated,
appreciated as the culinary marvels they are, precious
flavours from the wild.

Food is a central focus for life in general, but
outdoors it is even more important. On the trail, meals
provide us with energy, with enjoyment, and set the
routine of the day. Even the effects of the worst day's
travel will not long resist the restorative cheer of a
warm, hearty meal. Travelling in wild country demands
of us efficient cookery skills, a repertoire of recipes
carried in our memory and the ability to supplement
our finite supplies from the land.

Utensils and the wanigan

In terms of equipment, there is virtually no limit to
what can be employed, if you are prepared to carry it.
But in our camp you will find only the lightest, simplest
set of utensils. Carved from wood, they can be made on
the journey if necessary. In truth, you will need little
more than an eating spoon, two serving/stirring spoons
and a spatula. Take a long hard look at most cooking
outfits and you will find too many tools and gadgets.

Below Eating al fresco at the end of a hard day's paddling, this restaurant's stars are provided by the night sky.

'Flour, beans, lard, tea, and a certain amount of sugar, with salt pork, may be transported in sufficient quantities to suffice for all winter, in a single canoe, for a single man.'

Men of the Last Frontier GREY OWL

The wanigan has become a cherished tradition of Canadian canoe-tripping. Perhaps a legacy of the canoe brigades of the fur trade, the wanigan or kitchen box is a firm favourite of summer camps. It certainly has much to recommend it: the box is robust, can be made watertight, provides convenient storage for otherwise awkward items and is a welcome food-preparation

surface. Equally, it is popular as a seat, and is frequently a thing of beauty, embellished with poetry, art or just names of trippers. The disadvantage is that it is bulky, awkward to portage and relatively heavy.

We prefer a system inspired by the nomadic First Nations we have worked with, employing food pouches that are all contained in a lightweight dry bag. This is far lighter than a wanigan, watertight, lacks bulk and will reduce in size as the rations are consumed. The perfect wilderness larder, even a small food sack can feed four people for a week. The bulk of the supplies remains tightly stowed in the food pack or barrel, the wanigan being replenished as necessary. The system doesn't provide a work surface, but this is easily remedied by simply employing the blade of a paddle or the underside of a canoe hull to fulfil the same role.

With space always at a premium when winter camping, the food sack is ideal as it occupies less space in the tent.

The importance of salt

Salt has always been of great importance to wilderness travellers, particularly for those hunting and fishing and living for long periods in the wild. As a consequence, it was a highly valuable commodity. Salt was vital for the preservation of fresh meat and fish, and was also the principal seasoning used to improve their flavour when boiled. The sami reindeer herders even salted their coffee, carrying the precious crystals in salt flasks carved from burrs or tightly woven from birch roots.

Fishing

Although, sadly, the days when it was possible to carry a gun or rifle to supply game for the pot are long gone, it is still possible to fish, and the ability to muster food from the wild remains an important skill. Just last season I watched as floatplanes headed out in

Top left Salt flasks are carved from burrs that are hollowed inside with the use of a small chisel and later plugged with antler.

Top right The effort put into creating a hand-carved flask demonstrates the importance of salt in the wilderness.

the early morning mist to pick up parties of canoeists delayed by three days of terrible weather. One party was of particular concern to their outfitters as they had exhausted their food supplies before the storms hit and were not equipped with any fishing equipment. At moments like this you can sense the astonishment of the bushmen and women long past. More than sport, fishing is a fundamental means of obtaining food in the boreal forest, a way of extending our rations and of securing food in a crisis. Being able to catch a fish when necessary is the first step towards being able to *live* in the boreal forest, rather than just visit. Moreover, being able to catch and eat fish on a journey provides a deep spiritual connection to the land.

Fishing in the boreal forest need not be complicated. Although coarse fishing and fly fishing possibilities are excellent, it is spin fishing that is the most common. Plenty has been written on the subject of this method elsewhere. Suffice it to say that your fishing equipment should be strong enough to withstand the rough handling it will experience while being transported in the bush. A glass-fibre rod, such as those made by Ugly Stik, has proven to be excellent in this regard. As we are interested in catching fish for food rather than sport, strong, thin fishing line should be chosen, always equipped with metal leaders to prevent the loss of lures to toothy predatory fish. In terms of lures, spoons and spinners are good, but the most effective of all are jig heads with silicon worm bodies and Rapala crankbaits.

Right Being able to fish is an important skill, enabling us to supplement our staple rations with fresh food.

Try to fish predominantly in the early morning and towards last light. Choose places with steep drop-offs, such as cliffs that plunge into water; narrow places between islands or the shore and islands; where there is weed; at the foot of rapids; or where there is heavy vegetation overhanging water. Take time to read about the species you will be fishing for, and learn their habits and preferred habitats. In the middle of the day while travelling, rig your rod to troll the line behind your canoe.

In winter, it can be very rewarding to fish with a small ice-fishing rod using tiny lures specially designed for the purpose. It is important to dress warmly and to take a filled vacuum flask with you. For those who have the legal right, net fishing is the most reliable method of obtaining fish in the winter.

Above A typical northern fishing-tackle shop, and its proud owner, in Finland.

Left A fishing rod set up with a convenient clamp for trolling enables fishing to be carried out while on the move.

Right Ice-fishing.

Opposite A simple outfit of modern and traditional fishing lures that will cope with most fishing needs in the boreal forest.

How to prepare fish

The simplest way to cook a fish is simply to slit open the belly, clean out the entrails and then skewer it on a sapling. Carve the sapling to have two or three sides to prevent the fish from rotating while cooking, and push the skewer through from the mouth to the tail. This can then be set at an angle beside hot embers and rotated as necessary until the flesh flakes away from the bone. This is a quick and easy traditional method that requires no special skills.

Alternatively, if you have a filleting knife with you it is possible to remove the bones and the skin altogether. This is advantageous as it greatly reduces the chances of choking on a fish bone, a dangerous accident in remote spots far from normal medical back-up. Filleting and skinning fish also removes parts of the fish that can harbour pollutants. For filleting, invest in a good-quality filleting knife such as that made by Marttiini of Finland.

Top left Being able to fillet bony fish is an important skill on the trail.

Top right If you are unsure how to debone a fish, it is always possible to fall back on the simplest cooking methods.

How to fry fish

Top right
Dust chunks of fish
in flour seasoned
with salt and pepper.

Bottom right Fry in
a little hot oil in a fry
pan until crispy and
golden. Delicious.

249

How to fillet a northern pike

Pike are abundant throughout the northern forests. They are easy to catch and very tasty to eat, but despite this they are often avoided due to their reputation for being bony. They do have a set of so-called 'Y bones' that require special handling, but these can easily be removed following this method.

Opposite
1 Cut along the belly and around the pelvic fins.
2 Cut down to the spine, but not through it.
3 Cut towards the tail.
4 Stop before you reach the tail – don't cut through it.
5 Turn over the fish and repeat on the other side, removing the pelvic fins.
6 The head, spine and guts should now be free, as shown.
7 Cut away the ribs.

8 Once mostly separated with the knife, the ribs can be peeled away.
9 Using your fingers, locate the pin bones remaining in the fillet and cut straight down to them.
10 Cut following the angle of the pin bones to their tips.
11 Now cut behind the pin bones, following their angle.
12 The pin bones can now be pulled out.
13 Remove the fillet from the skin using a sawing action.
14 Voilà! A beautiful bone-free fillet.

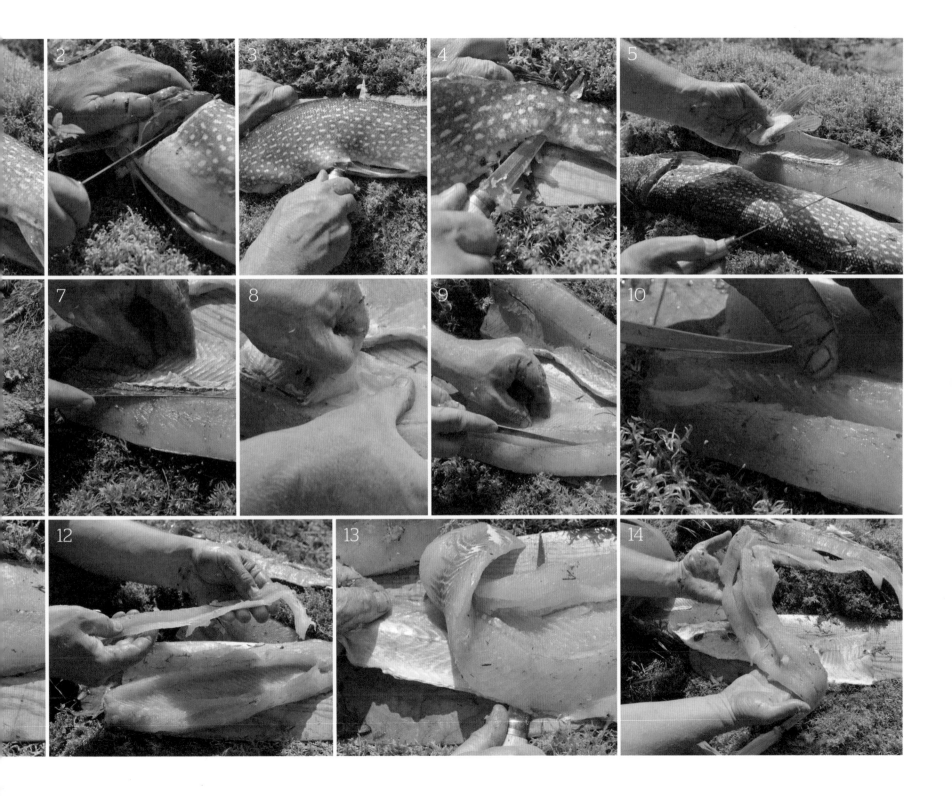

How to fillet Arctic char

This method can also be applied to trout and salmon. It is easy and, done carefully, will remove every bone.

Opposite

1 Remove the guts from the belly of the fish and cut away the dorsal fin.
2 Locate the pectoral fin and its supporting bone.
3 Holding the fin and the bone, cut away each pectoral fin in turn.
4 Slit the fish to the tail on either side of the anal fin, and remove it.
5 Cut down to the spine behind the gill on both sides of the fish. Do not cut through the spine.

6 Using your thumb, begin to separate the ribs from the flesh.
7 Use your fingertips to continue separating the ribs and flesh until you feel the top of the spine.
8 Repeat this process on the other side of the fish.
9 Lift the head and spine from the fillet.
10 Cut away the tail, leaving a large boneless fillet.

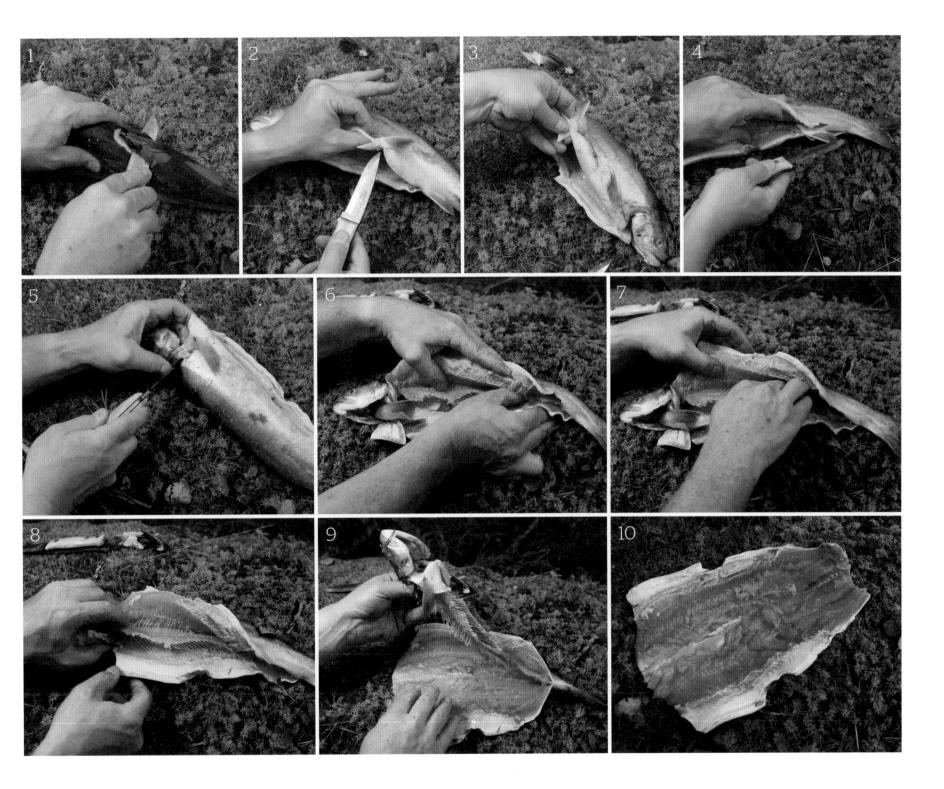

How to cook Arctic char

This simple, elegant native method can be used to cook all the delicious members of the salmon family.

1 Carve two pointed and flat green-wood sticks and skewer them through the fillet.
2 Place the skewered fillet into a split green-willow sapling.
3 Tie the split stick firmly shut using several strips of willow bark.
4 The fillet is cooked in front of a hot ember fire, angled over the coals.
5 Once cooked, the crispy fillet can be removed from the split stick.
6 To my mind, there are few dishes that come close to Arctic char cooked in this way.

How to dry fish

Fish were once a vital source of winter food, particularly for feeding sled dogs. From late summer and through the autumn, stockpiles were prepared and preserved ready for the winter, normally by drying. To achieve this, the fish was carefully filleted and then the flesh was finely sliced to speed the process and to ensure the flesh dried thoroughly.

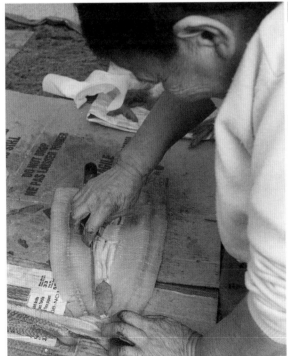

Above Fish drying in a Dogrib camp.

Far left Great care is taken to score and prepare white fish for drying.

Left Scoring ensures that the fish flesh dries quickly and evenly.

Willow grouse

Grouse have always been a part of the
menu in the Northern Forest. If you
travel widely enough in winter you will
certainly be offered one to eat at some
point. They are delicious but need to
be cooked gently since they are easily
spoiled by overcooking.

How to cook
a willow grouse

Take the breasts and season them with
salt and pepper. Ideally wrap each in a
strip of bacon, if you have it. If not, no
matter. Heat a little fat, ideally butter,
in a frying pan. Once sizzling, add the
breasts and brown, basting constantly.
Once well browned all over, remove
the meat to a warm billycan, cover
with a lid and leave to rest for at least
10 minutes before serving. Be careful
not to overcook the meat.

Right The willow
grouse has always
been an important
source of sustenance
in the north.

How to dress a willow grouse

Right
1 Pluck the feathers from the breast.
2 Split the skin by stretching it across the breastbone.
3 Peel back the skin from all around the breast.
4 Place your thumb under the sternum and lift up the breast from the carcass.
5 Break off the wings and any other attaching points.
6 The removed breast meat is now ready for cooking.

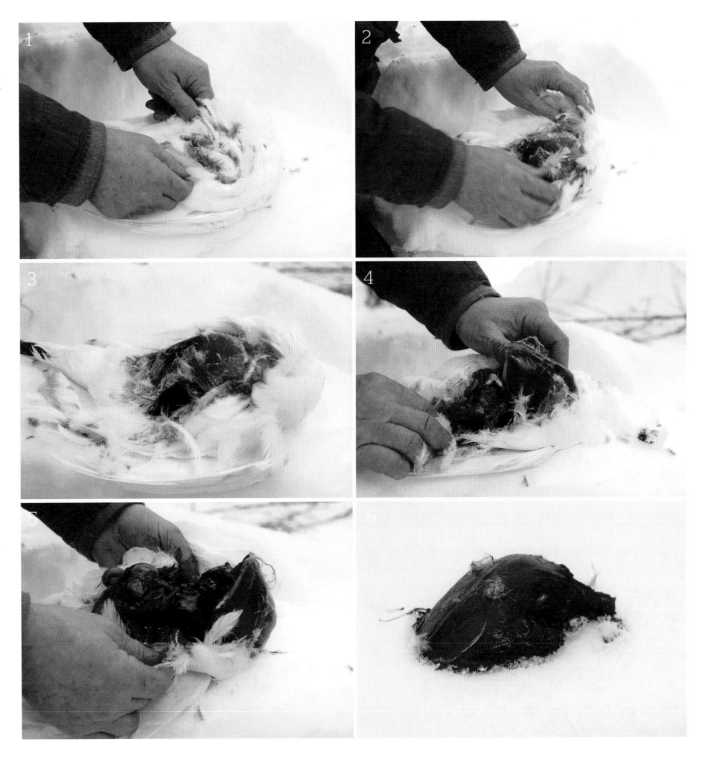

Drying meat

Meat is traditionally preserved by being thinly sliced and dried on racks suspended from the top of a tent or *laavu*. Meat dried until it is virtually brittle is still an important winter resource in northern communities. One excellent way to use it is to shred the dried meat by pounding it between a smooth, hard stone and the poll of your axe. This can be kept for long periods. Along with the meat, it is usual to store marrow fat. To obtain marrow fat, break reindeer bones into small fragments and then boil them in plenty of water. The fat liberated from the bones rises to the surface, where it can be skimmed off, collected and allowed to harden.

Dried reindeer heart

Reindeer heart is delicious and is easily preserved. Simply slice it in half lengthways and then dry it outdoors in the very cold spring air. It makes a great alternative to jerky.

Above Caribou meat being dried on a frame inside a heated winter tent.

Left Meat drying in an Indian camp.

Pemmican

Pemmican is well known as an iron ration on long wilderness journeys. To make it, dried meat is first shredded and then fried with plenty of fat. Dried pounded berries could also be incorporated. Once cool, the fat hardens and aids the preservation of the meat. In truth, it is an acquired taste and is rarely made today, as dried shredded meat tastes better and can be easily stored for long periods in zip-seal bags.

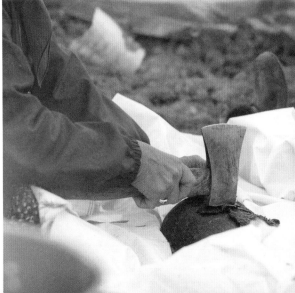

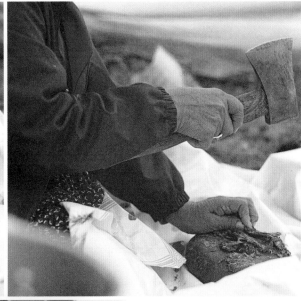

Top left Dried caribou meat is shredded by being pounded with the back of an axe.

Top right This is a time-consuming and tedious job.

Left Shredded dried caribou meat is mixed with fat to create pemmican.

Beverages

Teas

In the camp, the kettle is always available, usually with two or three teabags inside, cooking out the full measure of their flavour. But there is a number of wild teas that we can also utilise on the trail. These are important, not just for providing flavour to water but also for the vitamins they can contain; in the past, evergreen teas were an important source of vitamin C and were used to prevent scurvy.

To make tea, boil water and then infuse it with your chosen brew. Many plants can be dried for use in this way, including: mint, birch, wild raspberry, wild strawberry, blueberry, fireweed and bog myrtle (go easy here, it is very strong), to name but a few. Of immediate use on the trail we can look to the needles or leaves from the following trees: spruce, pine, cedar, Labrador tea and juniper. Note: these teas are potent and should only be used occasionally. They can be harmful if overused.

Right
1 Spruce
2 Pine
3 Cedar
4 Labrador tea
5 Juniper
6 Mint

Right Super-strength woodsman's coffee can be brewed directly in a kettle reserved solely for this purpose.

Coffee

Coffee is a perennial favourite trail beverage; in Scandinavia, it is traditional to carry a kettle solely for its preparation. No fancy gadgets here, just proper woods-brewed coffee strong enough to dissolve a birch-wood spoon. To make coffee in the old way, add 7 tbsp (105ml) ground coffee to 4 cups (1 litre) cold water. Stir it well, then place the kettle to warm on some embers for a few minutes before elevating it to the hottest part of the fire to boil. As soon as it boils, remove the kettle, place it on the ground and either add 3 tbsp (45ml) cold water to settle the grounds, or drum on the side of the kettle with a stick to agitate the contents and achieve the same result.

Inevitably, the kettle will soot up over time, and it is worth removing this frequently as it will slow the boiling time. Transport this kettle in its own cloth sack to avoid making everything else sooty.

Boullion

The best boullion is made by roasting bones for 30 minutes in a Dutch oven, then adding cold water and simmering for 1 hour. It makes a warming drink on the winter trail as well as a wonderful ingredient in stews and soups. However, when travelling in the winter it is more convenient to use dried meat in place of the bones. In Scandinavia, we always carry smoked dried reindeer meat purchased from Sami butchers, who leave a small amount of fat on their meat by tradition, in contrast to the popular lean jerky available as a trail snack today. This fat is important in the cooking.

Having pitched the tent and lit the fire, put some snow on to melt in the pan and use the time to organise your belongings. Once the snow has melted, slice in small slivers of the meat and leave it to cook on the stove while hanging your day clothes to dry along the tent ridge and donning dry clothes. Usually by now the warming boullion is ready. Simply add a pinch of salt and enjoy your drink with some crisp bread.

Breads

Summer bannock

Brought to Canada by the Orkney employees of the Hudson's Bay Company, bannock swiftly became a staple of the fur-trade and First-Nation camp. Despite its dubious nutritional value for everyday life, it is nonetheless a welcome bread on the trail, being easy to make and very versatile.

Below Bannock on sale in a bread shop in the Orkneys.

Ingredients (makes 1 bannock)

2 cups (500ml) plain (all-purpose) flour
1 cup (250ml) powdered milk (optional)
2 tsp (10ml) baking powder
½ tsp (2.5ml) salt
1 tsp (5ml) sugar
sufficient water
1 cup (500ml) dried fruit or fresh berries
oil or lard, for cooking

Method

1 Mix together the dry ingredients, excluding the fruit, being sure to loosen up the flour and stir in plenty of air with a spoon.

2 Add the water gradually, mixing it with your fingertips until you have a soft but not sticky dough. You may not need all of the water, so add it a little at a time. If the mixture is too wet, add a little extra flour.

3 This being done, fold in the dried fruit or freshly picked berries, if available.

4 Put your fry pan on the heat and add a little oil or lard. Once this is hot, add the dough, spreading it out with your knuckles until it fills the pan. It should be approximately 2cm (⅘in) thick.

5 Heat the fry pan directly over some slow embers until the dough starts to firm up. Do not burn the bannock. Eventually, the dough will be firm enough for you to be able to tilt the pan and set it upright to one side of your fire. In this way, grill the bannock, rotating it and turning it over as necessary, until a sliver of freshly shaved wood skewered into the centre of the bannock comes out dry.

Opposite
1 Aerate the flour and dried milk powder.
2 Add the baking powder, salt and sugar.
3 Add sufficient water to form a dry dough.
4 Add any dried fruit.
5 Heat some oil or lard in a frying pan.
6 Add the dough to the pan and spread with your knuckles to the full width of the pan.
7 Heat the pan over the fire, without burning the dough, and cook until the dough begins to firm.
8 Place the pan tilted towards the heat of the fire and cook until golden.
9 A kettleful of bush tea and a bannock are the key components of a classic outdoor meal.

> **Variation** A savoury bannock can be made without the addition of fruit and sugar. Place it under a fish grilling beside the fire to catch the dripping fat, which adds a wonderful flavour.

Winter bannock

This differs from its summer cousin in that it contains lard or oil, which will make the bread less likely to freeze hard in cold weather. Bear in mind it will still freeze in extreme cold. If you wish, milk powder can be added, and instead of fruit, cheese or sliced salami can be included.

Ingredients (makes 1 bannock)

Served with jam and a drink of black tea or with dried meat and marrow fat, this is the perfect winter treat.

2 cups (500ml) plain (all-purpose) flour
2 tbsp (30ml) lard or oil
½ tsp (2.5ml) salt
2 tsp (10ml) baking powder
sufficient water to make the right dough
1 cup (500ml) dried fruit

Method

The cooking method is the same as for the summer bannock. If you are camping in a tent with a wood-burning stove, the bannock can be started on top of this and, once firm, suspended on a sharpened stick to cook vertically close to the wall of the stove.

Twists

If you have no pan, you can cook bannock by forming it into a long sausage shape and wrapping it around a stick. Choose a green birch stick that is 2–4cm (⅘–1⅗in) in diameter. Using your knife, shave away the bark from the cooking end of your stick and add a point to the other end. Scorch the cooking end of the stick in the fire before wrapping it with your dough, then toast the bannock twist over your fire, rotating it as necessary. Do not rush the cooking or the outside will form a hard crust but the centre will be uncooked. It makes a delightful accompaniment to roasted goose, or can be served simply with maple syrup or jam.

Below In a Dogrib winter camp, bannock is started on top of the stove and finished held on a stick beside the wood stove.

Above Fry bread is
a calorific version of
a doughnut.

Fry bread

More common at a fixed camp, this is a delicious,
calorie-rich bread that is popular in Native American
and Canadian communities. We only recommend its
use for feeding camps engaged in hard physical activity.
It is a versatile food that can be eaten like a doughnut
dusted in sugar or with maple syrup, or as a savoury
accompaniment to stews or soups. It can even be used
as the bun for a high-calorie burger.

Ingredients (makes approx 4)

2 cups (500ml) flour (preferably bread flour)
2 tsp (10ml) baking powder
½ tsp (2.5ml) salt
sufficient warm water
½ cup (125ml) cooking oil

Method

1 Mix together the dry ingredients and ensure that
there is plenty of air in the flour by mixing lightly
with a spoon.
2 Add the water gradually, mixing it with your
fingertips until you have a dough that is soft but not
sticky. Do not knead it.
3 Leave the dough to stand in a covered container for
30 minutes.
4 Form the dough gently into 4 balls and stretch them
out flat, like mini pizza rounds. Make a hole with your
thumb in the middle of each round.
5 Pour sufficient oil into a fry pan to come to a depth
of 2cm (⅘in). Heat until hot. Test the temperature by
dropping a bit of dough in the pan and if it sizzles it is
the right temperature.
6 Carefully and gently add a dough round to the oil
and fry until the edges are golden. Turn and cook on
the other side, until it is golden all over.
7 Remove from the oil by hooking a stick through the
hole and drain it well before serving. Repeat the cooking
process with the remaining dough rounds.

Crisp bread

This is the classic Scandinavian hard tack. Crisp bread is easy to make, can be stored for a long time and is a first-rate lunch ingredient when travelling. In a cabin, you can attempt the classic round bread with a hole in the centre. This allows the crisp breads to be threaded on to a stick and suspended in the dry air above the fireplace. In the bush, however, it is more practical to make small biscuit-sized ones. The secret to good crisp bread is to ensure they are very thin.

Ingredients (makes approx 40 crisp breads)
2 cups (500ml) rye flour (or whatever you have)
1½ tsp (7.5ml) salt
sufficient water to mix

Method
1 Combine the dry ingredients and add water to form a stiff dough.
2 Take small balls of the dough, about 2.5cm (1in) in diameter, and pat out until they are very thin. Prick all over with the point of your knife. Alternatively, if you have a table, take a ball of dough the size of a golf ball and roll it out to a thin round about 10cm (4in) in diameter, then prick it all over or roll it with a knurled rolling pin. If you intend to make a lot of crisp breads you may enjoy carving your own rolling pin.
3 The crisp breads can be cooked one at a time on a hot surface, such as a hot, dry fry pan or even a flat rock. Cook the pricked surface first, until the edge starts to brown, then turn it over.

4 Continue cooking until the bread is very stiff, then remove from the heat and allow it to dry in the warm air at the edge of your fire while you cook the remaining dough in the same way.
5 To store, keep them dry.

Above Crisp bread is delicious and makes a good lunch on the trail.

> **Variation** Crisp bread can be flavoured by the addition of edible herbs – a good way to use the more bitter-tasting ones found in the forest. To do this, chop the herbs finely with your knife and add them to the dry ingredients before combining with the water.

Gahkku

Below *Gahkku* can be topped with various ingredients, or used as a wrap.

Gahkku is the delicious bread of the Sami. Being easily prepared in the *laavu*, lasting for a few days, not being prone to freezing and robust enough for travelling, it is a classic travel bread. The recipe calls for yeast, although it can be made without. Sometimes the bread is made with stock from boiled reindeer bones for added flavour. If this is the case, there is no need for syrup.

Ingredients (makes 6–8 flat breads)

5 tbsp (75ml) powdered milk
2½ tsp (12.5ml) fast-action yeast
3 cups (750ml) plain flour or strong bread flour
1 tsp (5ml) salt
5 tbsp (75ml) golden (light corn) syrup
sufficient water

Method

1 Combine the dry ingredients, then add the syrup.

2 Add water gradually to form a smooth bread dough.

3 Leave this to sit in a warm place in a covered bowl for 2 hours.

4 Divide the dough into 6–8 balls, then roll out each into a thin circle with a diameter of about 20cm (8in).

5 Prick each circle all over with the point of your knife.

6 Cook one bread at a time on a hot, dry fry pan or griddle until brown, then turn and cook the other side.

7 Transfer to a clean cloth and cover while cooking the rest. Serve with a stew or use to make a delicious wrap sandwich.

Pancakes

Pancakes make a hearty breakfast to start the motors on a rainy day. More than once we have laughed with canoeing pals as we tucked into pancakes with maple syrup, drowning in a bowl that was rapidly filling with rain. Add freshly picked blueberries or some sliced apple poached in maple syrup for added zing.

Ingredients
(makes 4 20cm/8in pancakes)
2 cups (500ml) plain (all-purpose) flour
2 tsp (10ml) baking powder
2 tbsp (30ml) dried egg powder
4 tbsp (60ml) powdered milk
2 tsp (10ml) sugar
sufficient water
oil for cooking

Method
1 Combine the dry ingredients, then whisk in sufficient water to form a batter with the same consistency as thick cream.
2 Heat a spoonful of cooking oil in a fry pan.
3 Spoon in sufficient mixture to cover the base of the fry pan.
4 Fry until bubbles form across the top of the pancake, then flip it and cook the reverse until golden.
5 Transfer to a plate and cook the remaining batter in the same way.

Left Pancakes are a hearty way to start a day's canoeing in remote country.

Dessert

Rice Pudding

This dish needs little introduction, and is delicious eaten hot or cold. It is incredibly easy to cook on the trail, made in its simplest way in a billycan. If you have access to one, an oven or a Dutch oven can of course be used instead. But truly there is little need – a billycan does an admirable job.

Ingredients (serves 4)

10–12 tbsp (150–180ml) milk powder
4 cups (1 litre) water
1 cup (250ml) short-grain pudding rice
1 tbsp (15ml) sugar

Method

1 Reconstitute the dried milk with the water in the billycan to make 4 cups (1 litre) milk.
2 Add the dry ingredients, stirring them into the milk.
3 Cover and hang the billycan high over the fire so that it will cook very gently – do not let the milk boil.
4 Gently stir the mixture occasionally, until the rice is cooked. If necessary, add extra water. In ideal conditions, cooking will take 30–40 minutes.
5 Serve the rice pudding with a sprinkling of sugar or some maple syrup. Alternatively add wild berries or a handful of dried fruit after 15 minutes of cooking.

Right Rice pudding sprinkled with brown sugar is an underrated and easily cooked outdoor meal.

Foraging

Compared to more southerly environments, the boreal forest is a poor supplier of edible herbs. Foragers with good knowledge and sharp eyes will of course find plants to eat, but the real foraging potential of the taiga is realised in the harvest of wild berries and fungi. For the traveller, being able to recognise a few of the tastiest and most common of these can really enliven the trail menu. If you decide to explore the world of edible wild foods you must equip yourself with the knowledge to clearly identify the edible plant, to know what it might be mistaken for, and to differentiate between them.

Berries

There are very many berries that can be encountered in the boreal forest, depending upon your location. Take a good field guide with you and take the time necessary to learn to distinguish between the berries. Bear in mind that the forest bears species of poisonous as well as edible berries.

> **Toxic.**
> **DO NOT EAT!**

Bunchberry Bland-tasting with a large seed, bunchberries are only really used as a survival food.

Kinnikinik Used by native people, kinnikinik are fried in fat or boiled in soups with caribou meat.

Lingonberry Easily identified by the pores on the underside of the leaf, lingonberries contain a natural preservative. Tart, the best way of eating them is as a jam or with reindeer meat.

Bilberry and Blueberry Eaten raw, these berries can reduce blood-sugar levels. They can also be cooked with sugar or dried and added to pancakes or bannock.

Wild strawberry Smaller and even tastier than the cultivated variety, wild strawberries are a delectable treat.

Arctic bramble Small and easily missed, this is the most delicious berry on the planet; one taste is all it takes for you to become hooked.

Rosehips Rosehips are packed with vitamin C. Remove the irritating hairy seeds prior to eating them, either raw or cooked.

Redcurrant These familiar currants are delicious little edible jewels of the forest that can be eaten raw or cooked.

Gooseberry and Raspberry Wild gooseberries are smaller and sweeter than the cultivated cousin. Raspberries every bit the equal of cultivated species.

Amelanchier Reddish-purple to dark blue when ripe, these berries were usually dried, or mashed and dried as a fruit leather. They can be added to soups and stews or added to bannock.

Rowan berry With a high tannin content, rowan berries are extremely bitter. They are best used to make jelly, with pectin and sugar, although in a crisis they can be deseeded, dried and added to bannock.

Twisted stalk This has been used as food by native people, but is probably best avoided since it has laxative properties and looks similar to plants of the toxic Veratrum genus.

Clintonia (*Left*) The blue berry of clintonia is TOXIC, but the leaves have been used raw or cooked and have a flavour reminiscent of cucumber.

Baneberry (*Right*) All parts of the baneberry are poisonous, most particularly the roots and berries. Severe poisoning can result in paralysis of the respiratory system and cardiac arrest. DO NOT EAT IT!

Red osier dogwood Although used by native people, the berries of the red osier dogwood are extremely bitter and generally not considered worth eating today.

Fungi

Fungi are flavoursome marvels for those who can recognise them. However, this is not an area of knowledge suited to home study with a field guide – expert tuition is required. Differentiating between fungi can be a subtle business in the field, requiring a thorough knowledge of fungus anatomy, the ability to differentiate by smells and taste, and a good knowledge of the vast range of species that may be encountered. The way to learn about fungus identification is to attend a course run by an expert field mycologist and understand that it is going to be several seasons before you really become competent. On a positive note, though, fungi are fascinating things to learn about.

Amanita brunnescens A poisonous member of the deathcap family, it is important to recognise the key features of this group of fungi: white detachable scales on the surface of the cap; the distinctive skirt around the top of the stem; white gills beneath the cap; and a bulbous base to the stem, in some cases emerging from the sack.

Puffball When edible, puffballs have pure-white flesh when cut through, with no signs of any developing internal features.

Chanterelle Most poisoning occurs as a result of the misidentification of chanterelles. Once proper identification has been learned it is easy to spot this delicious fungus, which has an apricot-like scent.

Hedgehog fungus Hedgehog fungus has spines beneath the cap, is easy to learn to identify, and makes delicious eating.

Forest bolete Boletes have a spongy underside to the cap. There are some poisonous family members, but also many delicious edible boletes, which are easy to learn to identify.

Nettles

Either stinging or stingless dead nettles can be used for cooking. If collecting stinging nettles, get them from a shady location – ones growing in the open are too bitter.

Nettle soup

This is a very ancient dish that is quite delicious if made well. If you have the benefit of an onion, some pancetta and a potato, it can be spectacular. The secret lies with choosing the best nettles, using a high-quality stock and seasoning the soup well.

Variation

Should you have a little pancetta, bacon or an onion, chop it finely and fry it until soft in the fat before you add the flour. Failing these ingredients, a little meat or fish can be substituted or even the white leek-like end of a cattail stem.

Ingredients (serves 2)

4 cups (1 litre) nettle tops
butter or cooking oil
enough plain (all-purpose) flour to make the roux
1 litre of stock
sufficient dehydrated potato or milk powder
salt and pepper, to taste

Method

1 Drop the nettle tops into 2 cups (500ml) boiling water and simmer for 5–10 minutes (this will neutralise any stings).

2 Lift out the nettles, reserving the cooking water, then chop them finely with your knife.

3 Melt the butter or heat the oil, then mix in the flour to create a smooth paste called a roux.

4 Add the stock to the roux, mixing it in slowly and thoroughly to prevent lumps forming.

5 Add the reserved nettle water and finely chopped nettle tops.

6 Allow the soup to reduce for about 10–20 minutes. In an ideal world we would thicken the soup with a potato or by adding crème fraîche, but on the trail it can be thickened with some dehydrated potato or a little milk powder.

7 Finally, season the soup to taste with salt and pepper just before serving.

Above Nettle soup is a tasty and nourishing delight, a wonderful soup produced from the least likely wild herb.

Survival

'FROM HER ACCOUNT of the moons passed since her elopement, it appeared that she had been near seven months without seeing a human face; during all of which time she had supported herself very well by snaring partridges, rabbits, and squirrels; she had also killed two or three beaver, and some porcupines. That she did not seem to have been in want is evident, as she had a small stock of provisions by her when she was discovered; and was in good health and condition, and I think one of the finest women, of a real Indian, that I have seen in any part of North America.'

SAMUEL HEARNE *A Journey from Prince of Wales's Fort in Hudson's Bay to the Northern Ocean in the Years 1769, 1770, 1771 and 1772*

Misfortune is no respecter of experience. Despite the fact that in all our preparations and actions we strive to avoid exposing ourselves to harm, there are many contrary forces that remain beyond our control. Extreme weather, injury, acts of war, harm by wildlife, mechanical failure, human error – the list is long, but serves to remind us that any one of us could find ourselves facing a life-threatening situation. The sober reality of traversing remote boreal forest is that the very isolation of our situation will assuredly complicate such scenarios, elevating the consequence of minor mishap

to potential tragedy. Think 'survival' and the mind automatically conjures up a plane crash or bear attack – we forget that even small events such as an allergic reaction to a wasp sting can trigger a nightmare struggle for survival in the taiga.

The one thing that we can predict about a survival scenario is that we cannot predict what the situation will be, and that almost certainly it will come as a surprise. Coping with a life-threatening event is massively stressful, particularly if we are surprised or trying to function with little time. Under these conditions, our sympathetic nervous system takes control of our body, adrenaline courses through our blood and we experience perceptual narrowing, our brain only paying attention to the sense that it perceives to be most relevant. For example, a canoeist trapped by a fallen

Below Some of our students training to survive in northern Sweden, where the temperature was -48ºC (-54ºF). No amount of reading or video-watching can replace hands-on tuition; only under these conditions will you fully understand the true importance of the basic skills for survival – building a snow shelter, making a fire and wearing the correct clothing – as well as comprehending how your body and brain react in cold weather.

Previous pages
When things go
wrong, remember
you can and you
will survive.

branch in a rapid may become totally focused on trying to extricate themselves from their dilemma, unable to hear the shouted commands of nearby potential rescuers. So serious can this become that they may experience a tunnelling of their vision, whereby they are only able to see their own hands, all other senses and peripheral vision denied by their stressed brain. In short, the stress experienced in a life-threatening situation can itself become a danger.

It is precisely under these circumstances that prior training can make a difference, the body going into autopilot as drills and well-rehearsed procedures kick in to meet the need. What we can learn from this is that training in all our skills needs to be progressive, realistic and include some degree of stress so that we inoculate ourselves against times of greatest need. No matter how experienced we are, we should all test ourselves in this way on a regular basis. For example, combining canoe-capsize training with the ability to subsequently swim

to shore, light a fire and dry our clothes. Such testing training inevitably reveals weaknesses in our methods and equipment. This is what we are searching for, our failings — it is far better to discover them in a practice session than reality.

One particular area of training that must never be ignored is the need for realistic, wilderness-appropriate first-aid training. Not only will this prepare us to handle a range of potential accidents, but it will also guide our selection of first-aid equipment and, most importantly of all, will raise our awareness of the threat posed by the potential medical hazards we will be encountering. Forewarned is forearmed: awareness of consequences is a vital element in our assessment of risk. It should also be noted that we have encountered many cases in which wilderness first-aid training has been put to life-saving use in the home to save the lives of friends and family, so it is always of benefit.

Survival mentality

Being cut off, lost or alone in the vast boreal forest is not a desirable state of affairs, but need not prove fatal. If you keep a cool head and a positive frame of mind there is little doubt that you can and will survive. In our professional lives, we have both made extensive studies of real survival episodes. This has taught us that, ultimately, survival situations are won or lost in our hearts and in our minds. For this reason there is no such thing as a survival expert, for even the best-trained, toughest individual may be overwhelmed if faced with a life-threatening situation when emotionally upset. Real life demonstrates time and again that survivors of extraordinary circumstances come from all walks of life – rarely are they the chisel-jawed hero of Hollywood. What they do have, however, is an internal ability to make their psychology work for themselves.

A survivor chooses to survive and, having done so, stubbornly refuses to do anything else. They find a personal focus, a reason to live. There is no obvious pattern here. For some it may be seeing a loved one again, while for another it may be a determination not to quit the mortal realm without having owned a car. Whatever it is, this personal focus becomes a fixed point of attachment to a mental lifeline that reaches beyond the circumstance of the survival situation to a more normal future. Visualising this future replaces despair, and gives hope and the necessary motivation to achieve a positive outcome. This determination reaches beyond the cerebral dimension, providing tangible stability and balance in the physical realm. Now, whatever challenges must be faced are dealt with as manageable steps towards a desired outcome.

In most survival episodes the immediate need is for medical aid, shelter from elemental threats, or water. Food is therefore considered a minor priority in the short term. However, given the remote nature of the boreal forest, if we do not have the means to summon assistance or rescue it is highly likely that we may be facing a long wait. In such instances, finding food becomes a far higher priority.

Below A First Nation man demonstrates a traditional lifting-bar hare snare. Perfected over thousands of years, skills such as these were essential to life for remote communities and remain a component of the cultural identity of forest peoples.

Living from the land

While we may be used to supplementing our rations with a fishing rod and therefore feel confident that we can feed ourselves, the reality of living from the land is a totally different proposition. There is no better reminder of this than the last diary entry of Leonidas Hubbard.

'SUNDAY, OCTOBER 18TH, 1903
…I believe we will all get out. My tent is pitched in open-tent style in front of a big rock. The rock reflects the fire, but now it is going out because of the rain.
I think I shall let it go and close the tent till rain is over, thus keeping out wind and saving wood. To night or to-morrow perhaps the weather will improve, so I can build a fire, eat the rest of my moccasins and have some more bone broth. Then I can boil my belt and oil-tanned moccasins and a pair of cowhide mittens.

I am not suffering. The acute pangs of hunger have given way to indifference. I'm sleepy. I think death from starvation is not so bad. But let no one suppose I expect it. I am prepared – that is all. I think the boys will be able, with the Lord's help, to save me.'

LAST PART OF FINAL DIARY ENTRY OF LEONIDAS HUBBARD

Finding food in the boreal forest has never been easy, a fact well reflected by the smallness of the human population historically found in this vast geographical region. First Nations in the boreal forest were highly mobile societies, spending most of the year in small family groups hunting and gathering widely throughout the forest. Only in the summer was there a sufficient abundance of resources for them to be able to congregate in greater numbers. Consequently, these summer gatherings were important social events, times for trading, ceremony, love and marriage. During the winter, they would be dispersed to the winter hunting grounds, often several families living and working together cooperatively under the leadership of whichever family's territory they were inhabiting. In this way, other areas could be left fallow for future seasons. Equally, the scant resources had to be husbanded, fathers teaching their sons just how many of each animal could be consumed each year, as taught to them by their fathers before them.

Apart from the significant late-summer wild berry harvest and wild rice where it was found, there were relatively few vegetable food resources to be found in the poor and cold boreal soil, so the diet was largely meat-based. Successfully hunting large game was not a foregone conclusion, however. Indeed, it was difficult to find in the forest, requiring a high degree of hunting skill and a large investment of time; parties of hunters could be away from their families for weeks at a time. Game, however, was vitally important to the community for more than just food. Moose and caribou/reindeer skins were converted into clothing and tent covers, the tendons into sewing threads, the bones and antlers into tools. As a result of the men's often-prolonged absence in search of the large game, the women were masters of the trapping of the small variety.

As is typical of hunting-and-gathering societies worldwide, the seasonal cycle dominated the life of the people, who had to place themselves in the right place at the right time. But here in the northern forest there was the added complication of needing to have the correct tools to traverse the landscape: canoes in summer for fishing, hunting swimming game and harvesting wild rice; skis and snowshoes in winter. To avoid mineral deficiency, First Nations utilised the fermented stomach contents of reindeer/caribou and hare, which enabled them to digest food sources such as lichen that would otherwise be inedible. The ability to preserve food was also a vital skill for survival. Meat and fish could be dried, smoked or pickled, while berries were preserved as fruit leathers, dried or, in the case of the cowberry/lingonberry, which contains its own natural preservative, stored in water.

Underpinning all of the considerable food-gathering effort was a simple principle: more calories needed to be collected than were expended in the gathering. The Hubbard party failed in this regard in several ways. First, they relied upon fishing rods – an energy-inefficient way of collecting fish – and when they had excess food they did not manage to preserve it. For First Nations, the much more effective fishing net was the most fundamentally important foraging tool. Here, then, are the keys for obtaining food in the boreal forest: correct use of the net and the snare. Both methods are heavily regulated or in some cases prohibited by today's game laws, according to the location, but if you are starving, a far higher court presides and these techniques may yet save a life.

The woman that Hearne encountered on his return from the Coppermine River in 1772 perfectly exemplifies the necessary abilities of a boreal survivor:

'The methods practiced by this poor creature to procure a livelihood were truly admirable, and are great proofs that necessity is the real mother of invention. When the few deer-sinews that she had an opportunity of taking with her were all expended in making snares, and sewing her clothing, she had nothing to supply their place but the sinews of the rabbits legs and feet; these she twisted together for that purpose with great dexterity and success. The rabbits, &c. which she caught in those snares, not only furnished her with a comfortable subsistence, but of the skins she made a suit of neat and warm clothing for the Winter. It is scarcely possible to conceive that a person in her forlorn situation could be so composed as to be capable of contriving or executing any thing that was not absolutely necessary to her existence; but there were sufficient proofs that she had extended her care much farther, as all her clothing, beside being calculated for real service, shewed great taste, and exhibited no little variety of ornament. The materials, though rude, were very curiously wrought, and so judiciously placed, as to make the whole of her garb have a very pleasing, though rather romantic appearance. Her leisure hours from hunting had been employed in twisting the inner rind or bark of willows into small lines, like net-twine, of which she had some hundred fathoms by her; with this she intended to make a fishing-net as soon as the Spring advanced. It is of the inner bark of willows, twisted in this manner, that the Dog-ribbed Indians make their fishing-nets; and they are much preferable to those made by the Northern Indians. Five or six inches of an iron hoop, made into a knife, and the shank of an arrow-head of iron, which served her as an awl, were all the metals this poor woman had with her when she eloped; and with these implements she had made herself complete snow-shoes, and several other useful articles. Her method of making a fire was equally singular and curious, having no other materials for that purpose than two hard sulphurous stones. These, by long friction and hard knocking, produced a few sparks, which at length communicated to some touchwood; but as this method was attended with great trouble, and not always with success, she did not suffer her fire to go out all the Winter. Hence we may conclude that she had no idea of producing fire by friction, in the manner practised by the Esquimaux, and many other uncivilized nations; because if she had, the above-mentioned precaution would have been unnecessary.'

SAMUEL HEARNE *A Journey from Prince of Wales's Fort in Hudson's Bay to the Northern Ocean in the Years 1769, 1770, 1771 and 1772*

Signalling

The general principle of signalling is to attract the attention of rescue authorities, either directly or through a third party. This may be achieved with your communication equipment. Ideally, you will have predetermined emergency procedures, contacts that can be reached 24 hours a day, and briefed every member of your party in the operation of the communication device you are using. If you are carrying a simple satellite device, such as a SPOT, which only allows limited messaging, the following predetermined messages may prove useful:

> SEND HELP
> EVERYTHING OK
> HOLDING FOR WEATHER
> AIRCRAFT DAMAGED

If your communication equipment is lost you may have had the forethought to carry an emergency personal locator beacon.

Without these hi-tech devices, you will have to work on the more hit-and-miss process of attracting the attention of a passer-by. In the remote boreal forest there is no guarantee of *anyone* passing by. This reiterates the importance of carrying modern communication devices and/or beacons.

Signalling for help requires you to attract attention by direct communication or by creating a signal that contrasts recognisably with the normal state of the environment. Active signals such as a flashing light are more likely to be noticed than passive ones, such as an S.O.S. made from stones. In a real emergency you will almost certainly need to use a combination of techniques. Consider the equipment you normally carry. Many can be used for signalling, including: whistle, torch, mirror in the compass lid, ferrocerium rod, camera flash, etc.

Below Signalling is a skill, and it needs to be practised. Always employ more than one method of signalling.

Your 'Guardian Angel'

Notifying someone of your plans before departure is of critical importance, but it is a survival tenet that is frequently ignored. The most reliable person is usually a loved one. We call this person our Guardian Angel. Perhaps the best method is to use your outfitter or another official as your Guardian Angel with a loved one as a back-up.

Arrange a time to report in and be certain to provide instructions for how your Guardian Angel should proceed should you fail to do so. There have been cases of experienced bush travellers getting into difficulties early on during a remote trip and having to survive for months until the alarm was raised. For this reason, we favour a Situation Report [SITREP] Schedule that involves using an inReach device to send a predetermined message on a regular schedule. Ideally sent daily, this message can simply be 'all ok' or may contain updates about the state of your party and future intentions. In this way, should your communications cease the alarm will be raised quickly and the search can begin close to your last known position. Your Guardian Angel should reply with an acknowledgement of your SITREP and, if necessary, can apprise you of important changes in the weather forecast.

Be sure at the completion of your trip to inform your Guardian Angel of your safe return and to thank them for their support.

DETAILS TO BE LEFT WITH YOUR GUARDIAN ANGEL

- ▶ Your expected date of return
- ▶ Instructions in case you are overdue
- ▶ Emergency contact details, ideally the name of a person to contact
- ▶ Local emergency-service contact details
- ▶ Your personal details (DOB, phone numbers including satellite-communications devices)
- ▶ Relevant medical details (fitness, medication required, allergies etc)
- ▶ Your physical description
- ▶ Your level of experience
- ▶ Your next of kin and their contact details
- ▶ A description of your transport (colour of canoe etc)
- ▶ A description of your tent (colour, type, brand etc)
- ▶ List of the clothing and equipment you are carrying
- ▶ How many days' rations you are carrying
- ▶ Map sheets carried

Communication equipment

There is a range of modern and traditional techniques for getting a signal to the outside world. Given the remoteness of the boreal forest, it is worth ensuring you have the means to employ more than just one.

Personal locator beacon (PLB)

Sailors have carried distress radio beacons called EPIRBs for many years. Now, in many regions of the globe these have been sanctioned for use on land as well and are referred to as a Personal Locator Beacon or PLB. Your device has only one purpose: to transmit a signal to the local government authority that you are in distress and require rescuing. It is intended for use when your LIFE, a LIMB or your EYESIGHT is in danger.

We favour a PLB that has an inbuilt GPS, which enables the device to locate its position, which information is then transmitted on the 406Mhz Satellite Search and Rescue network. Once received, the signal passes to the local rescue-coordination centre. Modern devices send a powerful 5-watt satellite signal for 24 hours or longer, and some also transmit a radio homing signal on 121.5Mhz that can be picked up by overflying aircraft or SAR homing receivers on rescue aircraft. Bought with a modest one-off payment and having a shelf life of six years, they are an excellent insurance policy for remote travellers. It is essential that you familiarise yourself with their operation before departure and ensure that you have registered your device with the local rescue authority.

Above A personal locator beacon should be securely attached to your body.

Above When deployed, point the antenna south towards the equator, wherever possible through a gap in the forest canopy.

Above These simple devices have saved many lives. They do not replace proper preparation but are certainly a good insurance policy.

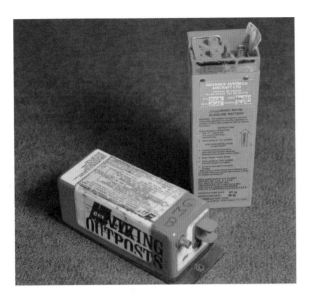

Above Aircraft Emergency Location Transmitters are fitted to aircraft.

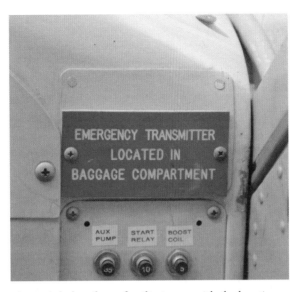

Above Ask the pilot to familiarise you with the location of the emergency equipment carried on board the aircraft. Normally a part of the pre-flight safety briefing, sometimes these details can be overlooked.

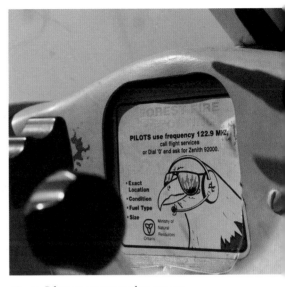

Above Pilots are requested to report forest fires. A signal fire may therefore be a good way to grab the attention of a passing pilot.

Aircraft beacon (ELT)

Should your floatplane crash, it is important to know that bush planes are required to be equipped with an Emergency Location Transmitter or ELT. These are designed to trigger on impact but can be triggered manually, too. These also transmit on the 406Mhz Satellite Search and Rescue network. Bush pilots carry basic survival equipment, rations and blankets, which may be salvageable after a crash.

The signal fire

Fire is a serious danger in the boreal forest. For this reason, all those who work in these regions keep a sharp lookout for smoke on the horizon. In some places, pilots are requested to report any fires spotted. Consequently,

it may be possible to attract the attention of a bush pilot by use of a signal fire. This should be constructed in an open area where there is little risk of sparking a forest fire, perhaps even on the shore of a small island, and where other signalling methods may be deployed. Consider marking out the letters S.O.S. with brushwood, or anything that creates a strong contrast with the background. Make the letters very large. Day-glow marker panels can prove to be very effective and can easily be stowed at the bottom of a pack.

If you signal to an aircraft in this way there is no guarantee that it will be seen. You should immediately prepare a new signal fire just in case. If a pilot does see your signal they may not be able to signal back to you, so keep going until you are rescued, just in case.

1 Construct a raised platform from green wood in a clearing away from dry combustible materials.

2 Atop the platform, construct a fire with the driest snapwood and small-diameter fuel. Charge the fire with shredded birch bark.

3 Cap the fire with a dense layer of spruce boughs. These will weatherproof the fire and create smoke once ignited.

4 Ignite the birch bark. The fire will burn quickly and hot.

5 Have extra fuel and spruce standing by as necessary. A correctly constructed signal fire burns with control.

6 Using a signal laser to reinforce the smoke signal.

Shelter

If you have been separated from your normal shelter you will need to find protection from the elements, wind, wet, cold and insects. This should be made as efficiently as possible; do not waste energy constructing a shelter that is over-specified for your needs. For example, if it is winter and the weather is stable you may be better off sleeping on a bed of spruce boughs between two fires or igniting the root ball of a fallen dead tree and improvising a seat in front of it. However, if you are caught out in the face of worsening weather you must find protection from the wind, wet and cold.

Above Open-front lean-to.

When constructing any shelter, work steadily, trying to avoid overheating and sweating into your all-important layers of insulation. The type of shelter you construct will depend on whether you have a fire or a sleeping bag.

Brushwood shelters

The boreal forest offers one great advantage to the survivor: an abundance of construction materials. Simple timber-frame shelters can be easily constructed and then thatched with evergreen boughs. Even without a cutting tool it is possible to collect dead trees, which can be propped over a rock or fallen tree and covered with spruce boughs broken off by hand. Ideally, though,

Above Brushwood *laavu*.

Above Emergency *laavu*.

you will be properly dressed for the forest, equipped with at least a belt knife and preferably an axe. In this case, more effective shelters can be constructed, which are comfortable enough for prolonged use.

Snow shelters

Snow in many ways inhibits our movement, chills us and makes us wet, so it is strange to think of using it to create shelter. It can, however, be excellent for this purpose, being our most abundant building material and composed of water crystals that trap air, meaning it is a brilliant insulator.

In the forest, the snow crystals fall gently to the forest floor undisturbed by wind. Consequently, they retain their individual nature and behave like salt. Indeed, at the extremely low temperatures common to the forest in the depths of winter, it is impossible even to make a snowball. For this reason, one cannot quarry large blocks of hard wind-packed snow and build igloos. Instead, we must adapt our construction methods to the soft snow of the forest.

The snow trench

This is the simplest forest shelter. It requires you to have a sleeping bag and bivvy bag and is usually used as a quick overnight shelter while on the move. If you have a tarp, so much the better. In its simplest form, simply dig out a trench from the snow that is large enough to sleep in without touching the sides. Insulate the base of the trench with spruce boughs, running some up the sides.

If you have skis, cross them above your face and arrange a cover with your windproof jacket to prevent snow falling on to your face. This shelter provides no warmth but does protect you from the chilling breeze.

To improve this shelter, stamp down a trench into the deep snow and dig out a sleeping shelf to one side. Insulate this with spruce boughs on its bottom and sides. Light a long fire in the trench. Roof the shelter with a tarp.

The quinze

This shelter is the forest igloo. There is an art to building it quickly and strongly, and this should be practised before it is needed for real. It is usually used to provide protection

Above A snow trench is improved by the presence of a warming three-log fire, which is quick and easy to build.

Above The quinze, constructed at low temperatures from powdery snow, is the forest equivalent of the igloo.

Right When you sleep in a quinze it is important to have good ventilation. We always use candles to help us monitor this; if the candle goes out, you know you are in danger from a lack of oxygen and can react accordingly to improve the ventilation.

from extremely low temperatures – we would not normally construct one in temperatures above -15ºC (5ºF). The great advantage of this shelter is the very stable temperature that is achieved inside. Although cold, it is considerably warmer than the ambient temperature outside.

Inside a quinze, no sound can be heard from outside, so should a storm blow up you will be blissfully unaware of the fact. For this reason, a watch should be organised to ensure that the critically important ventilation hole is kept clear of obstruction. Also, it is wise to keep a tool on hand for digging inside the quinze, in case of collapse.

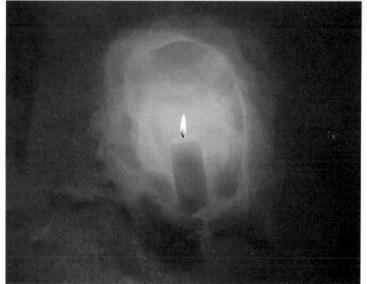

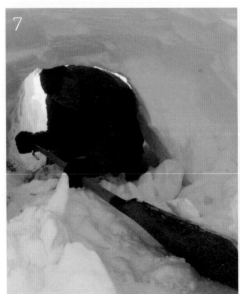

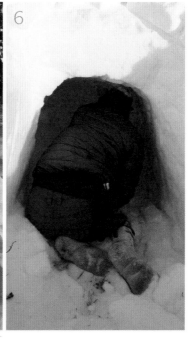

When we build a quinze we normally use an 'Indian snow shovel'.

1 Having established a campfire and put a kettle on, throw up the snow with sweeping movements (the snow crystals will mix in the air and freeze together more easily).

2 Pat down the final 30cm (12in) layer with the shovel to make it more firm.

3 Spread out damp clothing and put on warm, dry clothing.

4 Replace the moisture you have expended by drinking a warm beverage and, if possible, eat a little food. While the quinze freezes, collect insulating spruce boughs and firewood.

5–6 Hollow the quinze from two sides for speed.

7 Inside, the shovel provides good reach but you may need to finish the interior by scooping out snow with a cooking pan.

8–9 Block off and seal one of the two openings.

10 Insulate the floor of the quinze with spruce boughs.

11 Create a ventilation hole above the door.

12 The quinze provides a stable temperature a few degrees below freezing, while outside the temperature may be -40 – -50ºC (-40 – -58ºF) colder.

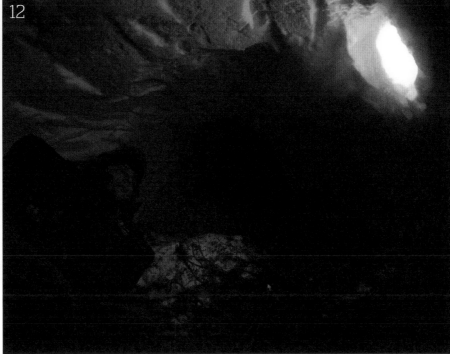

Water

Water is vital for life. Without it, our bodies cannot function efficiently and our ability to make sound judgements is impaired. Fortunately, in the boreal forest, we are surrounded by water in one form or another. Despite this, dehydration can be a serious concern, particularly in the winter when it is an important contributor to hypothermia and cold injury. The extremely low temperatures of the boreal winter result in very dry air. To enable efficient respiration, our body must humidify this air with each breath we take. This means that simply breathing has a dehydrating effect. In a survival situation, we may also find ourselves without the usual food supplies. In normal circumstances, the carbohydrate component of our daily diet provides a significant contribution of water, so when we are without food we should increase our water intake.

Snow and rain are safe sources of water and there are places in the boreal forest where the water from lakes and rivers is considered pure enough to drink directly from source. However, it is safer to always assume that the lake and river water is a potential font of infection and to purify it accordingly. Low temperature does not make water safe; bringing water to the boil for more than a minute does. Without a cooking pot this can be difficult. One solution is to clean out a rock hollow and to use it as a cooking pot, with hot rocks as the source of heat. Alternatively, it is possible to make either a temporary folded and pinned kettle from birch bark – usually the thin bark available in the late summer – or a *makúk* (container) of thicker bark that is sewn and has its seams waterproofed with spruce gum.

How to make a birch-bark kettle

1 A folded and pinned bark kettle held above embers on rocks.
2 Alternatively, a bark kettle can be suspended over the flames of a small fire.
3 To make a *makúk*, fold the bark to the desired shape, pin together the basket with small twigs and sew a thin wand on to the rim with split spruce roots.
4 Collect spruce gum and make a glue stick by heating the powdered resin with a scorched stick and building it up on the stick in layers.
5 Heat the resin on the stick to make it smooth. You now have a glue stick.
6 Heat the resin on the glue stick by the fire and paint the soft gum on to the seams of the *makúk*.
7 You can cook in the *makúk* using rocks heated in the fire.

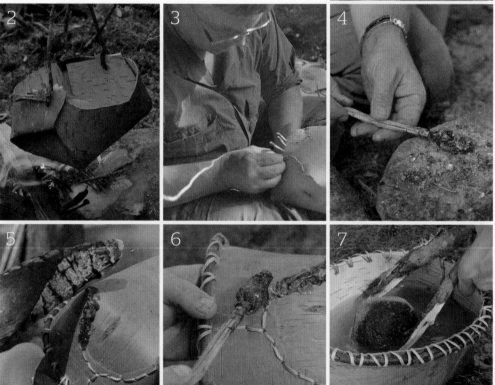

How to convert snow or ice to drinking water

When the land is in the grip of the winter freeze, water can be obtained by drilling or chiselling through the ice of a river or lake. If the necessary tools for this are not available, ice or snow can be melted.

Snow comprises much air, so ice is the preferable source for melting. If snow has to be chosen, look for the sugary snow crystals often found close to ground level.

Whichever you use, pack the billycan and suspend it high over the fire – aluminium pots can burn through if they are positioned too close to the hot fire, although stainless steel ones should be fine. Once the snow or ice becomes watery the pot can be lowered to speed the boiling. More snow or ice will have to be added gradually.

Without a cooking pot, snow can be melted easily by being placed in a porous bag improvised from a head net, T-shirt or other similar article. This is suspended in the warm air to the side of the fire. Alternatively, a Finnish marshmallow can be made and used in the same way. As the snow melts it is blotted up by the unmelted snow and at first nothing will seem to happen. However, once the snow reaches saturation point the marshmallow will drip water steadily, sometimes even developing into a steady flow. Try to keep the snow out of the smoke of the fire as this will taint the flavour of the water.

The Finnish marshmallow

Right A block of firm clean snow is pierced with a knife and supported on a stick in the warmth beside the fire. As it melts it will drip like a slow tap.

Left Once used throughout the boreal forest by indigenous people, this method has been forgotten in some regions.

Survival fire-lighting

Fire is a vital aid to survival in the boreal forest; with fire we have warmth, and a way to purify water, signal, cook food and dispel dangers. Fire also raises our morale. For survival, we need to have a new knowledge of fire-starting skills – one that understands how unrelated equipment can be used to make fire and how our ancestors conjured fire from natural means.

Electrical ignition

A snowmobile battery can be shorted out with ignition jump leads to create a spark that is sufficient to ignite a fine tinder bundle. Ideal for this is the fluffed-up cotton wool from a field dressing. A 9V radio battery can also be used to create fire if you short out the terminals with very fine wire wool. The wire wool will glow like a light-bulb element and begin burning. Prior to this, lace the wire wool with fine tinder and, once burning, blow it to flame, adding more tinder as necessary.

Flares

Flares intended for signalling are by their design a reliable source of ignition and hand-held ones are very viable as an emergency fire-starter. However, those designed to project into the air are dangerous to use for fire-lighting due to the energy they possess and are best avoided for this purpose. To use a hand-held flare, prepare your fire and construct it ready for ignition with plenty of kindling and tinder. Ignite the flare and use it like a candle to ignite the tinder, then step away. Do not throw the flare into the fire.

Bullet propellant [DANGER]

Hunters and soldiers may have access to shotgun shells or standard centrefire rifle cartridges. The propellant they contain has in times of extreme need been considered as emergency tinder. However, the risk of injury must be carefully weighed: this is only a technique of dire emergency. There are some important safety considerations. First, if the primer in the cartridge should detonate while disassembling the cartridge there is a high risk that you will be seriously injured. Second, some cartridges should not under any circumstances be tampered with, such as .22 rimfire cartridges. Because of their design, these are highly likely to detonate if you attempt their disassembly.

Bullet propellant is easily ignited with heat, so whatever method you employ to undo the cartridge should *not* generate heat. With a centrefire cartridge, the easiest method is to slowly loosen the bullet from the

Below left Grasp the bullet towards its tip with pliers and lever to loosen the neck of the brass case. Repeat the process, turning the case at each attempt, until the neck releases its grip on the projectile.

Below right The bullet should readily lift clear once it has been sufficiently loosened.

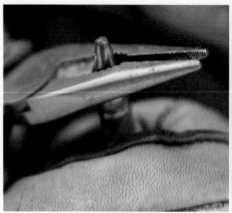

neck of the cartridge case using pliers. Under no circumstances apply any crushing or hammering force in the area of the primer. A shotgun cartridge is some-what easier to open. Score the plastic case just above the brass until it can be easily broken free. Depending on the load, you will have separated the cartridge in or just above the propellant.

Under no circumstances attempt to ignite the propellant with the primer: it is highly unlikely to work and, being explosive, is very dangerous.

Propellant can be ignited by a variety of methods. It burns quickly with an intense hot flame but is not of itself explosive unless confined. To convert the fast-burning flame to a 'reliable flame' you should ensure that you have some other tinder standing by, ideally a good feather stick.

The propellant can be easily ignited with sparks, but if you have the means to make sparks you do not need to run the risk of extracting propellant from a cartridge. Therefore, it is logical that you will need to employ another less-certain method. The easiest of these is to ignite the propellant by using a magnifying lens, perhaps that found on your compass or carried to assist in map-reading. If the sun is not shining,

Above Shotgun shell propellant can be accessed by carefully cutting through the wall of the cartridge above the brass.

FRICTION IGNITION OF BULLET PROPELLANT

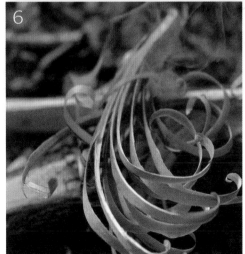

1 Fill a depression carved into a board with propellant.
2 Place tinder or a shaving cluster close to the depression.
3 Drill into the depression with a bow drill. DO NOT INHALE THE FUMES OF THE IGNITING PROPELLANT.
4 The propellant will quickly ignite from the friction heat.
5 Be ready to ignite the shaving cluster with the rapidly burning propellant.
6 Add more shaving clusters to build fire.

the propellant can easily be ignited by using friction from a fire drill. Failing these, if you have access to a piece of fencing wire then this can be vigorously rubbed back and forth around a log or rock until it is very hot and then immediately applied to the propellant.

Sunlight

The sun's energy can be harnessed with a condensing mirror or a lens that converges the rays to ignite tinder. This lens can be found in various items in your outfit:

Compass

If you follow our advice concerning the essential items in your outfit then you should never be without your compass, which hopefully you will have chosen for its inclusion of a magnifying lens. Even a tiny lens, just

ø15mm (⅝in), will work fine, although the larger the diameter of the lens the better. A Fresnel-type magnifying lens attached to your compass will not only help with map-reading but it is also a superb converging lens for fire-lighting. The secret to all fire-starting with sunlight is to employ a dark-coloured tinder such as charred cloth, dried fungus or an already charred log end.

Above and below
Many lenses can be used to concentrate the sun's energy. Here an 8 x 32 binocular and the small magnifying lens on a compass base plate. You should know which of the lenses you carry can be used for fire-lighting.

Binocular

It is not necessary to dismantle a binocular for fire-lighting. What is needed is a binocular with a small-diameter exit pupil – 4mm or smaller. The ideal binocular for serious use in remote areas is the 8 x 32, which works very well as a fire-lighter. Set the focus of the binocular to the closest setting and use just one lens tube to focus the tightest beam of sunlight that you can.

Rifle scope

Like a binocular, you need a scope with a small exit pupil. Just as for the binocular, set the focus to the closest setting and, if you are using a variable power rifle scope, set the magnification to the highest setting possible.

Reading glasses

Not all prescription lenses can be used for fire-lighting. If you are a spectacle-wearer, experiment to see if your lenses work. Reading glasses, however, function brilliantly to condense sunshine. Use them in exactly the same way as a standard magnifying lens.

HOT WIRE IGNITION OF BULLET PROPELLANT

1 The propellant from a bullet cartridge is poured into a small heap on top of some dry wood shavings. Containing it in the lid of a mess tin prevents spillage and the wind from blowing away the powder.

2 An 80cm (31½in) length of wire, fitted at the ends with toggle handles, is rapidly pulled back and forth around a piece of firewood until the wood smokes and scorches.

3 The hot wire is brought into contact with the powder, which ignites due to the heat.

4 Kindling is ready to ignited from the intense, short-lived flames. Do not inhale the smoke.

Condensing mirrors

It is not just lenses that can be used to focus the sun's rays; concave or converging mirrors can also be used. These can be purchased as an emergency fire-starting tool and are excellent for the task. They have no moving parts – just a polished mirror surface that should be protected from abrasion and scratches. The best designs are compact, strong and incorporate a cover.

It used to be relatively easy to improvise a converging mirror using the concave reflector found behind the bulb in car headlights and flashlights. Today, however, with the advent of sophisticated headlamp arrays and LED headlamps, this is more difficult. One alternative in very bright sun conditions is to polish the concave underside of an aluminium beverage can to act as a converging mirror.

To use a concave mirror, aim it directly at the sun and offer up a small piece of dark-coloured tinder in front of the mirror while taking care not to totally shade out the mirror. Move the tinder back and forth until you find the mirror's focal point – where a tight spot of sunlight occurs – and then wait until the tinder begins to smoke and glow. This can then be added to more tinder and blown to flame.

Fire by natural means

Prior to the availability of steel strike-a-lights there were two principal ways in which fire was created in the boreal forest. The first was by the generation of sparks from iron pyrite, and the other was by wood friction.

Fire by iron pyrite

While iron pyrite can be found in the boreal forest, it is unlikely to be available in a survival situation. Indeed, such is its scarcity that it was traded between the aboriginal communities and cherished, carefully carried in a tinder pouch. Should you have access to such a fire-lighting tool, you will need excellent tinder, such as chaga, char cloth or amadou, since the dull red sparks produced are cool compared to the other spark fire-starting methods we may employ. Sparks are scraped from the iron pyrite rather than being struck off, as is the case when using steel.

Fire by friction

Today, little evidence remains of the original friction fire-lighting equipment in use in the boreal forest. Organic materials decay rapidly, even if they have not been simply used as firewood once worn out. There is a number of

Left A condensing mirror igniting some chaga. Mirrors such as this are not prone to breakage even during hard travel.

Below The bow drill was traditionally the friction fire-starting method of the boreal forest. An efficient technique, it can withstand extreme cold, damp and snow.

methods that can be used to make fire by friction. The one most widely practised around the world is simply the twirling of a drill stick against a hearth stick between the palms. It is hard to imagine that this method would not have also been used in these regions at some point in time, particularly in warm summer weather. In winter, however, this technique, while still possible (one of the

authors once created an ember on top of a block of ice at -35°C (-31°F) just to prove the point), is definitely marginal. Unsurprisingly, it is in this region that the best-known fire-making method has its home: the drill-and-bow method.

Using a bow provides greater mechanical advantage, enabling a thicker drill to be spun. This results in the creation of a larger ember that more robustly copes with adverse weather. In the hands of an expert, the greater mechanical advantage also allows for the use of slightly substandard materials.

The great bonus with this fire-starting method is the wide availability of its constituent materials. The only problematic component is the cord used to spin the drill, although normally this can be easily carried or improvised from a bootlace or clothing. Failing this, a cord of sufficient strength and durability can be made from willow bark or twisted spruce roots.

Although anthropology tells us repeatedly that for this method hard wood and soft wood are used respectively for the drill and hearth or in the reverse combination, in actual fact we normally fashion both drill and hearth from the same wood, ideally from the same bough. Choice of material is critical: while theoretically fire can be produced from any species of wood, in practice we have discovered that some types are easier to use than others. Hence the old saying, 'Fire does not sleep in all trees'. In the boreal forest we have used all of the following woods: alder; aspen; balsam fir; basswood; birch; red and white cedar; elder; juniper;

1 The bow drill apparatus comprises a bow made with strong cord, a drill, a hearth and a top bearing block.
2-3 Drill into the hearth.
4 Create a notch joining the drilled depression.
5 Drill hard to produce thick smoke and dark powder, which will fill the notch.
6 The powder will eventually coalesce into a delicate ember.
7 Whisper on the ember to encourage it to grow.
8 At this point the ember can be transferred to a bundle of tinder and blown to flame.

maple; white and Scots pine; poplar; spruce; sycamore; tamarack; willow.

The wood chosen must also be in the right condition. It needs to be dead and dry, beginning to decay but not rotten and yet neither too hard. Ideally, you should be able to dent the wood's surface with your fingernail. When using natural cordage, time must be taken to select wood in the optimal condition at the softer end of the acceptable spectrum.

Carve the thicker end of the bough into a flat board and look for a straight, knot-free section of the correct diameter for the drill. The following dimensions are taken from one of our sets made from willow:

THE DRILL
ø 2.5cm (1in), l 23cm (9in)
Do not make it larger than 3cm (1⅕in)

THE HEARTH BOARD
w 4cm (1½in), t 2.5cm (1in), l 37cm (14½in)

BEARING BLOCK
Split from a green branch ø 5cm (2in), l 11cm (4⅓in)

BOW
ø 2cm (¾in), l 74cm (29in)
The bow should have little or no flex. It need only have a shallow arch.

Having made the bow drill apparatus, it must be bedded in. Carve a deep depression in the centre of the flat surface of the bearing block. This needs to be deep enough to prevent the drill top slipping out when in use. Carve a wider, shallow depression at one end of the hearth board. It is now possible to start drilling, with the intention of bedding in the hearth and drill. When drilling, locate the hearth under the arch of your forward foot. Twist the drill into the cord so that it will lie to the outside of the bow – this will enable the most efficient use of the bow.

Fill the depression in the bearing block with some green leaves to aid rotation, and support your top hand tightly against your shin. The top hand must be rock-steady. Hold the bow with your fingers grasping around the cord to aid stability and maintain tightness. Drill with a slow, steady, arm-swinging action. Try not to rely on strength here. Aim to keep the string parallel to the ground. Drill slowly, using all the length of the bow, maintaining a steady downward pressure and gradually increasing your speed. Smoke will rise from the drill tip. Drill until the drill has scorched a circle into the hearth that matches the full diameter of the drill.

Now that the drill is bedded in, the all-important side notch can be cut, to collect the friction dust that will form a coal. Like removing a one-eighth segment from a cake, cut a neat V-shaped notch from the side of the board extending to the centre of the scorched depression. The bow-drill set is now ready for use.

In dry weather, the tinder bundle can be placed directly beneath the notch, otherwise use a broad shaving under the notch to collect the coal that will be formed. Drill again, but now with more vigour.

Generally, speed is more important than heavy downward pressure, although not in every case, depending upon species and wood condition. As you drill, smoke will rise from the drill tip – watch for a fine dark powder collecting in the notch. As the notch begins to fill, drill energetically enough to cause smoke to billow from the drill tip. Stop drilling when the notch is overflowing with black powder that smokes independently of the drill.

Carefully, so as not to damage it, hold the ember in place with a small stick and roll the hearth away. You should be left with a marble-sized smoking mass of black powder. Gently whisper a breath on it to increase the combustion, and when you see it begin to glow transfer it carefully to your tinder. The tinder bundle should ideally be a mass of dry, finely teased plant fibres. This can be enhanced with the addition of some crumbs of charcoal or chaga. Pack the bundle tightly, place the ember on top and carefully fold it into the tinder, without crushing it. Now blow on the ember in the tinder bundle so that it grows and sets the bundle alight.

As you will discover, there can be a number of frustrating things that you will need to overcome before the knack is learned. Remember, though, that these frustrations are just the price we pay for learning one of our species' most ancient and important skills. And besides, a sense of humour is an essential tool for wilderness travel.

In snowy conditions, the hearth can be modified so that instead of a notch being carved in the side of the hearth board, a hole is first drilled deeply into the hearth and then a second hole is drilled alongside. By carving a gully to connect the two depressions, the dust ember can form in the first hole as the second is being drilled. This method was employed by the Inuit, who also frequently held the hearth board on their lap while drilling with a bow and bearing down with a block held between their teeth.

Survival food

In conventional survival training students learn that a human can survive for three minutes without air, three days without water and three weeks without food. The concept holds true: food is therefore a lower priority for survival than water. However, when food does become a concern, it becomes an overarching focus. This is particularly the case in the boreal forest, where easily gathered plant foods can be difficult to find and where the daily caloric requirement is magnified by the demands of the cold environment.

Ant larvae collection

During the summer months it is possible to easily gather the larvae and pupae from wood-ant nests. Requiring little effort to collect and being high in protein, these are an important source of survival food.

Opposite
1 At the height of summer the wood ants' nest is a ready source of emergency protein.
2-3 Collect together nest material, ants and their larvae into a tarp.
4 Spread out the tarp in a patch of sunshine.
5 Form a ridge around the edge of the tarp with small branches.
6 Turn the edge of the tarp over to create shade around its perimeter.
7-8 The ants will collect their larvae and move them into the shade.
9 After 30 minutes, roll back the edge of the tarp and harvest the edible ant larvae. When fried, they taste like shrimp, and they can be incorporated into all manner of meals to improve their protein content.

Fishing

Every wrinkle of fishing skill and experience can be used to assist you to catch fish in a survival situation. However, the most appropriate survival fishing methods are those that require the least activity. Principal among these is the gill net. While its use is strictly controlled in most situations, a small 10m (33ft) net can easily be stashed at the bottom of a pack for long expeditions in remote country in case of an emergency. Without hooks, we must fall back on more ancient methods, such as the use of gorge hooks, or hooks made from thorns, slivers of bone or metal nails. When ice-fishing, we can improvise tip-up rigs that enable us to monitor several fishing lines at one time, or we can set lines under the ice overnight.

Left and inset
A gillnet is often prohibited by law, depending upon local regulations. However, in a survival situation it can be a lifesaving tool. On the remotest expeditions, a suitable net takes up little space and can be tucked into the bottom of a pack in case of emergency.

Below Ice-fishing in winter is a popular sport today, but it's also an important source of food.

Improvised hooks

Below Traditional improvised fish hooks. Montagnais hooks made from split wood and sharpened nails were still in use in recent times.

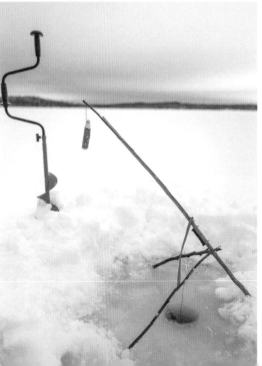

Left In some regions the law allows for two lines to be used simultaneously for fishing. A simple tip-up like this can be used for the second line. The baited hook is set beneath the ice, with a hank of cord to allow the fish to make off with the bait and thereby set the hook when the end of the line is reached. When this occurs, the tightening line dislodges a wire ring around the main stick, thus releasing the flag, which swings up under the force of the counterweight, indicating a bite that will need swift attention.

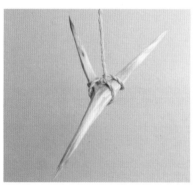

Above The use of a burbot hook made from a sharpened juniper Y-fork is the traditional way to catch turbot that was once widely employed in Scandinavia.

Survival
305

Trapping

Neither of us relishes the thought of trapping animals for food, but we understand the vast remoteness of the taiga. In a survival crisis, when starvation is a real possibility, trapping can make the difference between life and death. Between returning to loved ones or disappearing into the endless moss of the forest, vanished without a trace.

Below Typical materials and equipment carried for snaring. Snare wire has countless other uses besides snaring, such as repair and improvisation.

Above A spruce root attached to the end of a long spruce pole can be used to reach into branches and capture spruce grouse – an old trick of Canadian First Nations.

Above The *Ojibwa* bird snare can be used with thin thread, fishing line or a thin split root. The perch should be baited.

Above If there is no wire, small game can be snared using thread, but this must be secured with a lifting mechanism to prevent the prey from biting through the snare. This traditional set-up uses a slip-knot actuation for the trigger.

Left Willow grouse are still trapped using this method, in which gates holding a snare are placed into fences of small twigs bearing birch buds. The gates attract the willow grouse, which come to eat the buds.

Inset Strict rules and regulations specify the allowable materials and dimensions of the willow grouse snare.

Above A hare snare set with wire in summer requires no lifting mechanism since the wire alone is strong enough.

Below Hare snare set in winter.

Above and inset A hare snare, typical of that employed by the Tłı̨chǫ, was made either of sinew or carefully worked rawhide.

Left A deadfall trap set for squirrel, using a split log for the trap jaws, weighted for force and with a pole leading up towards the bait.

Inset A detailed view of the figure-4 deadfall trigger, baited for squirrel with a mushroom.

Below The kicking-bar deadfall trap was widely used in the boreal forest to catch medium-sized game. It can be made at almost any size, is actuated with a trigger bar and kills with a fast crushing force.

Long-range Bushcraft

'WET, HEAT, COLD, hunger, thirst, difficult travel, insects, hard beds, aching muscles-all these at one time or another will be your portion. If you are of the class that cannot have a good time unless everything is right with it, stay out of the woods. One thing at least will always be wrong. When you have gained the faculty of ignoring the one disagreeable thing and concentrating your powers on the compensations, then you will have become a true woodsman, and to your desires the forest will always be calling.'

STEWART EDWARD WHITE *The Forest 1903*

Previous pages Remote expeditions bring wonderful rewards – the opportunity to witness nature at her most beautiful and to feel the energy of our planet at work. However, despite the benefits, long-range travel does require the highest degree of self-reliance.

Opposite In long-range travel we learn to pay respect to nature and become pilgrims of the wilderness.

David Thompson, the great 18th-century surveyor of Canada, knew the value of travelling lightly, of being able to live from the country, and of superb craft skills. On his survey expeditions he carried with him a simple toolkit with which he was able to fashion boats, buildings and even tables that were so well made that he could use them as surfaces on which to plot his maps. To save weight, most of his tools were transported without handles. The first job, then, was to fit them with handles, fashioned with knife and axe from locally sourced wood, before any construction could begin. Thus, despite his superlative skill as a navigator, Thompson would never have realised his achievements without also being a master of what we call 'long-range bushcraft'.

While a lifetime can be spent enjoying the huge rewards to be found in static camping close to established routes of communication, or short-range travel, it is obvious that the boreal landscape will tempt the adventurous of spirit to go further or even to travel alone. The taiga provides wonderful opportunities for truly long-distance expeditions into areas that are incredibly remote from civilisation. The spiritual reward of such journeys can prove to be transcendental, but it must also be stated that the exposure to risk, both physical and psychological, posed by such excursions increases exponentially. Consequently, we advise novice travellers to extend the range of their journeys in pace with their growing level of skill. Many of the wilderness outfitters we have spoken to tell us that it is very common for trippers to attempt overly ambitious journeys, to fail to make proper allowance for the potential of bad weather, and for such trips frequently to end in disharmony.

It is no accident that we have left this topic until last. This is the finishing school of wilderness bushcraft; a school in which the student may advance but from which they will never graduate, a school of lifelong learning. Truly understanding long-range bushcraft requires prior experience of wilderness travel and competence in all that we have already covered. It is a skill in its own right, one that requires the highest degree of technical ability, personal honesty and sober thought. Self-delusion and overconfidence can get you killed when travelling in remote wilderness.

Long-range bushcraft demands that we become pilgrims of the wild, learning to live on the trail rather than just passing along it as tourists. To do so will develop an attitude of mind, the mastery of basic skills, and a more informed understanding of the forests themselves. This will draw its strength from the very limitations imposed by the necessity of travelling lightly on long journeys. For those prepared to set aside their

arrogance and keep a tight rein on their ego, long-lange bushcraft is highly rewarding; it will provide clarity of mind and a powerful confidence tempered in humility.

This type of bushcraft is a trail-based learning, predicated on independence and self-reliance. With serious consequences attending potential failures in preparation and weakness of mind, forward-thinking, attention to detail and mindfulness must be developed to a higher degree. On the trail, an iron-willed self-discipline ensures our outfit remains properly maintained and functioning while a strong spirit enables us to endure hardships with fortitude and humour. Over and above all of this, though, the most important attribute derived from long-range bushcraft is a heightened ability to make good decisions swiftly under difficult circumstances.

In terms of physical bushcraft techniques, all are enhanced but most particularly our craft and repair skills, which now need to be quick and efficient so that they can be relied upon to fashion the things we need or to replace breakages without the requirement that we carry many gadgets with us. Extending our range, we also discover the benefit of a deeper knowledge of nature and of being able to find alternative natural sources for the consumable items we carry.

With experience, those who choose to tread this path begin to see the landscape as their home and to travel like a native inhabitant.

Communication

Communication is a vital element of long-range bushcraft. Once a complicated process involving radios, modern technology – in the form of satellite phones and inReach satellite devices – has revolutionised our ability to communicate in remote regions. We only predict further enhancement and miniaturisation of this technology.

Battery life is the greatest drawback with these tools. On an expedition they must be used wisely. We employ a radio-age situation report or SITREP procedure (see Survival chapter) to minimise transmission time. While solar chargers are effective for topping up batteries, particularly when employed with an independent power cell, it is vitally important to have in place a lost communications procedure that has been agreed on by yourself and your outfitter.

Above The satellite phone has revolutionised wilderness communication. The device needs to be well protected in a watertight case.

Rght When talking to base it helps to have organised a schedule for communication, a fixed time each day when the remote party can make a situation report.

Below An independent power cell provides many advantages. The communication tool is not at risk of damage during the prolonged solar charging and you can effectively keep an instant power top-up to hand.

Right Solar panels provide the opportunity to top up batteries when the sun is shining. In the future, it may be possible to charge batteries with both gravity- and heat-produced power.

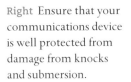

Right Ensure that your communications device is well protected from damage from knocks and submersion.

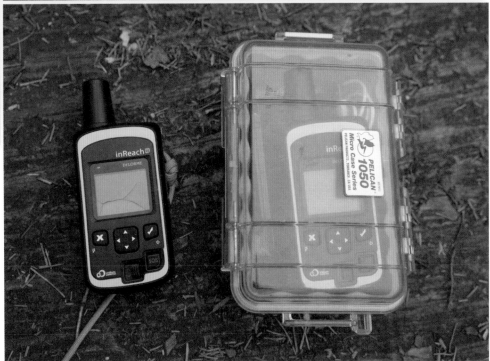

Pocket first-aid kit

Part of the mindset that comes with long-range bushcraft is making adequate preparations. For example, while we carry a comprehensive first-aid kit in our daypack, we know that most often minor injuries occur when you do not have this with you, for example when collecting firewood. For this reason, we carry a very simple cuts kit in a modified dry pouch that is watertight and small enough to be available always. The contents include: simple plasters, larger adhesive non-adherent dressings, adhesive sutures, antiseptic, friar's balsam, water-purification tablets, some miniature tampons and some anti-inflammatory painkillers. Of course we also carry a bandanna, which can be pressed into service in many ways.

Do not make this kit too big; the purpose is to have it immediately to hand. Minor cuts are a common injury but, cleaned and closed promptly, they heal well. Delays can result in slow healing and infection. Consider also that in a crisis the cotton wool of a tampon with the addition of some friar's balsam makes an excellent, long-lasting emergency fire-starter.

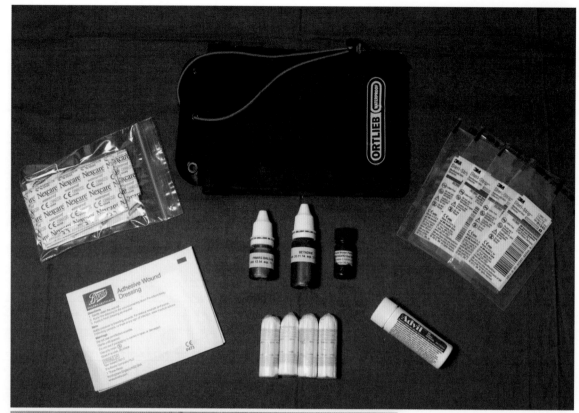

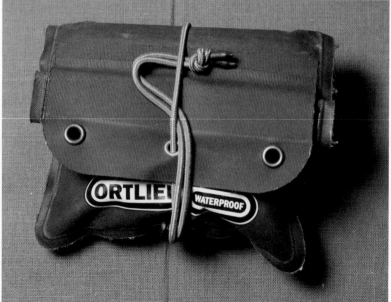

Above A very basic first-aid kit can be carried in a shirt pocket. This should enable you to treat minor cuts, abrasions etc without having to delve into your main pack.

Left The Ortlieb document pouch with some shot cord for convenience.

How to dress a wound

Here a cut is treated promptly, with the aid of a bandanna, a small tampon to help staunch the bleeding, antiseptic, adhesive sutures and non-adherent dressing. The dressings are made more adhesive by the use of friar's balsam around (not in) the wound and by warming the dressing with the hand once applied. A week of travel kneeling in a canoe later, despite having been subject to repeated soakings, the dressing has remained in place. This obviously helps the treatment, but it also reduces the burden on a limited supply of dressings.

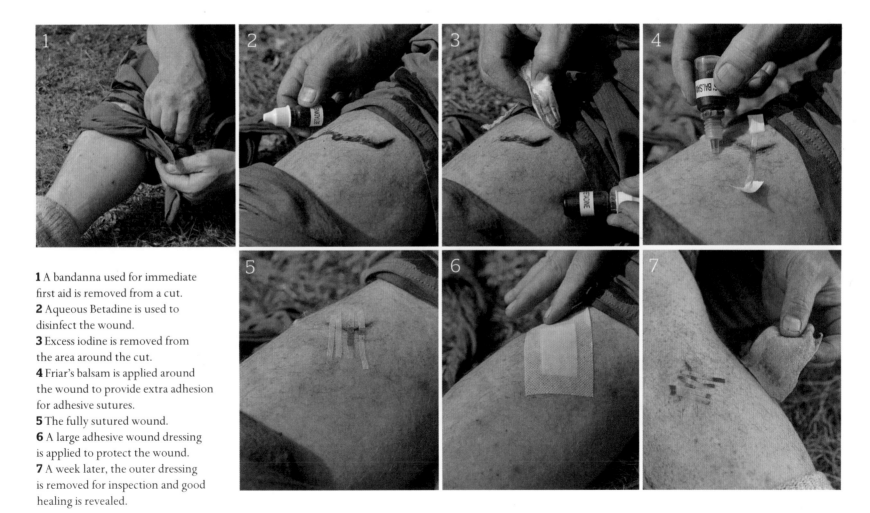

1 A bandanna used for immediate first aid is removed from a cut.
2 Aqueous Betadine is used to disinfect the wound.
3 Excess iodine is removed from the area around the cut.
4 Friar's balsam is applied around the wound to provide extra adhesion for adhesive sutures.
5 The fully sutured wound.
6 A large adhesive wound dressing is applied to protect the wound.
7 A week later, the outer dressing is removed for inspection and good healing is revealed.

Crooked knife

How to make a crooked knife

The crooked knife used by Canadian First Nations is an excellent candidate for inclusion in a long-range toolkit. Blades for these can be purchased today with relative ease, but it is more in keeping with the concept of long-range bushcraft to make your own from a worn file. This provides the added advantage of you being able to shape the blade to suit your specific need.

'We took up our abode at first on the floor, but our working party, who had shewn such skill as house-carpenters, soon proved themselves to be, with the same tools, the hatchet and crooked knife, excellent cabinet makers, and daily added a table, chair, or bedstead, to the comforts of our establishment. The crooked knife, generally made of an old file, bent and tempered by heat, serves an Indian or Canadian voyager for plane, chisel, and auger. With it the snow-shoe and canoe-timbers are fashioned, the deals of their sledges reduced to requisite thinness and polish, and their wooden bowls and spoons hollowed out. Indeed, though not quite so requisite for existence as the hatchet, yet without its aid there would be little comfort in these wilds.'

SIR JOHN FRANKLIN *Narrative of a journey to the shores of the Polar Sea, in the years 1819, 20, 21 and 22*

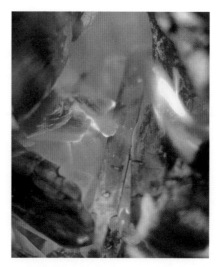

1 To soften the steel, the old file blade is heated in the heart of a small hot fire of seasoned wood until it glows cherry red. It is then allowed to cool slowly.

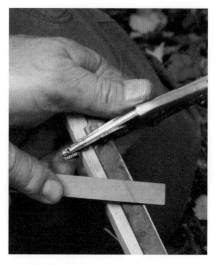

2 Clamped to a piece of wood that has been carved flat, the file can be conveniently held for shaping with a good file.

7 The blade is now tempered, reducing the hardness so it is not overly brittle. This is done by gently heating it on a fry pan over the fire – a delicate process, which takes practice. The steel will be heated until it turns a straw colour. Keep moving the steel to achieve even heating.

8 The moment the correct colour is achieved, quench the blade into warm oil.

3 The filing is nearing completion; the file has been smoothed on both sides and bevelled on the top surface to provide the necessary edge.

4 The blade is heated again until it glows red and is given the desired curve to the tip. This can be done by hammering it with the poll of an axe around a curved section of green wood or, as here, by carefully bending it using pliers. The tip is bent upwards by 90 degrees.

5 The blade is once more heated to cherry red and quenched immediately in salty water. This will harden the steel.

6 The blade is now brightened using emery paper or sand.

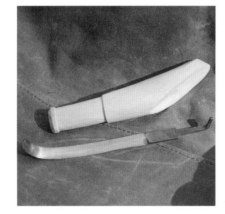

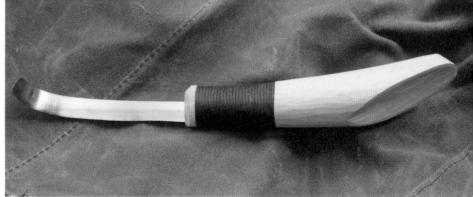

9 The finished blade. While the heat-treating will never be of factory quality, this technique is precisely how these tools were originally made in the forest, and the blade will be perfectly serviceable.

10 Carve an attractive and comfortable handle. Here, Norway maple is used, which is known to be good for handles as it does not cause blisters.

Above and left The finished crooked knife. All that is required now is sharpening and a strip of leather with which to wrap the blade for safety when not in use. Notice how the blade fits into a recess in the handle.

Bucksaw

The bucksaw is a wonderful tool, essential when travelling with a wood-burning stove in winter, although it can be bulky to carry. An alternative is to take just the blade and some bolts and to make the frame as necessary. The blade can be wrapped and transported coiled inside a cooking pot for safety. In Finland, the single-handed frame saw was used extensively. It is estimated that during the 1940s some 500,000 Finnish forest workers were engaged in cutting wood largely with the combination of axe and frame saw.

The simple bucksaw

Sometimes simplicity is beautiful. While we have encountered self-appointed experts of the woodcraft camp who claim that this type of saw is second-rate, the fact remains that they were once very common across the forests of Scandinavia, used by people who depended upon them and who certainly had the skill to fashion more elaborate models. They can still be seen in museums of rural life or adorning the walls of old cabins. The beauty lies with the ease and speed with which these saws can be made.

Repair kit

A comprehensive repair kit need not be large and heavy. Adhesive repair patches, duct tape, pliers and a hand vice will enable all manner of repairs to be made.

Above This kit contains a small square awl, a medium triangular awl and small chisel 9mm (⅓in) wide. All of these have been made from old files shaped and heat-treated in the field. With these items you can more easily make an astonishing range of tools, such as snowshoes, which require tenon joints.

Right Antique frame saw, Dalarna, Sweden.

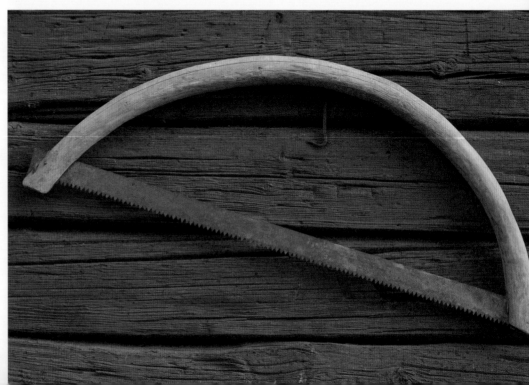

How to make a simple bucksaw

1 The quickest way to make a saw is to bend a sapling into a bow, as shown here. Begin by trimming a straight green sapling of birch, spruce or even pine.

2 Take care to bend a bow with a low arch, as this is more stable when in use.

3 (*Left*) Once carefully bent round, tie the curve and trim the ends to length. Cut notches to locate the fixing bolts and split the ends just deep enough to hold the saw blade. Fit the blade and then untie the binding.

4 (*Right*) A frame such as this can be made in just a few minutes; it will dry to shape and can be used for many years.

A Finnish bucksaw

During World War II, the Finnish army trained their soldiers to make these saws. They carried one blade, contained for safekeeping in a specially designed leather belt, per patrol.

We too can benefit from this saw-making skill, as the blade is very light and convenient to carry compared to the full frame saw. Making a frame saw is a simple task for a competent carver and is immensely satisfying. The key components, which must be carried, are: the saw blade; two bolts or suitable pins with which to fix the blade in the frame; 5m (16½ft) of cord for tensioning the frame.

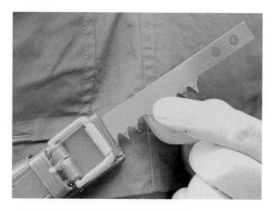

Left and below The Finnish saw is an excellent, stable saw and may give years of service.

Opposite If you have a toolkit you can drill and chisel holes. In which case, this style of saw can be easily made.

HOW TO MAKE A PADDLE

Misuse, poor manufacture or just sheer bad luck – whatever the cause, it is not uncommon to encounter broken paddles. Indeed, when choosing a paddle for remote travel it is wise to look for a sturdy design as the paddle will inevitably be subject to a degree of rough handling.

To fashion a paddle in the wild, search for a standing dead spire of spruce or cedar that is broad enough to provide a suitable width of paddle. The wood needs to have a straight grain and to be dry, but still sound in structure and not decaying. Cut the trunk to length and use gluts (wooden wedges) to split it in half. Choosing the half that seems best, hew it into a plank that is evenly rectangular in cross-section. Having done this, continue hewing the plank, but now so that it has a diamond cross-section, with a point at each end. The points and resulting ridge are the straight lines necessary to keep your work true and symmetrical. Where the blade is broad, flatten the diamond. Where the shaft will be round, hew it square. Once roughed out, finish the paddle with a crooked knife or belt knife.

If you cannot find dry wood, use living wood, even birch or alder. As the wood is drying, suspend it hanging free from the handle end to help prevent warping. Once finished, waterproof the paddle with cooking fat, oil or with tar from birch bark.

Left Requiring no holes to be drilled or joints to be cut with a chisel, the Finnish bucksaw relies upon the tension in the frame and the angle of the joints for its structural integrity.

Left Simple mortise and tenon joint.

'After having passed the carrying places, we encamped at the Dog River, at half past four in the afternoon, in a state of great fatigue. The canoe was again gummed, and paddles were made to replace those that had been broken in ascending the rapids.'
ALEXANDER MCKENZIE *Journal Account*

Axe repair

Should the helve of your axe become loose, it can be temporarily retightened by soaking the head in water overnight. However, this is only a temporary repair; when the wet helve dries out the head is, in most cases, looser than it was before the soaking. If this is the case, it will need to be replaced. Axe helves can also be broken by accident or through clumsiness, leaving you no option but to replace them.

Refitting a helve

Refitting a helve was once a task commonly carried out by all woodsmen, but in recent years – with axe helves being fitted by pneumatic presses – it has become an extremely infrequent occurrence. At home, where you have access to tools, this is a relatively simple process. The damaged helve can simply be sawn off below the eye and the remaining wooden helve carefully drilled until it is sufficiently weakened and can be driven out using a metal rod and a hammer. A replacement helve can usually be obtained at modest cost from a well-stocked hardware store or, in the case of good-quality axes, directly from the axe manufacturer or one of their appointed stockists. Failing this, carving a new helve from seasoned hard wood is a relatively simple task.

In the forest, however, far from the bench and vice of a convenient workshop, removing a helve will require forest-born ingenuity. Trying to remove the hard hickory helve from the eye using a knife risks damage

How to remove a damaged helve

1 First, polish the edge of the axe with a sharpening stone to a bright metal finish.

2 Bury the edge of the axe up to the eye in the ground.

3 Kindle a small fire of pencil-thick sticks over the top of the axe head that remains protruding from the ground.

to the knife or, worse still, the user. By far the best way is the old one: burning out the broken helve. This, though, is not as straightforward as putting the axe head in a fire. If the edge of the axe is heated to 200°C (392°F) its hardness will be affected and the axe consequently ruined. To prevent this, the edge of the axe must be shielded from the heat of the fire. This is because axes are only hardened at the edge and for a short way towards the eye, which means that so long as the edge is kept cool the eye of the axe can be heated without consequence.

Left In recent years it has been suggested that this method does not work and that the edge will inevitably be ruined by the fire. To test this theory, we returned to the factory with the axe head you see pictured and asked the technical department to test its hardness. The result was that the axe was still as it had left the factory and, indeed, apart from some soot on the back of the head, could be considered fit for sale.

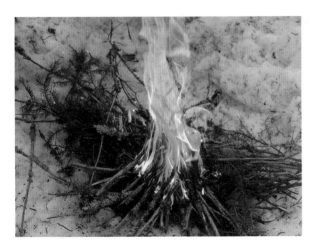

4 Being careful to keep the edge buried, let the fire burn until you are able to push out the charred remains of the helve with a stick. This will take about 20–30 minutes.

5 Clear away the embers and allow the axe to cool. If you prefer, remove the axe from the ground and cool it slowly away from the embers. DO NOT quench the head in water to speed the cooling. While the axe head is cooling, rake through the embers to salvage the metal staple. If you have been successful, you will see no colour change on the bright edge of the axe head.

How to make emergency snowshoes

1 (*Left*) Cut a straight birch sapling this long.

2 Trim off side branches and bend the sapling at its middle over your knee.

3 Anchor the ends in the snow and tie the arch.

4 Shave the ends of the sapling so that they can be bent as shown. These can now be tied off and the outside frame of the snowshoe will be complete.

5 The cross-member must be as wide as the frame plus two hand spans.

6 At each end of the cross-member, split down a hand-span length and carefully bend back each half through a 90-degree angle.

7 The T ends of the cross-member will locate inside the frame as shown and can be lashed in place.

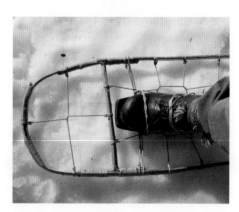

8 All that remains is to lace the frame and the snowshoe is ready for use

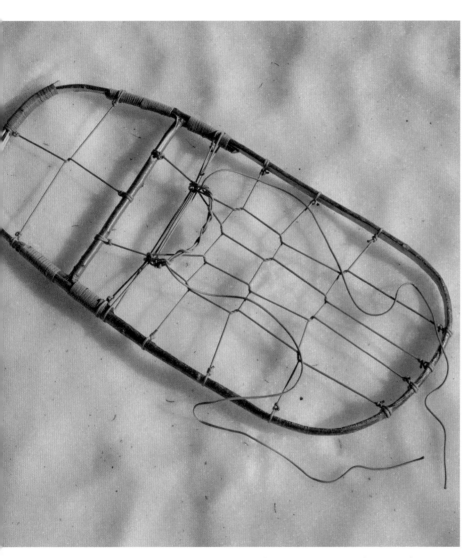

Above These emergency snowshoes are built to an ancient Chippewa design, but with nylon cord in place of the basswood bark that was the original lacing material. Although these are not the sturdiest of improvised snowshoes, they work well and can be made very quickly.

Repair

One of the most fundamental skills in long-range bushcraft is knowledge of how to repair the equipment we are carrying.

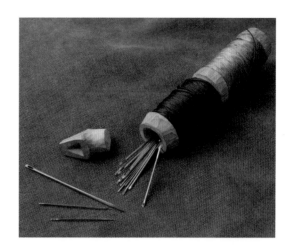

Sewing kit

Simple sewing kits like the one top right were found aboard the wreck of the Tudor warship *Mary Rose*. The design is ideal for wilderness travel.

Right Artificial sinew is an ideal thread to carry; it is waxed, very strong and can be split down to any desired thickness.

Repair clamp

A simple hand clamp made as shown can greatly assist in repairs, particularly when sewing leather.

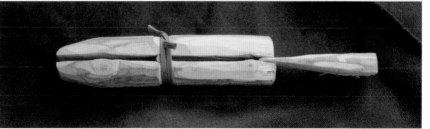

How to repair a tear

Without repair, a tear like this will only become worse, so it is worth knowing how to mend it.

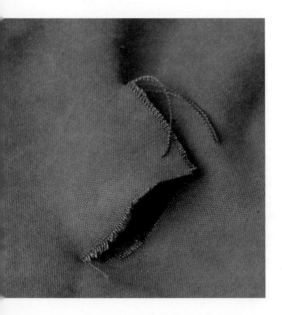

1 Trim away any loose fibres.

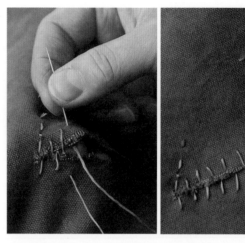

2 Bring the edges of the tear together with simple stitching.

6 Stitch the patch in place with a blunt needle.

7 This is how the stitches are made; keep it all tidy.

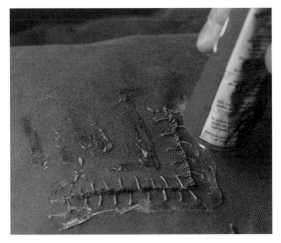

3 Cut a patch to size and apply glue to affix the patch.

4 The patch will be slightly larger than necessary so that the edges can be folded back.

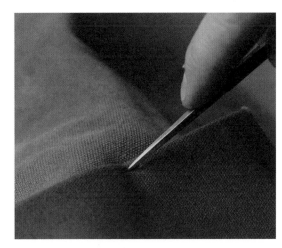

5 Tuck the edges back and use an awl to create holes for stitching.

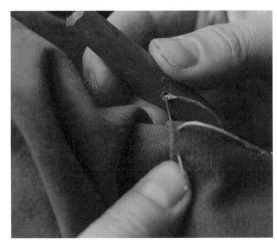

8 To help push the needle through the layers, use a small depression in the awl handle.

9 Finish off with an overhand knot tied tightly against the fabric.

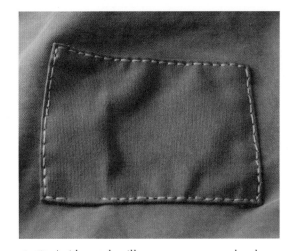

10 A tidy patch will ensure years more hard service. Note the gap in the stitching to prevent water becoming trapped behind the patch.

How to repair a loose eyelet

An eyelet pulled out from the corner of a tarp leaves the fabric weak and vulnerable to serious damage. Fortunately, it is relatively easy to repair.

1 Anchor the thread in the fabric on the reverse side of the tarp with two stitches.

2 Pass the needle through the eyelet.

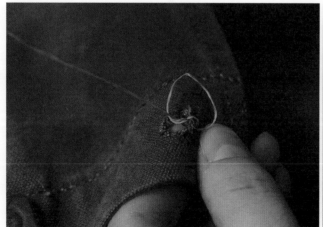

5 A knot will form on each stitch.

3 Begin stitching on the face side of the fabric.

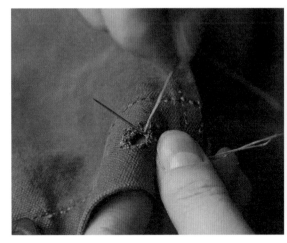

4 Wrap the thread around the emerging needle on each stitch.

6 Continue stitching in this way all the way around the eyelet.

7 Pass the needle back through the eyelet and finish off on the reverse side.

8 An eyelet repaired in this way will certainly see you through your trip and may last for many years.

How to repair a broken strap

A broken strap can be a real nuisance, but with the correct knowledge you can easily repair it.

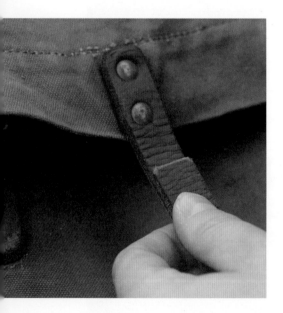

1 Trim the broken ends tidy and thin them slightly.

2 Pre-form the holes for stitching in one half of the strap using an awl.

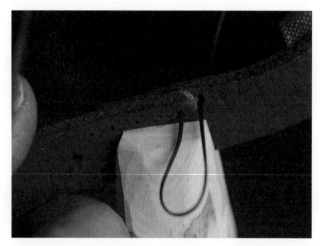

6 Ensure that a couple of stitches wrap around the end of the strap repair.

7 Stitch down the strap end.

3 Clamp the two halves together for ease of stitching.

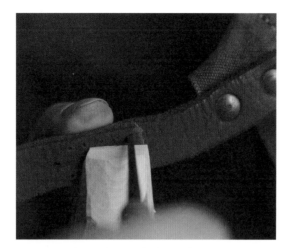

4 Using the awl, make holes in the unperforated half as you stitch.

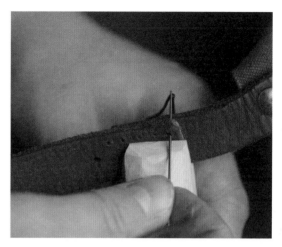

5 Begin by passing the needle through just one strap end to sandwich and conceal the stopper knot in the thread.

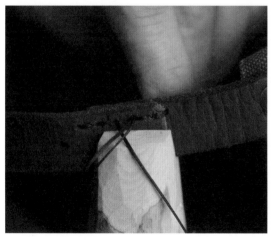

8 Stitch all the way back to the start to reinforce the repair.

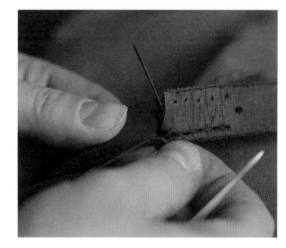

9 Pass the thread again between the layers of the repair to continue to stitch on the opposite side.

10 Repeat on the opposite side, finishing off with a couple of overhand knots pulled tight against the gap between the repair and the cloth. These can be forced between the layers for invisibility.

The forest as our friend

The forest can provide many of the things we need for life. Studying the traditional uses of the forest components is fascinating and absorbing, and an essential part of long-range bushcraft. Here are just a few useful things that the forest can provide:

Birch tar

It is relatively easy to dry-distill tar from birch bark. Called Russian oil, it serves many purposes – from waterproofing leather to making insect repellent and glue. To waterproof leather, it is rubbed in its neat form into moist leather and allowed to soak in. Insect repellent is made by adding the tar to a carrier, such as cooking oil or fish oil. Combined with rendered fat and beeswax, a waterproof leather dressing can be made. For glue, the oil can be heated and reduced to a wax-like consistency, forming thermoplastic glue that softens with heating and hardens as it cools.

Birch tar.

The only insect repellent available in many parts of Siberia was made from a mixture of three parts birch tar to five parts oil.

In Finland, bottles of birch-tar insect repellent were protected with birch bark during transportation.

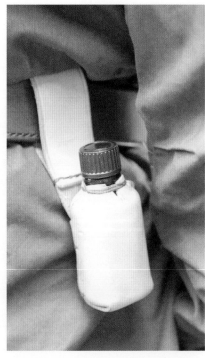

In Sweden, bottles of pine-tar-based insect repellent were carried in this way. The repellent is still sold today.

How to extract birch tar

1 Tightly fill a sealable metal container with birch bark.

2 Puncture a hole in the bottom of the container.

3 Make a larger hole in a second container; place the first tin on top of the second one.

4 Bury the tins in sand so that the top two-thirds of the first tin protrudes.

5 Burn a good fire over the tins for one hour.

6 Having allowed the fire to cool, carefully expose the tins, being careful to prevent sand from falling into the lower tin.

7 In the lower tin, you will have collected the birch tar.

Index

Italic numbers denote reference to illustrations